Against a Tide of Evil

MUKESH KAPILA with DAMIEN LEWIS

How One Man Became the Whistleblower to the First Mass
Murder of the Twenty-first Century

First published in 2013 by Mainstream Publishing.

This edition published in 2019 by Sharpe Books.

ISBN: 9781706663454

Table of Contents

'In this personal and moving plea, Kapila forces us to look directly into the face of genocide: the ashen mounds of twisted bodies, the hollowed eyes of mutilated women, and the insufferable silence of a system that treats some people as more human than others. He spoke truth to power and challenges us do the same to end such monstrous crimes.'
Lieutenant General Hon. Roméo A. Dallaire

'During one of the darkest periods in human history, Mukesh Kapila sounded the clarion call and stood firm in the face of the ultimate crime – genocide. Read his extraordinary story.'
Mia Farrow, actress and humanitarian

'This moving account of determination to fight injustice reads like a thriller. It reveals the chilling details of how the international community tried to silence Mukesh Kapila when he exposed the massacres in Darfur – and the price he paid for his courageous stand.' David Loyn, BBC international development correspondent

'Exposes how political expediency almost allowed the mass murderers to triumph in Sudan were it not for the unyielding spirit of Mukesh Kapila. It's precisely because "never again" all too frequently happens all over again that his book is essential reading.'
Lord Alton of Liverpool

'Keeps the Sudanese genocide alive in the hearts of the victims.'
Halima Bashir, author of *Tears of the Desert*

'A poignant and moving account of how one man stood against the tide of evil.'
Mende Nazer, author of *Slave*

'An eloquent testament to one man's efforts to blow the whistle and prevent evil from triumphing – a struggle that still continues across Sudan.'
John Prendergast, co-founder, The Enough Project

For the Red Cross and Red Crescent. They gave me the original gift of life.

And they opened up to let me in when all others had cast me out.

Mukesh Kapila

And for Roger Hammond A brother and a true friend.
Gone but not forgotten by all those who loved him
– you know who you are.
Semper fidelis.

Damien Lewis

AUTHOR'S NOTE

FOR MANY YEARS, I RESISTED TELLING THIS STORY BECAUSE I could not face the pain of recalling the memories and feelings that would be inevitably stirred up within myself. Only the constant nagging of friends that I had a duty to help others who faced the same dilemmas and despair compelled me to share what I have to say.

This book would never have been written without the inspiration and support of Holocaust survivors E.Z. and R.H., who, despite everything, refused to give up on humanity. My thanks particularly to Bayarmaa Luntan who badgered and badgered me until it was done.

In the process of writing this book, I have had to confront *who I am*. Inevitably this comes from both nature and nurture. Many family members, friends and colleagues have influenced my values and mindset. My maternal grandmother Vidya Wati brought me up never to forget *where I come from*. My early teacher Reverend Brother J.C. Drew at St John's School in India inspired me about *where I must go*. My subsequent mentors in England, Peter Waghorn at Wellington College and Sir Alec Cairncross in Oxford, made me believe that *I could do it*. In later life, Dr David Nabarro trained my mind *to make sense,* and Peter Penfold, former British high commissioner to Sierra Leone, showed me that *courage has a price*. Finally, my boss, the Right Honourable Clare Short, Britain's first secretary of state for international development, taught me that leadership is more about *doing the right things than just doing things right*.

Throughout my life, I have been fortunate in having many good friends and colleagues who have also delighted in being my harshest critics. They have not been reticent in pointing out my many limitations while somehow staying solid and supportive around me. In thanking them all, I would like to give particular acknowledgement to Nadia El Maaroufi and Isabelle Balot, my special assistants at the United Nations in Sudan, for their steadfast loyalty in most difficult times.

3

This book is written from my own personal recollections, from documents compiled at the time, and with the help of those colleagues who shared my experiences and were able to assist. Where necessary, I have changed the names of some people, to protect them from reprisals or to enable them to continue to operate in the humanitarian and peace-building fields.

Finally, any errors are purely of my own making, and I will be happy to address them in future editions.

Mukesh Kapila, Geneva, 2013

LIST OF ABBREVIATIONS

BBC British Broadcasting Corporation CNN Cable News Network

DFID Department for International Development (UK)

DPA Department of Political Affairs (UN)

ECOMOG Economic Commission of West African States Monitoring Group (African peacekeepers in Sierra Leone)

EPLF Eritrean People's Liberation Front

FCO Foreign and Commonwealth Office (UK)

FGM Female Genital Mutilation

GDSI Greater Darfur Special Initiative

HAC Humanitarian Aid Commission (Sudan)

ICC International Criminal Court

ICRC International Committee of the Red Cross

IDP Internally Displaced People

IFRC International Federation of Red Cross and Red Crescent Societies

IHP International Humanitarian Partnership

MOD Ministry of Defence (UK)

MSF Médecins Sans Frontières

NISS National Intelligence and Security Services (Sudan)

OCHA Office for the Coordination of Humanitarian Affairs (UN)

ODA Overseas Development Administration (UK)

OLS Operation Lifeline Sudan (UN)

OPOS Office for Placing Overseas Schoolboys and Schoolgirls in British Schools

PDF Popular Defence Forces (Sudan)

RPF Rwandan Patriotic Front

RUF Revolutionary United Front (Sierra Leone)

SABC	South African Broadcasting Corporation
SLA	Sudan Liberation Army
SLM	Sudan Liberation Movement
SPLA	Sudan People's Liberation Army
SPLM	Sudan People's Liberation Movement
SRF	Sudan Revolutionary Front
UN	United Nations
UNDP	United Nations Development Programme
UNFPA	United Nations Population Fund
UNHCR	United Nations High Commissioner for Refugees
UNICEF	United Nations Children's Fund
UNIDO	United Nations Industrial Development Organisation
UNSC	United Nations Security Council
WFP	World Food Programme
WHO	World Health Organisation

PROLOGUE

MY FATHER'S OLD SWISS FAVRE-LEUBA WATCH LIES ON MY DESK as I write. Before me, the window opens onto the Swiss Alps, majestic and snow capped on the higher peaks. It is winter, and I have just survived what by anyone's reckoning was an attempt on my life.

Early this morning, I had set out from Geneva to drive to a small studio set deep in the mountains. I was joining Damien Lewis, a professional writer, who was spending several days interviewing me to try to get the full story of my year in Sudan into some kind of shape and order.

We worked all morning, and then I suggested we take a break and drive to a beautiful valley nearby. It was a bitter January day, and even though it was bright and sunny it was freezing. We headed out in my battered Renault, and after a short drive I slowed to just above a crawl so that we could admire the scenery. We came to a low point where the road started to climb, and for the first time that day I found the sun shining directly into my eyes.

Instantly, I was blinded, the windscreen blurring into a thousand shards of burning light. Unable to see a thing, I slammed on the brakes and tried to steer for where I figured the roadside had to be. We came to a juddering halt, half hanging off the road. I cut the engine, and for a second Damien and I stared at each other in stunned silence.

'That was a... close thing,' I remarked, a little shakily. 'Lucky I was driving so slowly. Best we go clear the windscreen.'

'You didn't scrape your screen this morning?' he asked. I told him that I had but obviously not very well.

We searched around for something with which to scrape off the frost, then got to work. After a few seconds, Damien stopped. He held up his scraper and fixed me with a perplexed look.

'What on earth is this?' he asked, indicating a gooey brown mess sticking to the scraper and trailing gluey strings back to the windscreen.

I shook my head. 'I've no idea. Is it frost? It can't be.'

'No, it's not frost.' I saw him take a sniff. 'It's epoxy resin.' He had a dark expression on his face, a mixture of disbelief and alarm. 'Mukesh, what is epoxy resin doing on your windscreen?'

I shrugged. I didn't have a clue what epoxy resin was.

Damien proceeded to point out the spray marks criss-crossing the expanse of glass.

'Mukesh, someone has sprayed your entire windscreen with epoxy resin.'

'What is epoxy resin exactly?' I asked.

'Like liquid fibreglass. You use it to repair boats, that kind of thing. Incredibly sticky and impossible to get off. Dries hard like plastic.' He paused. 'The question is, why has someone sprayed your windscreen with the stuff?'

'Maybe an accident?' I ventured. 'Or vandalism?'

'Mukesh, no one accidentally sprayed your car. And if I wanted to vandalise it, I'd smash the windows with a brick, kick in the lights or get a can of spray paint. No one uses epoxy resin to vandalise a car.'

'So, what's going on?' I asked.

In answer, he stepped around to inspect the passenger window. 'They've sprayed this one, too.' He walked around the back. 'And the rear. Mukesh, someone has sprayed every window of your car with epoxy resin.' He glanced at the wing mirrors. 'My god, they've even thought to do the mirrors!'

He joined me at the front. 'So, Mukesh, what does this mean?'

'I don't know,' I replied. I really didn't have a clue what it might mean. It was so bizarre.

'OK, let's recap. It's a cold winter's day. There was a heavy frost this morning. You tried to clear your windscreen?'

'Yes. With the wipers and the screen wash, but I couldn't seem to get it clear. I just thought it was a bad frost and the heater would deal with it.'

'So, you drove out of Geneva heading west? The sun rises in the east. It just so happens that you didn't drive in the direction of the rising sun. If you had, you'd have been on the motorway when the sun hit your windscreen and you'd have been blinded. So tell me, if you had gone east and not west what would have happened?'

'Well, I guess I'd very likely have crashed.'

'You would. At speed on the motorway. As it is, the sun hit your windscreen at midday, here, where we were doing maybe 20 miles an hour and admiring the beautiful scenery.' He gestured at the drop into the valley below. 'And you just managed to stop before we went over that. How would you characterise events so far?'

'Well, I'd have to say we have been rather lucky.'

'We have. So back to my original question: why has someone sprayed your car with epoxy resin?'

'I suppose it has to be a warning...'

'At best a warning, at worst an attempt to kill either you or the both of us. Now, why would anyone want to kill you, as we have to presume you are the target here? And let's not forget all the death threats you've received over recent years.'

'Well... Sudan?'

'Yes. Sudan. Sudan, and more specifically I would imagine Darfur...' Using some de-icing fluid, we managed to clear a hole just about large enough for me to see through. Once back at the studio, he made me report what had happened to the diplomatic police in Geneva – as my work gave me diplomatic status – and other relevant authorities. An investigation followed, during which a Sudanese individual who had been acting oddly around me was thoroughly scrutinised. I have always made it clear that I have no argument with the Sudanese people. Quite the reverse: I hold them dear to my heart, and I have never been closed to working with Sudanese nationals in my humanitarian work.

Overnight almost, the individual under investigation slipped away from Geneva. Either she had returned to – or been recalled to – the Sudan. Those investigating the incident had no prior experience of epoxy resin being used in this way, but they recognised that in those wintry conditions, and with a low, winter sun, it constituted a potentially effective means to kill, injure or at the very least to warn. I was told to take certain extra precautions, and that was about all that could be done.

It was approaching ten years since I had held my post as the head of the United Nations in Sudan, and indeed the death threats had not come to an end. They were not so relentless these days, but just when I thought they had ceased I'd get the ring on my mobile phone and hear the sinister voice.

'Dr Kapila, we have not forgotten. We will never forget, and one day we will finish you...'

No matter how often I changed my number, the calls would keep coming. I figured it wasn't so hard to keep track of someone, especially if the stakes were high enough to warrant the investment in time and effort to do so.

And that perhaps is the point: some ten years after the genocide in Darfur began, the stakes remain incredibly high. They do so because this was genocide without end. In a sense, this was the world's most successful genocide, because the perpetrators achieved all they wanted: they exterminated hundreds of thousands of people; they spread absolute terror, and in so doing destroyed the victims' sense of identity to such a degree that they remain too fearful to return to their lands; and they wreaked physical destruction over their means of livelihood, so as to make such a return doubly impossible.

And so, a decade after the horror began, Darfur remains purged of its original peoples, some three million of whom are living as refugees or internally displaced people (IDPs). Moreover, the genocide was a success in the eyes of its architects – those at the helm of Sudan's governing regime – because not one amongst them has yet been brought to justice.

This is not to say that the events portrayed in this book

10

– when I broke all the accepted rules and blew the whistle over Darfur – failed to have an impact. Quite the reverse. My actions provoked a firestorm of international press coverage that turned the tide in Darfur. Just days after I flew out of Khartoum for the final time, the United Nations and powerful world governments were forced to act over Darfur.

And I presume it is *all of that* which the Khartoum regime's security services refuse to forget, and that is why on a winter's day in the Swiss mountains they sent me such a powerful warning. But, for whatever reason, it is not in my nature to be silenced. It was not in my nature back then, in the spring of 2004, when I blew the whistle over the horrors sweeping Darfur, and that remains the case now, a decade later as I pen these pages.

After my car was sprayed with epoxy resin, Damien asked me if I really did want to continue with this book. My answer was an emphatic 'yes'. Silence was not an option in 2004 and it is not so now.

For those of us who wish to ensure that 'never again' truly becomes a reality, silence can never be an option, even if speaking out may kill us.

ONE

Each back must bear its own burden.
My ancestor, the Sage Kapila (c. 500 BC)

THE ALARM SOUNDED AT 2 A.M. THE HOUSE WAS
DARK AND silent as I readied myself for departure, trying
not to waken my wife, Helen. After two decades spent jetting
into the world's trouble spots, I'd got into the habit of
travelling light and leaving silently in the night hours. I'd
packed just the one suitcase for my journey to my new
posting, in Sudan.

I poked my head around the doors to my daughters'
rooms and said my silent goodbyes. Our girls each have
an English first name, reflecting their British nationality,
and an Indian second name, reflecting their Indian
heritage.

The eldest is Rachel *Prakash*, which means 'light' in my
native language, Hindi. Rachel is the sensible, pragmatic
one. She viewed my going away to Sudan through her prism
of practicality: *this is just something that Dad has to do*. The
second is Lois *Vidya*, which means 'knowledge'. Lois is the
most instinctive of my girls, and she was hugely supportive
of my going off to Sudan, even though I'd be away for
months on end. She was proud that her daddy was going off
'to save the world', which was how my daughters
rationalised my missions to the ends of the earth.

Our third daughter is little Ruth. Ruth's Hindi name is
Maya – meaning 'illusion' – for she was something of a late
addition to the Kapila clan. Ruth was treated as the baby of
the family, though she was probably the wisest of all,
knowing instinctively that I was off 'doing good' somewhere
far away.

In my life, I'd spent many years working for the UK
government's Department for International Development
(DFID), so the girls had grown up with 'saving the world'

as a constant in the family. I'd often come home late from DFID's London office to find the kids in their dressing gowns eating Marmite soldiers in front of the TV. I'd cuddle up with them, and one of the girls would ask me how much of the world I had saved today. Or I might remark that I'd had a busy day, and my wife would say, 'Well, we've had to take the dog to the vet while you've been saving the world.' It was done with a mixture of pride, teasing and a little exasperation. *Dad always has time to save the world but not to take the dog to the vet.* It was a standing joke between us.

I'd been absent for so much of the time while the girls were growing up, and kids change so fast. I knew I'd miss them dearly while away in Sudan, but at the same time I couldn't wait to get started. I was hugely excited by my coming mission, which I sensed was going to be the most important of my life.

For two decades, I had borne witness to some of man's worst inhumanity to man – in Rwanda, the Balkans, Sierra Leone, Afghanistan and elsewhere. I'd taken aid, medical care, education and hope into some of the darkest corners of the world, only to see how the mass murderers invariably had triumphed. If ever I were in a position to stop it, I'd promised myself that evil would never triumph on my watch.

I was heading to Sudan to take up my highest-ever posting in the humanitarian field. At the age of 48, I'd been appointed the United Nations' resident coordinator for Sudan – in essence, the chief of all UN operations. For decades, Sudan had been wracked by a civil war, which at its simplest pitted a largely black African Christian and animist south against a hard-line 'Arabic' Muslim north. War had displaced millions of people, and feeding and safeguarding them had become the UN's single biggest operation.

If ever there was an opportunity to ensure that evil wouldn't triumph on my watch, then Sudan surely was it. Even more exciting was the imminent prospect of peace coming to the country. Under the Naivasha Accords, negotiations over a peace deal were under way, and a signing of that agreement was thought to be imminent. The prospect of ushering in such a historic peace deal during my two-year tenure as UN chief was one of the main reasons that I'd taken the posting.

I grabbed my suitcase from where I'd placed it the night before on the landing and lugged it downstairs. Typically, Megan, our beloved mongrel of a dog, was curled up on the living room sofa together with Tuppy – short for Tuppence – our ginger cat. We were hopelessly soft on the two of them, and many an evening was spent with the five of us crammed into the armchairs, while Megan and Tuppy stretched out luxuriously on the sofa.

It was ten years since the girls had first brought a tiny black puppy home, and over time Megan had grown to become my dog. She'd got into the habit of curling up under the desk in my study, and I loved having her there. Our little cottage – a former farm labourer's house in the Cambridgeshire fens – could be damp and chilly in winter, and I'd warm my feet on her tummy. Megan used to wait by the door prior to my coming home from one assignment or another. She had this incredible sixth sense and she always knew.

I glanced around the living room and thought about how much I would miss home. It was late March, and the garden was bursting with spring flowers. Our house lies beside a country lane with a stream running past. In summer, we'd have afternoon tea with a blanket spread on the lawn or stroll along the meandering riverbank. But this summer I would miss all of that, headed as I was into the heat and dust of Sudan.

I heard a soft toot from outside, which meant my regular taxi driver was there. Before unlatching the door, I checked in the outer pocket of my suitcase for my few personal effects. I pulled out the family photos, plus the one of Megan. I felt the lump of coal from the mine that my father had managed in Bihar state in India. That unremarkable rock had travelled with me when I first came to England from India, and I had carried it with me ever since, like a powerful talisman. If a penniless Indian boy could win the confidence of an English philanthropist and be educated at one of Britain's best schools, as I had, anything had to be possible in the world.

Lastly, I slipped my hand into my case and ran it over the two bits of reading material that I was taking with me. They were hardly a light-hearted or cheery choice. The reports on the UN's failure to stop the genocide in Rwanda and then Srebrenica (in Bosnia) made for a dark, sobering read. They explored the root causes of the UN's failings in 1994 and 1995 in an effort to prevent such spectacular failures being repeated. In a way, they were unfinished chapters for me, as in both places I had been very close to the darkness, with blood still running down the walls, and I felt the failures personally.

Late the previous evening, I'd thrust those reports into my luggage almost as an afterthought. For a moment, I went to remove them. Why was I taking them to Sudan? After all, I was going there to preside over the signing of a historic peace deal. But something with an almost spiritual forcefulness stayed my hand. As I gently closed the door to our cottage, I had no idea how important those two dry documents would become to me. They would become my touchstones and my bible as I wrestled with a choice of actions that could cost countless thousands – and perhaps millions – of lives.

'Good morning, sir, and where might you be off to today?' my cabbie remarked, as he lifted my suitcase into his boot.

No matter how unreasonable the hour, Harry, my regular taxi-driver, always seemed to be in good humour. I explained that I was catching a short shuttle to Frankfurt, from where I'd join a Lufthansa flight to North Africa, destination Sudan. At 6 p.m. local time, I would touch down at Khartoum airport, and a new chapter in my life would begin. A few hours after Harry wished me good luck on my mission, I was settling into my seat for the long-haul flight to Khartoum. Being on a United Nations posting of some significance, I had been booked to fly business class.

I was supposed to arrive well rested and ready to hit the ground running, and I was both excited and daunted by what might lie ahead of me.

Sudan was at this time Africa's largest country, being over six times the size of France. I was flying into Africa's longest-running civil war, one that had spawned more refugees and displaced people than perhaps any other. The only way to distribute aid across such a vast and undeveloped area was by air, and the UN operated the largest air force in Africa to do so. In a few hours' time, I would take charge of that massive operation, together with its thousands of workers.

Effectively, I would be running a mini state within a state, and my nearest boss would be thousands of miles distant in UN headquarters in New York. I would wield enormous authority over operations in the country, and yet I was acutely aware of how little experience I had working within the UN system. I had been brought in largely because my background promised to make me the most acceptable peacemaker to all sides in the civil war. From the outset, I was the UN outsider, and in time that would prove both my greatest weakness and my greatest strength.

I was a wild card for such a senior posting, for I wasn't steeped in the UN's procedures and I hadn't spent years learning how the game is played. Just a few months back, I'd been serving as DFID's head of conflict and humanitarian affairs, in charge of aid, conflict and disaster work for the British government. Over the years, I'd learned that most wars can only be brought to an end if one side is victorious or both sides run out of the energy to fight. A crisis has to be ripe for solving. Wars wax and wane, and you have to intervene at the right moment in the conflict cycle, or you might simply freeze it and in the long run make matters worse.

Sudan felt like it had arrived at the perfect moment to bring peace, with both sides having fought themselves to a standstill. Those who had recruited me persuaded me that I had the track record and background to help bring about an end to the war of all wars. My lack of prior history with the UN meant that I was seen as being neutral within the system, so not allied to any one UN agency. I had long ago taken up British nationality and so I was seen as being on side: I was part of the Western power bloc that wielded so much influence at the UN. But I was also of Indian origin and non-white, so I could be presented to the Sudanese as a fellow face from the developing world. And I was neither Arab nor African, which should make me acceptable to both sides of the conflict. In short, I was the perfect photo-fit for the job in hand.

My flight touched down in Khartoum on a sweltering late afternoon. The last time I'd been here was on a DFID aid mission four or five years previously. Each time, the city skyline seemed to change noticeably, as the country's recently discovered oil wealth fuelled a construction boom. The aircraft lurched to a stop and the engines powered down. It was 1 April – April Fool's Day – and as I went to leave the plane I had barely heard of a remote western region of Sudan called 'Darfur'.

In retrospect, my arrival was as bizarre and surreal as my departure was to be. I stepped out of the air-conditioned cool of the aircraft and the heat hit me like a furnace. Having been brought up in India, I'm a hothouse plant by nature, but as I walked the short distance to the terminal building it felt unbearably hot, not to mention dusty. It struck me as odd that there was no one to meet me, but I figured they'd be waiting for me once I'd cleared customs.

I joined the queue for passport control, but shortly I heard a voice calling my name. 'Dr Kapila! Dr Kapila! Where are you, Dr Kapila?' I turned to see a man dressed in a pristine white dish-dash (a full- length Arab robe) and turban. From my Indian appearance, he must have concluded that I was the elusive Dr Kapila, for he came hurrying over.

'Dr Kapila? Sir? You are Dr Kapila? But what are you doing here?' he demanded. 'Everyone is waiting for you in

VIP hall!'

I felt like asking him where was the sign saying: 'Dr Kapila, VIP, this way'. I settled for: 'But how would I know to go to the VIP area?' He brushed aside my question, and I allowed him to take me by the arm and march me back out onto the runway. Parked as close to the Lufthansa plane as possible was a sparkling white Toyota Land Cruiser. He took me to it, opened the rear passenger door and shoved me inside.

He shook his head in frustration. 'Dr Kapila... But this is your official car. How did you not notice the official car?'

I shrugged. There was something hugely comical about all of this. The car certainly hadn't been there when I arrived. Perhaps I had been too quick, so frustrating their plans to whisk me away from the aircraft's steps. Or maybe they were all running on 'Sudan time', which was something I'd experienced during my previous visits. All meetings – even scheduled public events – generally started a good half-hour late, and no one seemed to pay much heed to accurate timekeeping. I settled into the air-conditioned hum of the vehicle, and 30 seconds later it pulled up a short distance away at the terminal's 'VIP entrance'. The door to the vehicle swung open, and as I entered the building everyone rose to their feet. The VIP lounge was cooled to a fridge-like chilliness, and, amongst those that had risen to greet me, the Sudanese government officials were obvious in their crisp white robes. I figured the tired-looking white guys in their crumpled suits had to be my new UN co-workers.

The Sudanese government head of protocol ushered me to a low table surrounded by overstuffed sofas. My passport was whisked off to be processed, and I sipped my tea and nibbled on a date or two. The Sudanese officials lined up to greet me formally, followed by the *khawajas*, as white men are called in Arabic, the language of north Sudan. The polite chitchat went to and fro. *How was your flight? Did you manage to get some rest? What was the weather like in the*

UK? It is not too hot for you here in Khartoum?

My suitcase duly arrived and, my meet-and-greet over, I was hurried outside. Another white Toyota Land Cruiser was waiting, this one distinguished by having a blue UN flag flying from the right-hand side of the bonnet. Feeling as if I was in some kind of John le Carré novel, I was driven away from the airport in a convoy led by a Sudanese police vehicle complete with flashing light and wailing siren. As I'd exited the terminal building, I'd managed to get just a sniff of the smell of Africa – the dusty, spicy, hot scent – that I knew so well. It brought back conflicting memories – of the incredible generosity of people who seemingly had nothing, and of the unspeakable brutality of tribe pitted against tribe. I'd caught just a hint of that, together with the noisy cacophony of life going on all around me, before I was locked into the air-conditioned hum of the Land Cruiser. I was starting to sense that this was the cocoon of privilege with which I was expected to surround myself now, and that it would take some effort to break free from its suffocating constraints.

My Sudanese protocol friend had squeezed into the vehicle alongside me, but after five minutes we had exhausted any topics of polite chitchat. We sat in silence as we were whisked through the streets, the 'mee-maw' of the police siren beating out the rhythm of our passing. I gazed out at the myriad faces turning to stare. I couldn't help but think of a cold beer, but I was hardly likely to ask my protocol friend where I could find one. Khartoum was ruled by Islamic – *sharia* – law, and alcohol was banned. Even the one good hotel that foreigners tended to stay in, the Hilton, had a no-alcohol rule.

The Khartoum Hilton sits on the banks of the mighty Nile. It was going to be my home until I was officially accepted by the Sudanese president, at which point I might find myself somewhere more permanent to live. My room was on the ground floor, with a veranda opening onto the hotel's lush tropical gardens. Everything was spotlessly clean, but the place had a faded, slightly sagging 1970s feel to it. When I lifted one of the paintings of Arabian horse scenes, I could see an oblong patch where the wallpaper hadn't been so bled of its colour by the beating sun. Everywhere else it had faded to the hue of old newspaper, and somehow the room had a similar kind of smell to it.

I headed for the restaurant and grabbed some pitta bread and hummus, plus a non-alcoholic lager. An hour later I was back in my room, wondering what to do with myself. I knew I should try to sleep, for a driver was scheduled to arrive at 7.30 the following morning to take me to the UN office. But it was only eight in the evening UK time, and I wasn't feeling tired. I switched on the TV and surfed the news channels for a while.

I drifted off to sleep experiencing a mixture of emotions. A part of me felt an odd sense of displacement in time and space. Another part of me was gripped by a deep anxiety: *what exactly does a UN resident coordinator do?* I now knew that I got driven around in a car flying the UN flag, but other than that I had very little idea. Mostly I was trying to hold onto my sense of mission – that now was the chance to get this war sorted once and for all.

Yet there was also a part of me – maybe 10 per cent of my consciousness – that was clouded by this sense that it might not be so easy to achieve what I wanted here. My arrival had been wrapped in layers of privilege and protocol, and I sensed it might not be the best context in which to grasp the moment and achieve the extraordinary.

I'd been brought in as the outsider to help usher in peace, and to lift our sights beyond the war. If I was going to have to break the mould to get the job done, so be it. From my earliest years I'd been something of a non-conformist and a rule-breaker, and I guess it was hard-wired into my soul.

But the first rule breaking would come far sooner than even I expected.

TWO

Effects pre-exist, potentially in their causes.
The Sage Kapila

THE WORKING DAY STARTS EARLY IN KHARTOUM IN ORDER TO beat the heat. I was up for a 6.30 a.m. breakfast, dressed in what I figured would be the right kind of attire for my position – a sandy- brown suit. Recently, I'd visited New York to be briefed on what was expected of me in my new position, and I'd taken the opportunity to get two identical suits tailor made in a light and cool linen.

At 7.30 sharp, a Land Cruiser flying the UN flag pulled up at the hotel steps: no running on Sudanese time for the UN, it seemed. A tall, dignified-looking man dressed in Western-style slacks and shirt got out. He looked to be in his mid-50s, and he had the bearing of a person of experience and some standing.

'Good morning, sir,' he greeted me. 'I am Omer, your driver. I will be driving you. Please,' he held open the rear door, 'take your seat.' I did as I was told, and Omer set off west along the Nile Road, passing the presidential palace and the main government buildings. He didn't try to engage me in polite, meaningless chat, and I sensed that he and I were going to get on just fine. He pulled up at a run-down-looking building, whereupon uniformed guards swung the gates open and the car whisked me inside. We halted in a ramshackle-looking car park that was already half-full of Land Cruisers.

I went to open my door, but before I could do so Omer was there. I knew better than to object to any of this, regardless of how uncomfortable it made me feel. This was Omer's job, and to reject such treatment would be a real slight on my part. Being the driver of the UN chief in Sudan would be a prestigious position, and well paid by Sudanese standards. Omer clearly took pride in doing everything just right, and I would have to be careful not to disrespect that.

I glanced around the cluster of low-rise offices with the UN and Sudanese flags hanging limp in the still air. The first thing that struck me was how dingy everything looked. There was an air of dejection and neglect, and I vowed to do a tour of the entire place to see what might be done. Sudanese government policy was to try to minimise UN presence in the country, because international aid workers had a tendency to witness goings on that the regime would prefer to keep hidden. As a foil to that, we needed to take extra pride in our place of work or we'd rapidly degrade our morale.

I was received by a UN staffer and taken up the stairs to my office. We paused in the antechamber so I could be introduced to Mona, my secretary. Mona was a short, plump, motherly-looking Arab lady who appeared to be in her mid-40s. There was something of Queen Victoria about her, but a more warm and welcoming version. She smiled at me shyly, and I sensed that I would get to know and love Mona dearly during my time here.

The first thing I noticed as I walked into my office was the official portrait of Kofi Annan, the UN secretary-general, which dominated one wall. In UN terms, Kofi Annan was the equivalent of the head of state: nothing significant could happen in UN affairs without his blessing. In front of his portrait sat a massive teak desk with a set of deep leather armchairs opposite. The desk was polished to a mirror- like brightness and was completely devoid of clutter. It was the blank canvas upon which I was to stamp my identity.

On one side of the Kofi Annan portrait was a bookcase filled with all sorts of UN documents. I pulled out my few work things from my bag, including the Rwanda and Srebrenica reports. Feeling a little self-conscious, I added those to the bookshelf, then sat behind my desk and wondered what on earth I should do next.

Thankfully, Mona came to my rescue. Starting off a little nervously, she briefed me on what exactly was expected of me over the coming days. Until the Sudanese president had formally accepted my credentials, I wasn't allowed to go anywhere but the UN office or the Hilton. Everywhere else was off-limits. I asked Mona how long she figured it would take to get my credentials accepted. Mona didn't want to hazard a guess. All she could tell me was what had happened to my predecessor, Mike Sackett, an Australian. Mike had survived a hundred days before getting thrown out of the country, by which time he hadn't yet managed to present his credentials. Apparently, when Mike Sackett had decided to evacuate UN staff from a town in the south of the country for security reasons, the Sudanese government had used that as the excuse to get rid of him. It was hardly very encouraging.

After Mona's little talk, my next visitor was Shafi, a manager from the United Nations Development Programme (UNDP), one of the many UN agencies working in Sudan. We didn't exactly get off to the best of starts. After some polite chat, he informed me that my Mercedes was 'almost ready'. It was a top-of-the-range saloon, he told me proudly, being delivered direct from the showroom.

'But what's wrong with the Toyota?' I queried. 'I mean, why do I need a Mercedes? It's hardly as if I'll be driving around in both at the same time.'

The attempt at humour fell quite flat. 'There is nothing wrong with the Toyota, of course,' he replied, stonily. 'But maybe something more in keeping with your status would be suitable, don't you think, Dr Kapila?'

'It may boost my status,' I smiled, 'but not in a way that I'd want. It doesn't look good if the UN resident coordinator arrives and right away orders a brand-new Mercedes. I'm sure the money could be better spent elsewhere.'

Shafi pointed out that every UN chief before me had got a brand-new Mercedes. The car came with the position. I dug my heels in. I didn't need it or want it, I explained. I finally managed to get him to understand that I wasn't having it, and to cancel the order, so saving the car's

$25,000 price tag – a discounted price for diplomats, without taxes.

That done, I told Mona that I'd like to do a walkabout. If I was to be imprisoned here until my credentials were accepted, I might as well start trying to get the place sorted out. Going walkabout was also an excuse to meet all the UN staff, from the highest to the lowest. Under Mona's guidance, I proceeded to poke my nose into every nook and cranny, and to say a personal 'hello' to everyone, cleaners and guards included.

It was the kitchen and dining area that shocked me the most. It resembled nothing quite so much as the proverbial black hole of Calcutta. There were dark and dingy dining rooms with a clutter of ancient tables and chairs. One side was cordoned off to form a makeshift kitchen, equipped with an ancient iron range and some open fires. This was where the UN staff were supposed to eat, in spite of the fact that doing so looked like an invitation to food poisoning. In my experience, the kitchen and dining area is where the heart of an organisation beats strongest. It's the place where people gather socially and build an *esprit de corps*, and I decided there and then to use the $25,000 Mercedes money to renovate the place.

My next move was to call a meeting of the entire staff of UNDP. Along with OCHA, the UN's Office for the Coordination of Humanitarian Affairs, UNDP was the main agency under my direct control. The other big UN agencies in Sudan were the UN Children's Fund (UNICEF) and the World Food Programme (WFP), which focused on providing food aid to the millions of displaced people in the country.

With the northern, government-controlled part of Sudan at war with the rebel-held south, there appeared to be little cooperation between UN operations north and south. In effect, they were run as separate fiefdoms. Part of my reformist agenda was to unite those operations in preparation for the coming peace, so the UN could work as one coordinated body to help rebuild the entire country.

With peace would come huge expectations of development, not to mention millions of refugees seeking to return to their war-ravaged homes. If the UN wasn't ready to deliver, the peace might fail to take hold.

Some 40 UNDP staff gathered around a long conference table opposite my office. The room was a sea of Arab-looking faces, with hardly a black African amongst them. UNDP had no office in the south of the country, so the agency was in effect a north Sudan operation only, and the ethnic mix of the staff reflected that sad reality. There was a decidedly downbeat atmosphere, but I was determined to plough ahead with the inspirational talk that I'd prepared.

After the usual niceties, I got down to business. 'I look forward to working with you all as we welcome Sudan to a new and peaceful chapter of its conflict-ridden history. Our role is to develop the country in all areas, regardless of race, religion or ethnic creed, and to promote peace and harmony across all the peoples of Sudan. I know I can count on each and every one of you to help the UN in its mission, and I look forward to knowing you better in the coming days. Any questions?'

There was a polite but muted round of applause. Other than that, there was not a single spark of rapport, let alone any interest in what I had just said. If I hadn't known they all spoke English, I would have doubted whether they'd understood anything.

I excused myself and walked the short distance to my office, all the time wondering how morale could be any lower than it appeared to be right now. Perhaps they were just cynical and feeling as if they'd heard such grand words before from UN chiefs who rapidly came and went? Or perhaps their suspicions were more deeply rooted, as they worried that their comfy jobs might be turned upside down?

I was new and doubtless had a lot to learn, but of one thing I was certain. I'd been sent here to deliver on a reformist mandate, and deliver I would. Things would change very rapidly once peace came to Sudan. The UN had to be ready, which meant those people in that room coming very much to life. Millions of lives depended upon it, and anything less just wasn't good enough.

My last meeting of the day was with Roger Arsenault, the head of security for the UN in Sudan. Roger was a Canadian ex-Mountie, and he seemed to have worked in most of the world's conflict zones at one time or another. I figured he had to be in his early 50s, although with his lanky frame and weather-beaten, leathery face he probably looked older than his years.

I am around 5 ft 10 in. and a little portly, so Roger's lean form towered over me. With my thick beard and roundish face topped off by a whirl of pepper-grey hair, people often describe me as somewhat teddy-bearish in appearance. Roger and I couldn't be more unalike. We were the proverbial chalk and cheese.

Roger had direct links to the Sudanese government's security apparatus, the tentacles of which reached into just about every aspect of the nation's life. You couldn't so much as breathe in north Sudan without them knowing about it. He also had good contacts among the rebels and the militias. As a result, if trouble was brewing anywhere in Sudan that might impact upon UN operations, Roger was sure to be amongst the first to know of it.

My official title was 'UN Resident and Humanitarian Coordinator' in Sudan. In theory, that made me head of UN security and Roger's boss. But it was soon clear that he viewed me only nominally as such. 'Sir, the secret in Sudan is not to be in the wrong place at the wrong time,' he told me. 'It's my job as UN security advisor to manage threats, and it's your role to weigh up the consequences of my advice. If I advise you to batten down the hatches, rest assured I'll have good reasons for doing so.'

'Roger, it would be unheard of for the boss to go against his chief of security,' I reassured him. 'I don't think I'll ever have cause for doing so.'

'Sir, that's good to hear. Trust me, I know what I'm doing.

I'll brief you first thing each morning, and that way we can keep permanently abreast of the threat.'

Roger rounded off with a joke. He sported a long ponytail, which he assured me was a security measure. It enabled all sides to identify him in the field, so there was less chance of getting shot by accident. There was one final point that Roger wanted to brief me on, but he remarked, somewhat obliquely, that he'd prefer to do so at my hotel. It was an odd request to make, almost suggesting that we couldn't speak freely in my office, and I wondered what might lie behind it. It would be a couple of days before Roger would drop by the Hilton, and I would find out.

Apart from my driver, Omer, and my secretary, Mona, Roger struck me as being the first UN staffer that I'd met with a strong commitment to the job that he was doing. I detected a potential ally in him, and perhaps someone who might offer a modicum of companionship, for I sensed already that the position of UN chief was going to prove a lonely one.

It was past six by the time Roger and I were done. I gathered up my few things and went to leave. As I did so, Mona grabbed a walkie- talkie lying on her desk and mouthed into it a few words. By the time I'd reached the bottom of the stairs, Omer was there with the Toyota's door held open for me. I slid into the air-conditioned coolness and let him whisk me away.

I noticed that he was taking a different route to return to the Hilton, and I asked why.

'Never to take the same route twice in one day, sir,' he remarked, somewhat cryptically. And then, proudly: 'I learned this on my diplomatic driving skills course.'

We drove past a building that was familiar to me, being part of Khartoum University's medical school. My first ever visit to Sudan had taken me on a placement to that medical school, which was a renowned centre of tropical medicine and primary healthcare, and seeing it brought the memories flooding back to me.

At the age of 18, I'd won a place to study medicine at Oxford University. At that time, I still believed that I wanted to be a doctor, a life decision inspired by a book that my father had given me as a young child. He'd taken out a subscription to the Reader's Digest Condensed Books series. They arrived through the post at our home in India with titles like: *I am John's Heart*, *I am John's Lungs* and *I am John's Brain*. Reading about how each organ in John's body functioned, it was as if a light had been switched on in my head. I suddenly knew what I wanted to be: I was going to be a medical doctor.

Years later, I won a scholarship to study in the UK, and one of my Oxford University professors, Bent Juel-Jensen, had arranged for me a placement at Khartoum University. Its tropical medicine faculty was largely Oxford-trained, and there were regular student exchanges.

In the spring of 1979, I'd caught my flight to Sudan to begin my three-month posting. Professor Juel-Jensen had a secondary agenda in sending me. At that time, Khartoum was headquarters to the Eritrean People's Liberation Front (EPLF), something of a cause célèbre in the West. The EPLF was fighting for an independent Eritrea, and Juel-Jensen was a supporter of their cause. He sent me to Khartoum with a number of letters to deliver to the Eritrean resistance.

As a 24-year-old exchange student, I was housed in the Khartoum University dorms, but I had to keep my role as a go-between with the EPLF a strict secret, which was hugely exciting. My instructions from Professor Juel-Jensen were to stand outside the American Cultural Centre in Khartoum on one particular day, and to remain there until an EPLF contact made himself known to me.

I did as I'd been instructed, and eventually a car with darkened windows drew up. A door opened and I was told to get in. I was driven around the back streets before finally being delivered to the EPLF's office. I delivered my letters to the rebel leaders and listened to their stories of the armed struggle while trying to help them better plan how to treat the casualties of war.

All of that cloak-and-dagger stuff appealed to the rebel within me, and there is a long tradition of resistance within the Kapila clan. In the 1960s, my father had travelled from India to Europe to work for Krupp, a German company that had been a major arms manufacturer during the Second World War. It had reverted to heavy engineering, and my father was sent there to learn about mining and excavation equipment.

When he returned home to India, he regaled me with stories of his covert activities in post-war Europe. At that time, the U-bahn still connected capitalist West to communist East Berlin. Hailing from a neutral country like India, my father was allowed to travel freely between the two sides. India was then a newly independent country with strong socialist leanings, so the East Berlin border guards never searched my father. As a result, he was able to smuggle in food parcels and deliver letters between divided family members.

My father revelled in being able to help those families torn apart by war and in striking a small blow for freedom. His stories from that divided city had fuelled my childish notions of romantic, dangerous liaisons in far-off lands, and a decade later I had found myself doing something similar in the exotic setting of Khartoum. The late 1970s was a time of relative peace in Sudan, and I left the country having formed a deep affection for the Sudanese people and their culture.

I returned to Oxford and read General Gordon's tales of colonial times in the Sudan, and Winston Churchill's accounts of fighting colonial wars there. I studied the ancient history of the country, which stretched back several millennia to the time of the great Nilotic civilisations. I learned that the little-known pyramids in Sudan rival those in Egypt in terms of number and age. Sudan was truly an ancient and mysterious country rich in history, one peopled by the descendants of the original 'Black Pharaohs'.

During my first visit, I had formed a romantic, deeply affectionate view of this ancient civilisation upon the Nile. Now, I was here again as the UN chief, and I hoped very much that I could help bring peace to this captivating land. But my initial experiences were going to prove entirely more prosaic.

Once Omer had dropped me at the Hilton, I freshened up and headed for the coffee bar. I wanted to take stock of my first day in post here in Khartoum, but no sooner had I settled down to enjoy a pot of coffee than my mobile started to ring. I was surprised to get a call, for this was my Sudan mobile, and I'd given the number out to hardly anyone. Roger had it. So did Mona and Omer. But that was about all.

'Mukesh Kapila,' I answered.

I heard a soft female voice. 'Hello...' It was followed by something that I couldn't quite catch.

'Hello, this is Mukesh Kapila,' I repeated. 'Is that Mona?'

'Oh, excuse me,' the voice purred. 'I think I have the wrong number.' The mysterious woman hung up. She'd sounded very much like a local, and I thought little more of it until a few minutes later my phone rang again. It was the same caller, and again she apologised for getting the wrong number. By the time she called for a third time,

I was starting to doubt that she was doing so by accident.

'Sorry, I've got the wrong number again, haven't I?' the voice giggled. 'But now that I'm speaking to you, I'm curious... Would you maybe like some company?'

'Well, no, thank you, I'm not in need of any company. I have many friends...'

'Oh well, it was nice talking to you,' the voice replied, before ringing off.

How on earth had this mystery caller got my number, I wondered. The phone rang for a fourth time. 'Mukesh Kapila,' I answered, warily.

'It's me again,' the voice said. 'I hope you don't mind me calling, but I think you've just arrived in the country?

You must be lonely. You are sure you don't...'

'No, really, I'm fine on my own,' I interjected. 'And, please, don't call again. I'm not in need of any company, thanks.'

I rang off thinking this was all very strange. Who had given her my number and encouraged her to call? For sure, someone must have. And what might lie behind her doing so?

I threw myself into my work, spending the next few days examining how the various UN agencies were being run. What I uncovered was far from encouraging. Each agency had a fleet of Land Cruisers assigned to it, but there was no pooling of vehicles. So if one UN agency was unusually busy, it couldn't call on the vehicles and drivers of a sister agency. The costs in terms of hiring extra transport and drivers were exorbitant, and I sensed that someone was running a nice little scam here. One of my first actions was to do away with that system and pool vehicles as a unified fleet. It caused enormous ructions and not a little bad blood.

Worse, I discovered there were scores of 'ghost projects' within UNDP, wherein once bona fide development projects had never been officially closed. As a result, vehicles allocated to those projects remained so seemingly forever. On weekdays, there were scores of 'UN' vehicles being used to do the school run. I ruled that all such ghost projects had to be closed. This caused huge upset amongst a nexus of Sudan government officials and UNDP staff taking advantage of what was in effect a massive free lunch.

But most disturbing of all was the fact that for several years UNDP's Sudan accounts hadn't been given a clean bill of health. Repeatedly, the external auditors had found themselves unable to sign off on a budget of millions of dollars. Contracts to supply vehicles and other hardware were being arranged as 'inside jobs'. In short, UNDP was rife with petty corruption and profiteering. It had a dispirited culture wherein people tried to do the minimum possible while making as much as they could on the side.

I was shocked and appalled.

The UN's track record was little better in terms of its supposed *raison d'être* in Sudan – delivering aid and development across the country. The approach was chaotic and piecemeal, each agency working in isolation from the others. I drew up a map of where each operated, and it soon became clear that areas deemed 'too difficult' were being ignored. There was a mass of activity around Khartoum and a mass of programmes in the south, but the east and west of the country were largely off-limits.

As a result, vast areas were being all but totally neglected, including a remote western region called Darfur.

THREE

The great majority of us are required to live a life of constant, systematic duplicity.

Boris Pasternak

I DREW UP A PROGRAMME TO CUT WASTE AND CORRUPTION, and to get people motivated. I drew up plans for a one-country approach, with an outline of how each UN agency fitted into the bigger picture. At our Khartoum office, I encouraged staff to eat together in the canteen – which was already on its way to being refurbished – to help build one cohesive team. I stressed how vital this was in view of the coming peace, after which our role would rapidly change.

But I was barely a week into my posting when I received the first worried phone call from UN headquarters in New York. After asking politely after my welfare, the caller cautioned me to think carefully before making changes. I was warned – albeit obliquely – that I was treading on too many toes within the big UN agencies and that complaints were being voiced in New York. I was disrespecting long-held privileges and rights, and I was making enemies.

I told the caller that many of those rights and privileges were well past their sell-by-date, and they were unjustifiable. In Sudan, the UN's name was being misused and abused. I reminded him that I had two decades' prior experience running major aid programmes and that I hadn't been hired to make myself popular. My task was to reform the UN in preparation for when peace was declared in Sudan, and it was a task that I was driven to achieve.

That evening after work, Roger, my security chief, paid me his promised visit at the Hilton. We took our kebabs plus cold (non-alcoholic) beers into the hotel garden, where he figured we could talk in private. He proceeded to give me his unofficial security briefing – the one that he hadn't felt able to deliver at the UN office.

He told me that most, if not all, of our local staff – Omer, my driver, included – worked for the National Intelligence and Security Services (NISS), more commonly known as the *Mukhabarat*. They were either full-time Mukhabarat employees, or they were held on a retainer to report anything of interest. Moreover, I should act on the presumption that the UN offices were comprehensively bugged. Anything I said or did would be monitored or intercepted, or reported by human means.

Roger suspected that the Hilton was equally well wired, which is why we were having our chat in the garden. He told me that there was little we could do about any of this. In Sudan, the Mukhabarat was the real power behind the president, and nothing of significance happened in the country without its blessing. I thanked Roger for being so frank, and we lapsed into an uneasy silence, the rhythmic chirp-chirp of the crickets in the gardens echoing all around us.

Khartoum had an altogether more sinister feel after everything he told me. I knew from my New York briefings that Sudan was pretty much a police state, but I hadn't expected to be quite this closely bugged and spied upon. It was eerie and strangely unsettling, especially for someone coming from a country like the UK, where individual freedoms are taken almost for granted.

The following morning, I took a phone call from William Patey, the British ambassador to Sudan. In his booming voice he offered me his welcome, and I asked him what exactly was the form prior to having my credentials accepted. Was I really trapped in the UN office or the Hilton? William advised me that going out for social occasions should be fine, and he invited me over for dinner.

Omer drove me to his residence, where a fine spread had been laid on. The French ambassador, plus the Dutch and American chargés d'affaires had also been invited. I found them hugely receptive to my message that with the advent of peace, the UN had to be ready to step up to the mark in Sudan. With peace it would no longer be enough simply to hand out relief aid and keep people alive. With peace would come the driving need to address the underlying causes of poverty. Only by doing so could we rebuild the dignity of the suffering, and that had to be the ultimate aim of humanitarian work – to restore people's sense of self-worth.

We couldn't simply give people a piece of bread; we needed to discover why they were hungry and empower them to address the underlying causes of that hunger. This was something that had a deep personal resonance for me. It was a lesson that I'd learned repeatedly during my years as a humanitarian worker, and I had experienced it for myself in the earliest years of my childhood.

I was about seven years old when I first became aware of the existence of poverty in India. My father managed a factory making mining machinery in Bihar state, one of the poorest regions of India. Each week, he would drive my mother and me into the local town to stock up on supplies. I would get down from our Mahindra jeep dressed in my smart shorts and shirt, and all around me would be half-starved locals. Women had babies clutched to their shrivelled breasts. Kids thin and scraggy would be tearing all over the place.

I would be treated to ice cream and Coke by the local storekeeper while my mother shopped. At this time there was still food rationing in India, and the country was receiving massive amounts of overseas aid. My mother would get her ration of wheat flour from a sack stamped with a symbol of stars and stripes clasped in a pair of hands. One day I asked my mother what that symbol meant. I always put such questions to her, for I was a little daunted by my father's impatient ways.

My mother explained to me that this was the flag of a country called 'America'. Stencilled around the flag were the words: 'A gift of the American people – food for peace', plus the code 'PL-480'. Public Law 480 was a piece of US legislation that allowed for food aid to be sent to India in the 1960s. I asked my mother why we were eating food from a far-off land. She told me that India was not producing enough to feed itself and that we were a 'poor country'. I remember feeling shocked. I thought to myself, *but how can India be poor?*

I had just finished my first term away at school in Chandigarh, a city in the north of India, and I'd begun to devour books about India's rich history and culture. I learned that some two millennia ago, India's wealth accounted for a third of total global GDP. In other words, a third of the world's entire income was generated in India. I read stories about Ashoka the Great, the enlightened emperor who ruled nearly all of modern-day India at that time. Ashoka was a devotee of Buddhism, non-violence, love, truth and tolerance, and he'd reigned over a greater India in a golden age of peace.

I read about how India had thrown off the yoke of British colonial rule, winning her independence. Yet at the same time I now knew that this noble and ancient nation was surviving on handouts from a country called America. I didn't know what to think. On the one hand I was amazed at how great this 'America' must be. On the other, I felt shame and anger that we needed its help.

At the end of the school holidays, I travelled back to Chandigarh, making a 48-hour train journey from Bihar to the Punjab. The railways of India are where you witness all of life. The train stopped at countless stations and, now that I actually looked, India did indeed appear poor. There were stick-thin kids on the verge of starvation seemingly everywhere. They sat in the dirt and fought over food scraps thrown from the train windows.

Those images were seared into my brain. This was my country, one that I had believed was an ancient and exalted land. Now I knew the truth: we were forced to survive on handouts given by a people halfway around the world. If there was a moment when my childish pride took a pounding, this was it. And somewhere in my heart I knew that we didn't need America's food aid alone: we needed to be given the tools, the skills and the resources to feed ourselves. As a nation, we needed to be given back our dignity and self-respect.

I doubted if any of the diplomats assembled around William Patey's dinner table shared such direct experiences of poverty and indignity, but they did seem to share my passion for bringing peace and true development to Sudan. In this we appeared united, which was a welcome contrast to my recent experiences within the UN. I ended the evening cheered by fine food and fine company, and having decided that William Patey was going to prove a great ally on whatever journey lay ahead, as would his fellow diplomats.

It was 19 April, so approaching three weeks into my stint as UN chief, when I received a surprise early-morning phone call. I was being invited to meet the Sudanese president to present my credentials. I couldn't wait to get this over and done with. Omer brought the car, and I told him to make for the president's palace. Upon arrival we were waved into a small, modest-looking compound – his private residence.

I was ushered into the lounge area and offered a seat on one of the comfy sofas. I had my credentials clutched in my hand, consisting of a letter on beautiful parchment signed by Kofi Annan, introducing me to the president and begging his acceptance. It was bound in a fancy leather case and it looked very impressive and formal.

A figure arrived with surprisingly little pomp or ceremony. I knew little about President Omar Al Bashir, other than that he was a former army officer who had come to power in an 'election' that was largely boycotted. In spite of this, he was the internationally recognised head of state and deserved all the respect that position conferred. He was slender and ascetic looking, with fine features, although his pristine white *jalabiya* and turban probably made him look taller than he was.

It felt decidedly odd handing this man a leather-bound document as opposed to shaking hands, but I knew that was what was expected of me. He took it without reading it and passed it to his assistant. We sat, and tea was served.

'Dr Kapila, I'd like to bid you welcome to Sudan,' the president began. He was surprisingly softly spoken, and if you didn't listen carefully you might miss what he was saying. 'I hope you will have a long and peaceful stay here. I think you are not unfamiliar with our country?'

I smiled. 'Mr President, I am very pleased to be back. I have heard it said that those who drink from the Nile are fated to return, and it seems to be true.'

The two of us shared a moment of laughter.

'Indeed,' he agreed, 'so it is said by many. We certainly are glad to have you here.'

'Mr President, my secretary-general, Kofi Annan, has asked me to pass on his warm regards and to inform you that the UN is at the service of Sudan to help in every way possible.'

'Thank you. Please convey my gratitude for all the food aid, clean water and medicines that the UN is providing. These things are greatly appreciated.'

'Mr President, I'd like to ask you how you see the future unfolding for your country and what key piece of advice you might offer me during my tenure here. I'm particularly keen to hear your views on the ongoing

Naivasha peace talks and how the UN might further the cause of peace.'

The president stirred his tea pensively. 'Dr Kapila, I have very great hopes for Naivasha. I am optimistic a peace agreement can be signed. I am particularly hopeful because then we can begin to talk about real development – as opposed to emergency aid – and how to improve our infrastructure, water supply and healthcare, and how to advance the country more generally. This is what all Sudanese people want, Dr Kapila, as I'm sure you know.'

'Mr President, I'm so pleased to hear this. This is what the UN is here for, and we are at your disposal.'

At that moment a figure appeared at his shoulder and a few words were exchanged in Arabic. I knew instinctively that this was the signal that my time was up. The president rose to his feet and uttered his apologies, but other commitments meant that he had to leave. He offered me his hand and then he was gone. I had felt no searing connection with him, no compelling bond, but at the same time I had felt that this was a man with whom I could do business.

As Omer drove me back to my office, I reflected upon my good fortune. *Twenty-one days* – this was a record in terms of time taken by any UN chief to get their credentials accepted. It now remained to be seen how long I would survive, for my post was seen as being something of a poisoned chalice, one subject to impossible pressures from within and without. But for now at least I'd got the president's blessing, and I felt like I could fly. I could attend conferences and public events, I could travel the country and I could go into the field. And at last I could move out of the Hilton!

A house was found for me in a leafy Khartoum suburb. It was a large concrete slab of a thing, with a massive, echoing sitting room and a dining area off to one side. There were six bedrooms on two floors, so it was far too large for me alone. But at least the lounge opened onto a high-walled garden, which would be fine for holding open-air receptions, entertaining being an important part of my post. Roger gave the place the once over and ordered some extra security.

Wire grilles were to be fitted to all external doors and windows, and a reinforced door was to be placed at the top of the stairs leading from the ground to the first floor. That way I could lock and isolate the top floor from the rest of the house. Khartoum felt like a safe city to me, and it all seemed rather over the top, but Roger insisted that these were the standard security precautions for anyone in my position.

In the basement was a whole separate world of stores and staff accommodation. I hired Mary as my housekeeper, a black African woman who hailed from the south of the country. Mary had five children, but to me she only looked to be in her mid-20s. She was absolutely striking, with fine ebony features, and she held herself with a proud, dignified poise.

Some years back Mary, her husband and their children had come to Khartoum, fleeing the war. Mary's husband had gone to work in Libya, but he had subsequently abandoned her and the children. Mary was a Christian, and she had learned to speak good English at the school that she'd attended in the south. I offered her and her children a home in the basement, and she quickly took charge of my household. My cook, Ahmed, was an Arab from the north and he was a Muslim. I hired him on the basis that he had served as chef for other internationals, but all I can say is that they must have had stomachs lined with iron. He proved to be an awful cook. He knew how to prepare three dishes: fried meat, fried vegetables, or *baba ganoush* – a creamed aubergine and onions concoction, also fried of course.

His baba ganoush was just about edible, but the other dishes were not. At first I tried to educate him, but Ahmed was immovable. In his book, oil was good. He was a muscular, body-builder type, and I guess he was good looking in a nightclub-bouncer kind of way. He was married, but fairly quickly I realised that he had taken a shine to Mary. It showed in the extra flexing of his muscles whenever she was around. I began to wonder if love was blossoming under my roof, and I took to teasing Mary about it gently.

'So, Mary, dear, how is Ahmed today? I hope he's been looking after you? If you get a chance, try to teach him how to cook, will you? He's drowning me in oil.'

As with many southern Sudanese, Mary proved to have a great sense of humour – once I'd got her to understand that even a UN chief was human and not averse to a bit of joking. With Ahmed, there was too much muscle-bound Arab manliness to ever partake in a good dose of English teasing. As for Ahmed's infatuation, Mary was having none of it. As far as she was concerned, Ahmed hailed from the Arab north, and it was his kind that had killed her grandmother and oppressed her people for decades.

Having set up my home, life fell into a pattern. I'd rise at 6 a.m. with the muezzin's call for prayers echoing from the nearby minaret and sit down to a plate of rubbery white bread and eggs swimming in oil, washed down with Ahmed's barely drinkable tea. Omer, my driver/spy, would arrive at 7 sharp, propel me into my seat at the right rear, and 20 minutes later I'd be at work.

In the days following my acceptance by the president, I redoubled my efforts to revamp UN operations in Sudan. To me, the urgency of such change was paramount. Having been briefed that a peace deal would be signed in the next few months, the UN had to be ready. So many times in recent history we'd won the war but lost the peace – Afghanistan post-9/11 being the prime example. We'd routed the Taliban, then rushed off on a misguided adventure to invade Iraq, and in so doing had failed to do enough to make the Afghan peace take hold.

Believing peace in Sudan to be just around the corner, I drove my agenda of change relentlessly, but in doing so I made powerful enemies and only a few friends. Due to my position, no one felt able to be rude to my face, but behind my back the rumour mill was working overtime. I detected this in the odd bit of gossip I overheard, and I was totally unprepared for how vicious and vituperative the UN system could be.

I was doing one of my weekly walkabouts of the UN premises when I noticed a young woman shunted into a dark corner. What drew me to her was that she hadn't rushed over to greet me, as many did. She sat there working on her laptop, quietly getting on with things. I asked to be introduced to her, and I enquired as to what exactly she was doing. Her official job was to collate field reports, but I sensed that she was hopelessly underutilised and bored.

Nadia El Maaroufi was half-New Zealander and half-Moroccan. She looked calm and somewhat librarian-like with her severe wire- rimmed glasses. From the briefing papers I had received on arrival, I already knew that she had good report-writing skills and a fine knowledge of Sudan. My instinct told me that she would make a great special assistant, which is a professional post of real trust and confidence. I had been looking for one ever since getting here, and I made her the invitation right there and then.

'If you accept, you're going to work with me for six months intensively,' I told her. 'As UN chief, I am on-call twenty-four hours a day, seven days a week. Your role will be to help facilitate that. You will open, read and prioritise my mail, and you'll keep a watch on my email. If I go to conferences, you'll be at my side. When I go to field projects, you'll travel with me. I guarantee you'll be totally exhausted within six months, at which time I'll get you another job so you can recover.'

Nadia jumped at the offer. She soon proved my instinctive faith in her to be justified, as it was she who first alerted me to the coming storm in a remote, semi-desert region of Sudan called Darfur.

It was 25 April 2003 – so not yet fully a week after getting my credentials accepted by the president – when Nadia popped her head around my office door. She had a somewhat worried expression upon her face.

'Mukesh, we're getting scattered reports of a rebel attack in the far west of the country. If true, it's significant, because the rebels claim to have destroyed a number of Sudanese military aircraft at one of the state capitals in Darfur.'

'What's the source of the reporting?' I queried. 'The rebels? Or do we have independent verification?'

'I've seen a couple of very short articles in Khartoum's Arabic press, plus the odd report filtering in by email from the rebels. It's a group no one seems to have heard of, calling themselves the SLM.'

'SLM? SLM stands for?' 'Sudan Liberation Movement.'

'Probably over-exaggerated,' I told her. 'Aircraft destroyed? I can't believe the Sudanese military are that vulnerable. But thanks for alerting me. We don't have any people down there, do we, to verify?' 'We have a couple of local UNICEF staff based in El Fasher. I'll ask them what they've heard, shall I?'

'Yes. Perfect. Keep me posted. Oh, and get Roger to give me a security briefing when he's free.'

Darfur was one of the areas least covered by UN operations. Basically, we had zero presence there. I made a mental note to see how we might increase our footprint, just in case real trouble was brewing, and then I turned back to more pressing matters, like the coming round of peace negotiations. A few hours later, Roger put in an appearance, and I asked him if there was any substance to the reports from Darfur.

'My sources confirm there has been a military skirmish,' Roger said. 'Apparently, government forces were caught by surprise by the rebels, so possibly this is another front opening in the war. The question is, is it SPLM-backed? At this stage, we don't know. But the government lost several helicopters and aircraft, which suggests a real military capability on the rebel side.'

SPLM stands for the Sudan People's Liberation Movement – the rebels of the south who'd fought the government forces to a standstill. It was between the

SPLM's political leaders and the Khartoum government that the peace was now being brokered. If this Darfur rebel group had the backing of the SPLM, they would be a force to be reckoned with. Opening up a new front in the conflict would not be good for the peace negotiations, and Roger and I decided we'd have to keep a close eye on Darfur.

I grabbed a map so that we could take a good look at the area. Darfur is a vast stretch of semi-arid desert and mountainous terrain approximately the size of France. It was clearly unacceptable that the UN had almost no presence there, although I hardly found it surprising. If there was trouble brewing in Darfur that might derail the peace process, then we needed to be there to help defuse it. I told myself that just as soon I could get onto it we'd have to boost our visibility.

But I had no idea how fast things were going to start moving now in Darfur.

FOUR

Every tomorrow has two handles. We can take hold of it by the handle of anxiety, or by the handle of faith.

Unknown author

NADIA STARTED TO RECEIVE INCREASING NUMBERS OF REPORTS of civilians fleeing Darfur and turning up at the main urban centres – El Fasher, Nyala and El Geneina. If civilians were getting caught in the crossfire between the rebels and government forces, this was a worrying development. As the lead humanitarian agency in the country, it was the UN's responsibility to safeguard civilian life, and as UN chief it fell squarely upon my shoulders to ensure that we did so.

I felt a burning desire to live up to that responsibility. While I'd trained as a medical doctor, I'd been drawn to humanitarian work as my life's vocation. This was rooted in a deep-seated desire to help others, especially those in the developing world who had little access to life's opportunities. Indeed, I had been one of those individuals myself, for as a 16-year-old Indian schoolboy I'd been given the opportunity of a lifetime when granted the best education in England. My parents were reasonably upwardly mobile, and the most important thing for them was getting their children a good education. By age seven, I'd exhausted the learning opportunities in Bihar. My parents couldn't afford to put me into a private boarding school, so the only option had to be a mission school. Although they were strict Hindus, they had few qualms about sending me to St John's, an Irish Christian Brothers' school in Chandigarh. Luckily my grandparents were living just nearby, so I could stay with them during term time.

St John's may have been Catholic in name, but any overtly religious teaching dealt with all faiths, including our own Indian belief systems chiefly Hinduism, Buddhism and Islam. It was heavily subsidised and only cost 45 rupees a month, or the then equivalent of US$5. That was just about affordable to a middle-class family like my own, but not to the great majority of Indians.

The Brothers wore starched white smocks that must have been sheer torture in the heat. Brother Drew was my favourite. To me, he seemed at least 100 feet tall and 100 years old, and he smoked like a chimney, but he was mild-mannered, softly spoken and kind. After my Bihar schooling, I started off as one of the weakest pupils, but under Brother Drew's tuition I rapidly improved. I graduated from St John's with pole position in the leaving exams.

It was 1971, and that summer in Chandigarh was baking hot. I took refuge in the city library, which was blissfully air-conditioned. I'd cycle there in the morning and spend the day surrounded by books and magazines, and that was how I came across a short advert by the Office for Placing Overseas Schoolboys (OPOS), a small trust based in somewhere called Pinner, England.

'Scholarships available to come to Great Britain for A Levels,' the advert read. 'Write to this address for an application form.'

The magazine was six months old, and the deadline for that year's applications had long passed. But I purchased an aerogramme anyway and penned a short letter begging for a place. It was written from the heart, and by sending it I'd wasted nothing but a few pennies for the postage.

Having sent it, I promptly forgot about it, until days later a telegram arrived. In India, telegrams normally signalled bad news. If there was a death in the family, sending one was the only quick and reliable way to inform distant relatives. But when we ripped it open, this one turned out to be from OPOS: 'Scholarship still available. Stop. Please cable reply soonest.'

It was late August, and one of the OPOS scholars had just dropped out. By chance, my letter had arrived at exactly the right time. I sent a telegram in response: 'Scholarship accepted. Stop. What do we do next?' Five days later, a package of detailed instructions arrived from England.

That evening we sat outside the house, while the neighbours weighed in with their advice. How to get 'Babloo' – an affectionate nickname that everyone called me – to school in England had become a community effort. My father pointed out that we would have to move super-fast. I had no passport and no visa, and in India such documents usually took months to acquire.

My father duly related the entire story of the scholarship

to the passport official, a grand-looking Sikh. He was clearly very impressed. 'There is no question about it – the boy has to go!' he announced, twirling his magnificent moustache. Within 72 hours, I had my passport. In the meantime, the project to 'get the boy to England' had taken on a life of its own. The women were busy knitting thick woollen jumpers of hideous designs. Ancient magazines had been unearthed in the hope of finding the types of patterns that would be in vogue in England.

Lastly, we went to the travel agent and brought a ticket on Pan Am Flight 001 for 3,000 rupees, or $400. There were no cheap flights back then, and it would be the equivalent of some $5,000 today. My father had to take out a loan to cover the cost.

When filling out the OPOS forms, I'd been asked to choose what school I wished to attend. I recognised the world-famous 'Eton', and I'd also heard of 'Harrow' because India's Prime Minister Nehru went there. I told myself that I didn't want to go to any common school that everyone had heard of, so I wrote on the form: 'Any school but Eton or Harrow.' And so I was allocated to a house of learning called 'Wellington College'.

My father had travelled to Germany in 1959 by ship, departing Bombay via the Suez Canal and Italy, and travelling onwards by train to Berlin. Grandma now packed his ancient wooden trunk full to the brim, leaving precious little room for my personal possessions. I picked up the piece of coal from my father's mine, wrapped it reverently in a handkerchief and placed that inside. At the last minute, he decided that I needed a watch. He unbuckled his beautiful Swiss Favre-Leuba, one that he had purchased when working in Germany, and gave it to me.

That watch would last until 1994, when I was one of the first to travel into Rwanda in the immediate aftermath of the genocide. In that year-zero moment, when I came face-to-face with unspeakable hatred and horror, my father's watch stopped working once and for all. Yet I'd guard it forever as a keepsake, for it symbolised to me two precious things: my parents' love and my absolute conviction of the need to fight against man's inhumanity to man.

The 2nd of September 1971 was the day of my departure to England, and I watched my father's wooden trunk disappear towards the waiting aircraft with all its shipping labels still attached. Then I stepped forward to present my passport. There were few security checks back then, and I passed quickly through departures feeling more than a little lost.

Pan Am 001 was a brand-new Boeing 707, which started in Hong Kong, then routed via Delhi, Karachi, Tehran, Istanbul, Frankfurt and on to London. Some 48 hours after boarding that flight, I stepped through the grand gates of Wellington College with a fiercely beating heart. Here I was at long last about to start what I hoped would be my dream education.

As I had been given the chance of a lifetime at age 16, so I believed that others across the developing world deserved such golden opportunities. And as chief of the United Nations in Sudan, I figured I was in a unique position to start delivering on such convictions.

Within days of hearing those first worrying reports from Darfur, Roger and I decided to send a team to investigate. We'd need clearance from the Sudanese government to do so, for all humanitarian agencies had to clear proposed travel via the Humanitarian Aid Commission (HAC), part of the ministry for humanitarian affairs. Roger had briefed me that HAC was largely staffed by Mukhabarat agents, so in effect I would be seeking clearance directly from the country's security services, but there was no way around that.

The system for seeking clearances was horribly convoluted. I would need to send a manifest to HAC, detailing the names and passport details of all personnel intending to travel, their destinations and any specialist equipment carried. If I was sending a UN radio operator, he or she would need to be accompanied by an HAC 'counterpart'. That counterpart would be able to listen in on all our radio calls, which was most convenient for the Mukhabarat's purposes.

The HAC office was a good hour's drive from our office. It was a run-down, crowded place lacking in air-conditioning, and it was a baking-hot hive of intrigue. My key point of contact there was Sulaf Udeen, a tall, imposing character who was in his early 40s and balding. He wore Western-style dress, unless he was attending an official HAC function, wherein white turban and jalabiya were de rigueur.

I'd had a handful of previous dealings with Sulaf, and he'd proven polite, charming and urbane at all times. He spoke excellent English, and I figured he was the acceptable face of HAC – the front man for the Mukhabarat's hard-liners. By contrast, those at the inner core of HAC were renowned for being devious and manipulative. They never directly refused access, for to do so would be tantamount to frustrating vital humanitarian work. Instead, they simply failed to process an application, or they would use 'insecurity' as an excuse not to allow people in. Occasionally, they'd wait until a particularly troublesome member of staff had gone overseas on leave and fail to issue them a re-entry visa – therefore getting any unwanted UN personnel out of the way.

Dealing with HAC was like playing a game of cat-and-mouse. I was fully expecting the same treatment over our request to send a team into Darfur, so I was pleasantly surprised when Sulaf secured our permissions more or less without delay. The government appeared to have been wrong-footed by the rebel uprising in the far west of the country, and perhaps they felt getting the UN in might help shed some light on what was happening.

Our team flew in only to discover that the number of civilians fleeing the conflict was on the rise. Small informal camps were springing up around the main towns as people congregated for safety. There were water and food shortages in the region, and competition over scarce resources appeared to be driving the fighting. In short, there appeared to be a low-level humanitarian emergency unfolding in Darfur.

I held meetings with my key UN agencies to see how we might boost our presence in the region, so as to assess needs and strategise our response. But the reaction from my agency heads was that in sending our people into Darfur we would risk compromising relations with the Sudanese government. In effect, they were saying they'd prefer to keep things sweet with Khartoum, regardless of the humanitarian needs in the remote west of the country.

Their response didn't exactly surprise me. It was the same old story. Any attempt to change the status quo – or to shake up vested interests – was going to be fiercely resisted. I figured I needed some kind of feint to get us into Darfur, some strategy to lever open access. But as I set my mind to thinking what kind of form that might take, the situation took on an altogether more sinister dimension.

Around the outskirts of Khartoum there were a series of long- established camps for internally displaced persons (IDPs). The decades of fighting in the south of the country had forced millions to flee. Some had moved into refugee camps in Kenya and Uganda, but many had fled north and ended up clustered around Khartoum. With the prospect of peace now firmly on the agenda, those people were hopeful of returning to their villages and re-establishing long-abandoned lives, and part of the UN's function would be to help them do so.

But in the first weeks of May 2003, we started to receive reports of a new influx into the Khartoum camps. Whole families had come on foot, or partly hitching lifts on trucks, making the epic journey of 1,000 kilometres or more to escape the troubles in Darfur. As soon as we learned of these new arrivals, I knew that things had to be far more serious in Darfur. People only fled such a distance if there was some real, tangible fear driving them onwards.

As May ground on towards June, the numbers of new arrivals increased. At the same time, Roger was hearing increasing numbers of reports from his sources of the true nature of the conflict unfolding in the region. There were stories of villages being bombed by aircraft and of bands of marauding gunmen on horseback.

I raised the issue with William Patey, the British ambassador, plus the French and American diplomats based in Khartoum. They were sure to have excellent sources of intelligence, and I wanted to know if they were hearing similar things. Gradually, a more coherent picture began to emerge. This no longer appeared to be random skirmishing due to drought and food shortages; there was some kind of organised and targeted fighting going on in Darfur.

More than ever now I needed a ruse to jack up our presence on the ground in Darfur, for only then could I find out what was really going on there. I decided to seek help from someone outside the UN system. I asked a friendly donor government to put forward a suitable person, and I got Daniel Christensen, a smart young Dane with considerably more political nous than many aid workers. Daniel didn't have a great deal of humanitarian experience, but he did have a sharp brain for sifting fact from fiction, which was exactly what I needed. He flew out to Khartoum, and I set him up in my office to head up my newly formed 'Darfur Crisis Unit'. I had no idea yet what this unit would do, but simply by the act of forming it we were taking the initiative. Via Sulaf, my contact at HAC, I got permission to send Daniel to visit the three main towns in Darfur. My brief was simple: I told him to get behind the UN jargon and the government security-speak, and establish ground truth. What was the root cause of the strife? Who was attacking the villages? What specifically were the civilians fleeing from? And what could the UN do about it?

Daniel returned to Khartoum after a journey into Darfur lasting just a few days. I already felt that I could trust him completely. I brought him into my office and shut the door. The only other person present was Nadia, my special assistant, who I was coming to rely on more and more as my sounding board. Of course, the Mukhabarat was probably listening in via electronic means, but I figured it was good for them to know what we knew.

'So, what did you discover?' I asked him.

'First off, there are large numbers of IDPs around the major towns,' Daniel began. 'That, sir, I can absolutely confirm...'

'Mukesh, Daniel, it's Mukesh,' I reminded him. 'Go on.'

'Well, they're getting very little help, and they seem frightened of being attacked again. I tried to get to the heart of who attacked them, but bear in mind I had government minders with me at all times. They told me they'd been attacked by people who came in the night on horseback. "Nomad Arab horsemen" is how they explained it. But why those "nomad Arab horsemen" are doing it, and who's behind them, no one seemed willing or able to tell.'

'Anything else?' I prompted.

'Yes. I heard repeated reports of aircraft attacking villages, and at Nyala and El Fasher I noticed that there were military aircraft on the airstrips. The situation is chaotic and fast moving, but, needless to say, sir – sorry, Mukesh – only the government has aircraft.'

Under the circumstances, Daniel had done a fine job of clarifying things, and I couldn't have expected more. I told him as much and asked him to draft a detailed trip report. I double-checked all that Daniel had told me with Roger: was the Sudanese government using aircraft to attack villages in Darfur? A little reluctantly, Roger confirmed his sources indicated that indeed they were.

I read Daniel's report with a growing feeling of unease bordering on dread. He estimated that some 200,000 people had fled the conflict, and that refugees were starting to spill over into neighbouring Chad, which meant that this had now become an issue with international dimensions. I decided to raise this with Sulaf, my liaison at HAC. Sulaf received me in his cramped cubicle of an office, and once tea was served I got down to business.

'Sulaf, my good friend, I need you to tell me what's going on in the west of Sudan,' I ventured. 'I hear alarming reports. What exactly are your boys up to in Darfur?'

We had this curious way of communicating, which reflected the fact that Sulaf's English had a slightly dated and formalised ring to it, as if he'd learned it during colonial days.

'Well, Dr Kapila, I'm glad you've brought that up,' he replied. 'I believe there are some brigands and outlaws that are attacking villages and stealing things down there. But rest assured, the government is investigating and trying to bring security to the area, and to get these lawless bandits under control.'

'My point is, Sulaf, do we have a serious humanitarian situation? My fear is that we do. All the reports that I'm getting suggest this, and if so I'll need to increase the UN's presence, for humanitarian crises are our chief concern.'

'No, no, no, Mukesh, it's nothing like that,' Sulaf smiled. 'No need for the UN to go rushing down there like mother hen. I will find out more and let you know, but, believe me, it is certainly not a humanitarian problem of any great significance. Don't worry, we'll soon have it all under control.'

Sulaf gave me a solemn promise that he'd check and get back to me. I had little option but to take him at his word, yet I wasn't particularly comforted. The last time that I'd come across desperate civilians fleeing their homeland they were running from a threat of chilling power and malevolence, and I feared that something similar was unfolding now in Darfur.

In the aftermath of the 1990 Gulf War, the then US president Bush had called upon the Iraqi people to rise up and topple Saddam Hussein. Saddam had responded by unleashing his dogs of war on the forces of the Iraqi resistance, chief amongst them the Kurds. As Saddam's forces began massacring the Kurds, so they had fled ever deeper into the northern mountains. It was the winter of 1991, and conditions were bitter and murderous on the higher peaks.

When television news pictures filtered out of that remote region showing old women and young children freezing to death in the snow, there was a massive public outcry. Here were the very people that we had urged to topple Saddam Hussein, and yet they were squeezed between his guns and the unforgiving mountains. It was the British government's then aid agency, the Overseas Development Administration (ODA), that spearheaded the resulting relief effort, alongside the British military.

I was at home in our Cambridgeshire cottage reading my youngest, Ruth, *The Wolf and the Seven Little Kids*, when there was a call from my boss at ODA. Dr David Nabarro was somewhere in the remote Kurdish hinterland, and via the echoing void of static over the satellite phone link he told me, 'It's bad here, Mukesh. Very bad. Get me lots of people. And get yourself here. *Now.*'

He asked me to gather together as many doctors, nurses and emergency workers as I could. And so I launched this bizarre recruitment effort whereby I phoned around every hospital, fire station and police station I could think of. Within 48 hours, I'd recruited 80 volunteers, united by nothing more than a common sense of purpose and huge amounts of goodwill. We first came together at a Stansted airport hotel, wherein I used the ballroom to brief them on the mission. From there we flew to Incirlik Airbase in southern Turkey before heading off in a convoy of buses, complete with a Royal Marines military escort. On the border with Iraq, the Marines had established a tented camp, but it wasn't until the morning that we realised what lay before us: we truly faced the humanitarian challenge of a lifetime. Eighty very green volunteers were now suddenly frontline 'aid workers', and there were thousands of old women, pregnant mothers and young children stuck on perilous, snow-bound slopes.

As many as 50,000 Kurds were freezing to death, and

the snow was still falling. To have scaled those peaks in such harsh conditions was itself testimony to the horror that Saddam had unleashed upon them. We didn't have the capacity to fly them all to safety, so we decided to establish 'way stations' providing hot food and drink at five-kilometre intervals up the mountain. We divided into teams of four, each consisting of a nurse, a fireman, a mechanic, plus one soldier. In that way, we managed the seemingly impossible: getting those terrified civilians to stumble down from the peaks. Within 48 hours we'd managed to get everyone off the mountain, with the Marines providing a vital security screen and warplanes enforcing a 'no-fly' zone overhead.

Every few months thereafter, I travelled into northern Iraq to assess the ongoing humanitarian needs of the Kurds. The Kurdish rebels took me to visit Halabja, the scene of a horrific attack.

Saddam's forces had dropped chemical weapons on the town, and many hundreds had died. Every second person seemed to have some kind of deformity: their eyes were bulging, their skin was burned off, or their hair was falling out by the handful. The deformities in children were the most disturbing: babies were born with their limbs twisted, their heads misshapen and with their brains not developed properly.

The Kurdish rebels had taken me to Halabja to show me the kind of horror that had forced old women and pregnant mothers to scale an impossible mountain in the midst of a treacherous winter. I learned the extreme levels of brutality required to force these people to flee from places they had inhabited for generations. Such people would never abandon their homes unless their very lives were under threat. That was the case in the 1990s in Kurdish Iraq, and I feared the same a decade later in Darfur.

Over repeated visits to Kurdistan, I got to know the rebels well, shaking hands with the leaders over the aid that we were delivering. The Kurds had their own TV cameras, and they filmed and broadcast news of my visits.

Eventually, Saddam must have decided that enough was enough. He took a case against me in the Iraqi courts, wherein I was charged *in absentia* with 'illegally entering the country and fomenting insurrection against the Iraqi state'. I was sentenced to death, and a price of $100,000 was put on my head, dead or alive. My first reaction upon hearing the news was to take great umbrage that I was only worth $100,000. But the menace was very real. This was the first death threat against me, and it made me realise that doing good for the suffering people of a country could land one in deep water.

In many conflicts, it is the rebel movements that are the means of freeing a nation and ushering in democratic change. Iraq showed me that taking aid to them would attract the wrath of those in power, who had the will and the means to kill.

FIVE

Hope is the poor man's bread.
George Herbert

IT WAS EARLY JUNE WHEN I DECIDED TO FLY SOUTH TO VISIT the chairman of the Sudan People's Liberation Movement (SPLM), the southern rebel leader Dr John Garang. I had already met those on the government side of the peace talks, and I needed to make the acquaintance of the other side. Equally importantly, I wanted to discover the southern rebels' perspective on Darfur. I could get no further sense out of Sulaf, other than that the trouble was being caused by 'anarchic bands of brigands' and that they would soon have it under control.

I flew from Khartoum to Kenya's capital city, Nairobi, and from there northwards to Lokichoggio, a massive aid outpost on the border with Sudan. 'Loki' was the de facto headquarters of the UN's southern Sudan operations, and it was from here that our fleet of transport aircraft flew north to do airdrops of food aid.

I had initiated the meeting with Garang, and before leaving Khartoum I'd had to file a flight plan. As UN chief, I had to make my meeting with the rebel leader as open and transparent as possible. The government had made it clear that they weren't happy about it but there was little they could openly do to stop it.

Garang was known for being a visionary and an intellectual, as well as a fierce liberation leader who had fought the forces of the government to a standstill. He now controlled practically the entire south of the country, which was no small achievement for a rebel leader who had started out with a rag-tag band of fighters in the bush. I was excited at the prospect of getting to meet him.

I was flying in with my head of southern Sudan operations, a Norwegian called Bernt Aasen. For years now, the UN's southern Sudan aid programme had been known as 'Operation Lifeline Sudan', or OLS for short, and OLS was Bernt's baby. Bernt struck me immediately as being the type of guy I could work with. He appeared to play none of the Machiavellian games that seemed so common to our northern Sudan operations.

The rendezvous with Garang was scheduled to take place at his rebel base near Rumbek, a tiny settlement in the midst of the bush. I had Nadia with me on this journey so she could receive, sift and prioritise calls or emails while I was busy with the rebel leader. The flight droned on for several hours, itself testimony to the sheer size of the country. I found myself feeling surprisingly relaxed, and I had a sense of what a historic meeting this might prove.

We touched down on a dirt airstrip that had been carved out of a flat expanse of vegetation. In contrast to the arid north, southern Sudan receives high rainfall, and the surrounding terrain was almost jungle-like in places. As I stepped off the aircraft, I got my first sight of Garang's rebel army. The Sudan People's Liberation Army (SPLA) is the military wing of the movement (SPLM). Rebel soldiers had thrown a cordon of security around the airstrip, not that they would greatly fear being attacked by government forces here.

The nearest 'enemy' troops were several hundred miles away, across the indistinct border that divided north from south Sudan. The rebel fighters were dressed in a hotchpotch of camouflage fatigues, and most were wearing flip-flops as opposed to proper army boots. Yet they struck me as being a disciplined fighting force, and mostly they were armed with modern-looking AK-47 assault rifles. Some looked remarkably young, and I suspected that when peace was declared the UN would have to prioritise disarming and rehabilitating a large number of child soldiers.

Once we'd disembarked the light aircraft, the soldiers covered it with cut branches, to camouflage its gleaming whiteness from the air. Bernt explained that this was a standard security precaution to try to prevent government forces from discovering the whereabouts of Garang's bush headquarters. If they found the rebel leader they could kill him, so he shifted his location regularly. It was also sensible to hide our aircraft in case a trigger-happy pilot fancied taking a pop at such an obvious target.

A ten-minute drive delivered us to a simple camp of wooden huts.

Beneath a grove of spreading acacia trees was gathered a group of black African men dressed in neat army fatigues. I recognised Garang immediately from the photos I'd seen of him. The entire entourage rose to their feet, and we shook hands. Garang's massive paw enveloped my own, and I couldn't help but notice what a huge bear of a man he was. His skin was of an incredibly dark hue, almost blue-black, and his eyes were deep-set and burning with a fierce intensity.

His grip proved as firm and powerful as I expected, and I sensed here an individual of genuine physical and intellectual stature – a true leader of men. His gaze met mine with a look of curiosity bordering on suspicion, as if he was trying to fathom the nature of the new man at the helm of the UN. By contrast, he greeted Bernt with genuine warmth, their handshake quickly becoming a bear hug of an embrace. I took the white plastic garden-style chair that was offered me – Garang and his entourage were seated likewise – and we were served tea beneath the trees. The usual polite chat went to and fro for a while before I decided it was time to get down to business. We had to fly in and out during daylight, which left us only a couple of hours here on the ground.

'Dr Garang, if I might be so bold as to come directly to the nature of my visit, for I know time is short…'

He held up a hand to silence me. 'It is often said that Khartoum has long ears.' His voice was incredibly gravelly, like low, rumbling thunder. 'You never know who might be listening.'

He asked everyone else to leave. Chairs were removed to

the opposite side of the acacia grove, leaving him and me facing each other. Garang poured some more tea and told me that he hoped we were safe to talk freely now. For a second, I wondered who it was in our delegation that he didn't trust, or perhaps this was his standard security procedure when meeting a stranger.

'Tell me, how is Khartoum?' he ventured. 'I haven't been there for such a long time.'

'It's becoming a modern city,' I told him. 'It's a rich city, and it is developing fast. But there are still few good restaurants and nowhere to get a cold beer!'

He threw back his head and let out a deep, booming laugh. 'I shall make sure we have some cold Tusker next time you come.' Tusker is a popular brand of Kenyan beer, and like most consumer goods it would have to be smuggled cross-border into southern Sudan. 'Then we can raise a toast to you taking up your new post.'

Garang glanced off into the distance. He was quiet for several seconds, as if lost in thought. His whole demeanour had changed. He was no longer chatty and jovial, and I sensed that maybe that was his public face. He looked lost in his memories and wistful.

Eventually, he glanced back at me. 'You know, I would like to see the city again one day.'

'I would like nothing more than to welcome you to Khartoum,' I told him. I knew that he had been educated at university there before coming to the bush to found the rebel movement. 'As soon as the peace deal is signed, I'll look forward to welcoming you as the vice-president.' The peace agreement under negotiation allowed for him to be vice-president under Omar Al Bashir – the former enemies serving alongside each other in a government of national unity. 'That will be a great moment. When do you think it might happen?'

'I don't know,' he mused, 'but on our side we would like to do a deal as soon as possible. Everybody wants peace to come.'

'How can we help get both sides to a position where they

can sign? "We" as in the UN, I mean.'

'We in the south would like help developing a programme for after the peace, and by that we mean peace and development for the entire country.'

'You don't favour splitting the country into north and south, as some seem to?'

He shook his head and smiled. 'I think you know my position. I believe in the New Sudan, the one Sudan, so keeping the country whole, but within that framework equality and rights for all, regardless of race, colour or creed. Do you think that is realistic, Dr Kapila? It is what I have been fighting for all these years.'

'I think it's very possible. We'll look at how the UN can prepare for peace as one united country, working with all parties. And as part of that process we'll look at how we can best develop the south to bring it up to the standards of the north.'

Quite suddenly the mood of the conversation shifted again, and I sensed for just an instant what a fearsome adversary Garang would make were I his enemy.

'Dr Kapila, these are fine words, but how do I know I can trust you? Your last predecessor to visit sat here and promised to help us with development in the south and to open a UNDP office here. And then, nothing. The first thing to do is to honour the agreement made between the UN and the SPLM all those years ago.'

'I didn't know there was an agreement, or that it was broken,' I told him, truthfully. 'I'll look into it. And of course we need a UNDP office here if we're going to help your people develop. I've only been in post a couple of months, and I'm still learning.'

'Hmmm...' Garang looked doubtful. 'In Africa, we have a saying: if you want to talk peace, carry a big stick. It means that only he who speaks from a position of strength will be taken seriously. You need to show the people that the UN can deliver in the south, if you want them to take you seriously.'

'Trust me, I'm serious. Just give me the time to prove it.'

'Dr Kapila, you strike me as being the kind of person we

can work with. I hope I am not wrong in my assessment. I will give you whatever time you need, but, please, do not let us down again as the UN has before.'

I assured him that I would not.

He waved his hand at a nearby table that was being set with various dishes. 'There is perhaps one other matter we should talk about before lunch. You have heard about the troubles in Darfur?'

I told him that I had and that I was concerned.

'Many of my people don't share my conviction that Sudan should remain one nation,' Garang continued, 'but I'm going to do my utmost to keep the country whole. I didn't fight for decades in the bush just to look after my people here in the south. The struggle is about oppressed and marginalised people across the country, of which those in Darfur are a prime example.'

'What is it exactly that the Darfuri rebels want?' I asked. 'It's a question that vexes us all.'

'I'm not exactly sure, but it is reasonable to assume that they're fed up with the way they're being treated by Khartoum, which treats black Africans as second-class citizens. They rule the country from the capital with no development or empowerment for peoples with skin the colour of my own.'

'How are you interacting with the Darfuri rebels?' I queried. 'What are your relations like?'

'It is no secret that the SPLM has given advice to the rebels. Clearly, what started as a rebel movement in Darfur needs a philosophy to underpin it. We have a philosophy in the south based around our liberation struggle. We are sharing that with those in Darfur in an effort to help them work out what they stand for. Plus we have given them some material support.'

Garang paused for a moment, as if carefully choosing his next words. 'But rest assured, Dr Kapila, if matters in Darfur get a great deal worse then I will not be able to sign any peace deal with the north. If I do, I will be signing a deal with those who are responsible for crushing the people of Darfur, and that would go against everything we have fought for.'

'So, showing solidarity with Darfur is a priority?' He nodded slowly. 'It is. Solidarity.'

At that moment, we were interrupted by one of Garang's aides, signalling that lunch was served. We ate a simple but hurried meal of curried chicken, vegetables and rice beneath a spreading acacia tree. We had spent longer on the ground than we had allowed for, and the pilot was anxious to get airborne and to reach Loki before nightfall. The airbase had no landing lights, and if a flight did come in during the hours of darkness a series of kerosene torches had to be ignited to mark the location of the runway.

We said a hurried farewell, and I promised to visit again soon. On the flight out, I briefed Bernt on what I had learned. He told me that no one from UNDP had been to the south for many years. As for Operation Lifeline Sudan, it was largely a food aid and humanitarian mission. Instead of finding out why people were hungry and empowering them to help themselves, OLS simply kept people alive. It did little or nothing for their dignity and self-respect. It was no wonder that Garang was frustrated, and Bernt and I agreed that we simply had to get UNDP up and running here.

Before leaving the south, I wanted to see for myself the degree of poverty of the people. The following day, Bernt and I joined a UN flight heading for an airstrip that was little more than a patch of rough earth hewn out of the raw bush. The pilot managed to get us down regardless, and all around us was a thick wall of vegetation. At first, the place seemed utterly deserted. Then one or two raggedy kids poked their heads out of the vegetation, followed by a couple of adults – our reception party.

Our pilot – a very professional Kenyan guy wearing a crisp white uniform – bade us farewell, with a reminder as to what time he'd be back to collect us. It was an odd, lonely feeling seeing our aircraft flying low and fast over the trees before disappearing into the sky.

We followed the locals on a narrow path snaking into the undergrowth. Nadia went ahead of me, and I could tell that she thrilled to the sense of going into the unknown. We continued for a kilometre or more until we reached the village. It was little more than a collection of conical, mud-walled huts with reed-thatched roofs. Each was surrounded by a circular fence made of thorny acacia branches, within which the household kept their few goats and cattle. We'd come to visit Médecins Sans Frontières (MSF – Doctors Without Borders), the global medical charity that ran a makeshift clinic here. We'd brought in medical supplies, and Bernt wanted to assess how the UN might better assist with their work. In theory, I was simply an observer on the mission, but upon hearing that I was the new UN resident chief, the MSF worker took it upon herself to brief me on the needs here.

As I listened, I began to appreciate the abject poverty of virtually everyone in the south: 99.9 per cent of the population lived a hand- to-mouth existence, with war and disaster an ever-present threat. Malnutrition was universal amongst children. Infants were underweight and suffered stunted growth, and basic diseases were endemic. Malaria was rampant, and water and sanitation were practically non-existent, as were healthcare and education.

I was taken to visit the house of a typical villager. There was next to nothing there: an earthen floor, one battered cooking pot, a fireplace to cook over, a few rags of clothing. We only had two hours on the ground, but this short visit opened my eyes. As I made my way back to the airstrip, I reflected upon what I had learned. Amongst all my visits to the most poverty-stricken parts of the world, nothing had come close to this, and Garang's anger at the UN's inaction made a lot more sense to me now.

We reached the airstrip to find our pilot standing to attention by the aircraft's steps. These bush pilots were amazingly skilled and professional, using map and compass to navigate across hundreds of miles of seemingly featureless terrain. We boarded, the turbines fired up, and the pilot trundled down to the far end of the airstrip. We turned around, the propellers spooled up to speed, and we had just set off when the pilot spotted someone waving wildly at us to stop. He aborted take-off and we dismounted. To one side of the strip, a group of locals were gathered around a figure lying prone on the ground. He was a 6 ft 7 in. incredibly slender fellow, and I could tell at once that both his legs were broken. The bones were poking out in odd directions, the knees at impossible angles. He looked to be in his early 20s, and he must have been in complete agony, but he wasn't making the slightest complaint. It was only from the twisted grimace on his face that I could tell how much pain he was feeling.

The man had taken his cattle to a watering hole, the locals explained. There was a skirmish with a rival tribe, and during the fighting the guy had had his legs broken. Our flight was heading back to Loki, where the International Committee of the Red Cross (ICRC) operated the world's largest field hospital for war-wounded. The locals wanted us to fly the injured man there for treatment.

In theory, one had to secure prior permission to evacuate war-wounded, and the pilot asked me if I was willing to carry him without. I didn't hesitate for an instant, but the problem was how to manoeuvre him up the narrow fold-down steps into the cramped confines of the aeroplane. We managed to manhandle him up the steps, but there wasn't enough room to lay him prone on the floor. We tried with his legs stuck out of the door, but the pilot couldn't fly like that. We tried with his legs poked between the rows of seats, but the aisle proved too narrow. Eventually, we had to tuck the poor guy into a foetus-like position with his broken legs folded under him. The flight back was a good three hours, during which the injured man remained fully conscious but completely mute. I knew that every jolt caused by the turbulence would be agony, but he never once so much as let out a cry. The incredible stoicism of the people of this country was humbling.

We deposited him at the ICRC hospital – a huge, tented

area set to one side of the airbase. Once he'd been operated on and his leg bones set, he'd need some weeks' rest and recovery. They'd likely fly him back to his home village on crutches, having taught him how to use them at the hospital's rehabilitation centre. But if our flight hadn't been at the airstrip that day, I hate to think what would have happened to him. With his broken bones sticking through his skin, infection would have rapidly set in, and that would likely have been the end of him.

In the close confines of that light aircraft, I'd become aware of the injured man's smell. I'd caught a whiff of it at the airstrip, but it was more powerful in the hot, stuffy interior of the aeroplane. There was no running water piped into people's homes in south Sudan, so water had to be collected in earthenware pots and buckets, and it was generally reserved for drinking or cooking. It was a precious resource, and as a result people might not have washed for days. Generally, they took on a musky, salty aroma of sweat, mixed with the animal odour of their livestock and the barbecue smell of cooking fire smoke. It was a unique, signature scent, but it wasn't one that I found offensive. In any case, after just a couple of days flying around the south I'd become aware of my own body smell. While constantly on the move you had to learn to accept being less than scrupulously clean. If I had to live as the locals – in abject poverty and with few opportunities to wash – I dreaded to think what state I'd be in. I'd probably end up smelling like my dog Megan after a day spent in the ditches of the Cambridge fens.

I was also no stranger to hardship or adversity. Since the days of my earliest childhood I'd lived with real poverty and need.

SIX

All it takes for evil to triumph is for a few good men to do nothing.
Edmund Burke

IN THE INDIAN CASTE SYSTEM, MY FAMILY ARE BRAHMIN, SO from the privileged, priestly caste. If you are not a Hindu, you are viewed as being caste-less in India, so all non-Indians and non-Hindus are caste-less. But far worse is to be an outcast, which is the lowest of the low in Hindu tradition, and it was the outcasts, or the 'untouchables', who traditionally did all the worst jobs.

Our family name also indicates that we are direct descendants of the great Sage Kapila, or Kapil Rishi. In the Bhagavad Gita – the Hindu equivalent of the Christian Bible or the Muslim Koran – Kapil Rishi is depicted as the grandson of Brahma, the Hindu creator god. The Hindu sacred texts tell that many aeons ago there was a mighty battle in which 60,000 people were turned to ashes. The earth dried up and without water there could be no life. The sainted Kapil Rishi decided to travel into the Himalayas, the domain of the Hindu gods. There, he begged the Trinity – Brahma the Creator, Shiva the Destroyer and Vishnu the Preserver – to restore life-giving water to earth.

The gods sat there looking imperious, but they listened well to his pleas. They told him that they had heard him and that they would send a great river to quench people's thirst. But they warned that it would flow with enormous power, and the only way to prevent it from drowning everyone was to send it via an intermediary. That river was the holy Ganges, and the gods decreed that it would flow through the locks of Shiva's hair, so tempering its power.

The Ganges duly flowed forth and saved 'the world', which at that time consisted of India only. And so it was that

Kapil Rishi had saved humankind. To this day, his descendants bear the name Kapil or Kapila. Unsurprisingly, my parents were strict Hindus, burning incense and praying daily at the shrine in our home to our family god – Shiva, the Destroyer.

The caste system tended to give Hinduism a bad name, and thankfully it is now much changed. Gandhi renamed the untouchables the *harijans* – the beloved of God. India's modern constitution defines everyone as equal, regardless of caste. There is even an affirmative- action programme to ensure that lower castes have access to the best education. But during my childhood, the caste system was still very strong.

Our nearest neighbours in Bihar were an 'outcast' family. While we had a concrete-walled house with a fine tin roof, they lived in a mud hut. In spite of this, I was friendly with our neighbour's daughter, Arti, because my parents were very liberated for the times. We were around the same age, and the one thing Arti loved more than anything was my toy train. It consisted of a black steam engine with several carriages, and it came complete with a battery pack that connected to an oval-shaped track, so powering the engine.

My father had brought the train set back from Germany, and most in India had never seen such a wondrous thing. Arti would sit and stare at the train for hours on end as it chuffed around in circles. To her, it was pure magic. One day she and I were out playing, and my mother told me to go and put a jumper on. It was winter and there was a chill in the air.

I left Arti by the train set but came back to find her squatted beside our outside tap. Khadari, our cook, had been washing the rice for dinner, and a few grains had spilled out of the pan. I watched as Arti picked up the hard grains from the dirt and proceeded to eat them. I asked her why she was crouched there eating raw, dirty rice. She told me that it tasted nice.

I didn't understand, so I went and asked my mother, 'Why is Arti eating rice out of the drain?'

She looked uncomfortable. 'Arti's probably hungry after

playing for so long. We should invite her in for a bowl of dhal, don't you think?' I went and fetched Arti, and we ate a dinner of dhal and rice together. Arti acted as if it was truly heaven-sent, while to me it was the same kind of food that I got every weekday. Yet somewhere within my childish mind was lodged an important lesson, one about showing compassion to those less fortunate than ourselves.

I knew already from my parents' and grandma's teachings that giving charity to those in need was a key pillar of Hinduism. Hinduism is in many ways an enlightened philosophy of living as much as it is a religion. It embodies a code of life, with rules for the division of property, the rights of widows and for the conduct of war. During balmy evenings after school in Chandigarh, Grandma would read me the *Ramayana* and *Mahabharata*, two of India's most-celebrated epics. Dating to some 2,000 years BC, they are in part historical records from an ancient, glorious past when good always overcame evil and where people suffered but were finally saved by brave leaders.

In the *Ramayana*, a battle takes place wherein the god Ram fights Ravana, the devil, over the fate of Sita, Ram's queen. Ravana goes around killing, raping and pillaging, and eliminating whole communities in the ultimate story of good versus evil. In a sense, Ravana perpetrated the first genocides, as a terrible darkness and evil stalked the land. The tale ends with good triumphing over evil, as India is blessed with 1,000 years of peace, and the land flows with milk and honey.

Ramayana embodies rules for the conduct of a society during war and peace, and maps for leading good lives. It outlines a set of social mores promoting tolerance and accepting people for who they are. *Ramayana* and *Mahabharata* together constitute a treatise on the rules of war – dealing with prisoners fairly, being generous to the defeated and treating women and children with care. In a sense, they are a very early form of the Geneva Conventions.

As a result of Grandma's storytelling, I had those epic tales of good versus evil imprinted onto my soul. I also had it impressed upon me how I, a Kapila, held a special position in the web of life. I was traditionally one of the protectors of the poor and the oppressed, and it was my responsibility to live up to the lineage of Kapilas who had gone before me. And so it was that the growing disquiet that I was feeling over the situation in Sudan – and in particular in Darfur – troubled me greatly.

I returned to Khartoum after my visit to the south, pondering on all that I had learned. Garang's warnings over Darfur had struck me powerfully. If the situation in the remote west of the country worsened, it would derail the peace process – Garang had been absolutely clear about that. So, whatever evil was spreading across Darfur, we needed to redouble our efforts to stop it. The UN had to intervene to stop the conflict, if for no other reason than to save the wider peace.

Once back in Khartoum, I hit the ground running. I set up a Common Sudan Fund to finance development across the entire country, north and south, which would address one of Garang's key concerns. The Dutch and American governments – long-time supporters of the south – kicked it off by pumping in $2 million. The heads of the main Khartoum agencies – UNDP and UNICEF foremost amongst them – were incensed. I'd broken their cartel on fundraising for their own, largely Khartoum-driven, projects. But I pushed it through anyway, at which stage the Sudanese government went through the roof.

I was summoned to see the minister for international cooperation, someone with whom I'd already crossed swords. He was a small, shrivelled-looking man who was perpetually sour faced with me. Perhaps it was only to be expected: his ministry was the official partner to UNDP in many of the ghost projects that I'd shut down. I'd deprived his cronies of the UN vehicles that they had taken as their own, and in doing so I'd cost him a great deal of face.

He didn't waste any time getting to the point. 'Dr Kapila, we have heard all about your Common Sudan

Fund, but what do you think you are doing? You cannot simply do this, and certainly not before checking with my ministry.'

'With respect, Minister, I beg to differ,' I answered. 'This is purely UN business, and as the UN resident chief it is wholly within my remit.'

'It is not!' The little man thumped his desk angrily. 'We have the power to stop this, and trust me we will.'

'Sorry, Minister, but it's a done deal. I can't undo what's already done even if I wanted to, which I do not. Two very important donors have already kicked it off with several million dollars, and it is very much up and running.'

'Well, we'll just see about that,' he fumed. 'And I have also heard you plan to open a UNDP office in the south of the country. Rest assured, Dr Kapila, that will not – I repeat, NOT – happen. We will see to it!'

The confrontation ended in a none-too-polite argument, and I left sensing that I hadn't heard the last of the minister. I had already earmarked a significant proportion of the fund's $2 million to setting up UNDP in south Sudan, and I vowed to accelerate that process. I wanted it done and dusted before his ministry might try to stop me. With my promise to Garang part fulfilled, I turned my attention to Darfur. I decided to raise my concerns at the highest level of the Sudanese government, alerting them to how Darfur threatened to derail the peace process. I went to see Omar Al-Arabi, a senior advisor within the president's office. Omar was a smooth operator who spoke fluent and cultured English. He was young and talented, and looked like he was going places, so I figured he was my best route in to the president.

After the usual chitchat, I came to the point. 'As you know, I have recently returned from visiting Dr Garang, the chairman of the SPLM and your counterpart in the peace talks. I know your government wishes to sign the peace agreement as soon as possible, but it appears that the single greatest obstacle to that may now be Darfur.'

I outlined exactly what Garang had told me. I was

expecting a reaction revealing a degree of concern or surprise on Omar's part. Instead, he waved his hand dismissively. 'Yes, yes, of course, Dr Kapila, we know all of this already.'

His tone was of the worldly-wise, urbane technocrat being told something that was certainly nothing new. I probed further. This was too important an issue to leave to generalities or to dismiss so easily. 'I take it that the chairman of the SPLM's position on Darfur is already known to you?' I probed. 'You were aware already?'

'Yes, Dr Kapila, we know.' A theatrical sigh, somewhat bored. 'And we know we have to sort this out. That is why we are anxious to implement the final solution in Darfur. We can only move ahead to sign the peace agreement once we have implemented that final solution.'

I felt a chill run down my spine. *The final solution.* It was such a sinister choice of phraseology. For someone with such a fine command of English, surely he couldn't have used that phrase inadvertently. Surely he must have known how resonant it was with an utterly loathsome evil. It almost felt as if he was deliberately quoting from Hitler, but perhaps I had misunderstood him. Surely I must have done. If I gave him a chance to retract, surely he would.

'Sorry, but surely you use that phrase – "*the final solution*" – unintentionally?'

He sighed again. 'No, not at all. Clearly, Dr Kapila, the lawless elements in Darfur have to be brought under control. The government of Sudan will take all necessary measures to crush the rebels and bring peace. We will not tolerate any resistance. Ergo, a final solution will be found.'

So now I knew. He had chosen those deeply sinister words deliberately, knowing what connotations they would have for me. This had been a conversation between two educated internationalists, in which a senior presidential advisor had chosen to inform me what their intentions were regarding Darfur: *it was to seek a final solution, with no compromise.*

I left that meeting feeling punch-drunk. I followed up with visits to the ministry for foreign affairs and my old sparring partners at HAC. At each juncture, I discovered that the language had changed over Darfur. It was now entirely belligerent and confrontational. At every turn, I found people proclaiming they would 'take all necessary measures' and 'crush the lawless elements' before the UN would be permitted access to give aid.

Never had I heard such sentiments expressed openly and at such a senior level of government, and with zero talk about negotiating or hearing people's grievances. In similar situations – Sierra Leone, Afghanistan, Bosnia even – there had always been a subtext about the two sides getting together to solve their problems. But not here. Here, there was nothing, no room for compromise. Quite the reverse, in fact: there was room only for a *'final solution' in Darfur*.

The sheer horror of hearing that phrase used openly and with reference to the present day impacted upon me deeply. Worse still, it was being used with reference to people under my jurisdiction as UN resident chief and for whom I bore heavy responsibility. I was shaken to the core, especially as I felt the impact of that phrase so personally. The horrific reality of those words – 'the final solution' – is hard-wired into my soul, for my family is also one of genocide survivors.

In 1947, as British India gained independence from Great Britain, it was split into two nations, becoming India and Pakistan. Nearly all Hindus in Pakistan were forced to move into India, and many Muslims in India were forced to migrate into Pakistan. But over time, what became known as 'Partition' turned increasingly chaotic and bloody. Violence swept across the entire subcontinent. In India, Muslims were being rounded up by the mob and killed, and in Pakistan the same was happening to Hindus. In early August, my grandmother on my father's side was forced to abandon the family home in Lahore and flee southwards to Delhi. She did so with her ten children, one of whom was my father, but without my grandfather, for he had gone ahead of her to prepare a Delhi home.

Together with my teenage father and nine other children, Grandma Kapila boarded a train to travel south to safety. As it inched forwards in the boiling heat, the land all around her was in turmoil. A locomotive approached from the other direction, but it was pulling a terrifying ghost train. Apart from the driver, everyone else had been slaughtered. It passed, piled high with bloodied corpses, and with it Grandma saw the fate that awaited her and her children.

Inch by inch they crawled forwards, and when they ran out of water Grandma resorted to urinating in a pan so that her children could drink it. But her real fear wasn't dying of thirst: it was of the mobs. A very young-looking white man from the International Committee of the Red Cross had been assigned to accompany the train in an effort to safeguard its occupants. That man, who was Swiss, sat with the driver at the front of the train carrying a huge Red Cross flag.

At each juncture wherein they were halted, he stepped down to confront the wild crowds armed with guns and swords, with only that flag to protect him. Somehow, that man's extraordinary bravery kept the train and its occupants safe until it crossed over the border to the Indian side. In so doing he had saved my grandma's life and that of her children. Thus it is that if it were not for the Red Cross I would not be alive today.

Over a million people died in the violence of Partition, spawning the first genocide since the 'final solution' of the Second World War. In India we lost 'only' one million – as opposed to the six million souls killed in the Holocaust – but we did so in a far shorter time. The mass slaughter had taken but a matter of days.

My father was very lucky to be alive: those most often killed during Partition were young men of his age. My family rebuilt their lives in Delhi, but they never forgot how one good man had stood against the darkness as it stalked our land. As far as we are concerned, one man stopped the 'final solution' from becoming our own destiny. And so it was that the use of that macabre phrase – *'the final solution'* - by the ruling powers in Sudan had so shaken me.

As UN resident chief, I knew that I had no political mandate. My role was largely humanitarian. But there were those within the UN who could take the political initiative and raise such an issue on the international stage. I wrote to the heads of the main agencies in New York, alerting them to what I had learned. I warned them that the Khartoum regime was seeking a *'final solution'* in Darfur, and I sought their guidance on what we should do.

They responded that this was a political issue, and that my mandate was purely humanitarian. I should concentrate exclusively on getting aid into Darfur. Strictly speaking, they were right. But practically, I found this anathema. Perhaps it wasn't my position as a humanitarian figurehead to act, but who then within the UN system would make a stand? It was deeply unsettling.

I raised the issue privately with New York: *who, then, is going to act?* The only response I received was a wall of prevarication and silence. I remembered how often I had sworn to myself that *not on my watch would the evil-doers triumph*. But if I was to act – and whatever form that action might take I didn't yet know – first I would need evidence. Words were one thing; I'd need proof they were being acted on.

I would need incontrovertible proof that the 'final solution' was being executed in Darfur. I would need hard facts, raw data and statistics. And, perhaps most importantly, I would need to go to Darfur so that I could speak from direct experience.

I would myself need to step into the darkness.

SEVEN

You can discover what your enemy fears most by observing the means he uses to frighten you.
Eric Hoffer

IN LIFE, IT'S WISE TO CHOOSE THE BATTLES YOU WISH TO FIGHT carefully. When I had won my scholarship to study in England, I ended up going to one of the top public schools in the country: Wellington College. I hadn't been there for long when I took up the sport of fencing. I had no burning desire to demonstrate my skill with the blade. I did so purely as a defence against the bullying.

For a somewhat pudgy, bespectacled, studious Indian schoolboy, I proved myself to be a remarkably adroit swordsman. None of my fellow students had expected me to be able to fight, let alone to make the highly regarded school fencing team. They were shocked when they learned that I had claws and could use them, and it did act as a foil against the worst of the school bullies.

Likewise, I had yet to show my claws with the leadership in Sudan, and I was happy to let my benign exterior mask the cold steel within. It helped on numerous levels, not least of which was enabling me to secure clearance to fly us into Darfur.

It was early July when I met with Sulaf, my HAC liaison, once more. I told him we were going in with a purely humanitarian agenda and with no view to the underlying causes of the conflict. I told him it would look very bad if they blocked the UN when all we sought was access to give food, water and medicines to the suffering.

Sulaf assured me that he'd do his best to get us in. It was several days and much tough negotiating before clearance was finally granted. I would be flying in with my security chief, Roger, plus some minders from HAC. I was leaving Nadia in Khartoum to oversee the work of the Darfur

Crisis Unit, along with Daniel Christensen, my key researcher and investigator.

Tom Vraalsen, Kofi Annan's special envoy on humanitarian affairs in Sudan, wanted to join me for the trip, and I hoped very much we might use his presence to up the ante within the UN on Darfur. As he was Norwegian and based in Oslo – as opposed to Khartoum – I also hoped Tom might convey a tough message to the Sudanese government to draw back from its 'final solution' in Darfur.

Tom was bringing with him Isabelle Balot, a mature and elegant Frenchwoman and the Sudan desk officer at OCHA headquarters in New York. Isabelle was tall, slender and hazel-eyed, and she was very up to speed on Sudan. She would go on to play an absolutely pivotal role in the unfolding crisis in Darfur and one for which I am eternally in her debt, but all of this was yet to come.

The day prior to our scheduled departure, I went to check on my supplies of insulin. I have diabetes, which is something that had hit me a few days short of my 40th birthday. I had travelled into the heart of the Rwandan genocide, and over a matter of days my hair had gone from a glossy jet-black to a snowy grey. I had also lost weight until I was stick thin.

My wife, Helen, is a doctor, and she decided to test my blood sugar when I was back in the UK, which was how I discovered that I had diabetes. My single greatest fear upon hearing the news was that it might prevent me from going back into the field. I went to a local hospital to learn how to prick my finger, to test the blood-sugar level, and inject the right amount of insulin. Being a doctor, I'm used to injecting others, but to do so to myself was a different thing entirely. The nurses at the clinic warned me that if I didn't get it right, I could die.

I met my diabetologist, Jonathan Roland, and asked him to draw up a plan for how I might manage my condition in war, conflict and disaster zones. It would need to account for the possibility of kidnap and being held hostage without access to insulin. We figured I could cut out certain foods – chiefly sugars – and eke out any existing supplies of insulin I might have. If I combined that with exercise, I might survive for three months or so. My eyes, legs, fingers and toes would begin to seize up, and then I'd start to experience kidney failure. But three months would be doable. Any longer, and I would be dead. Ever since then, I had treated my diabetes on a need-to-know basis.

I had feared people would see me as weak and vulnerable if they knew about it, and restrict my ability to go into the field. In Sudan, I made sure to inject myself where I wouldn't be seen – so in the toilet at my UN office or my bedroom at home. But the greatest challenge was how to keep injecting when travelling, and how to keep my insulin cold in temperatures of over 50 degrees. If insulin is exposed to extremes of temperature, it is completely ruined.

I discovered something called a 'cryo-bag', which is a pouch made of certain crystals. When dunked in water, the crystals become a freezing mass, acting like a mini fridge. The cryo-bag would keep several phials of insulin cold for 48 hours, after which I'd need to dunk it again. And so far, having my cryo-bag with me had enabled me to travel pretty much freely in the field.

At home in Khartoum it wasn't an issue, or at least it shouldn't have been. I had several months' supply of insulin stored in the fridge. Even if I had a power cut, there was a back-up generator, so those supplies were pretty much invulnerable, or so I had thought.

It was the absolute boiling heat of the summer as we prepared for our journey to Darfur. I went to the fridge to fetch my supplies of insulin only to discover them gone. Ahmed, my sometime cook, had decided to choose this moment to defrost the fridge. While doing so, he'd loaded everything, including my supplies of insulin, into the freezer.

By the time I'd discovered what he'd done, every single phial was frozen solid and ruined. In a sense, it wasn't

Ahmed's fault. I hadn't told him I was a diabetic, but it had never once crossed my mind that he might choose to take all my insulin and freeze it!

The only saving grace was that I had a few phials stored in my office fridge. At a pinch, it would be just about enough to get me through Darfur. After that, I'd have to go overseas to secure a fresh supply. I would only ever pick up subscriptions from the UK, for there is a massive trade in fake drugs going on around the world. If I were given fake insulin, it would be the death of me.

Very early on the morning of our departure for Darfur, I had Omer drive me to the office so I could quietly retrieve my few precious phials of insulin. I wrapped them carefully in my cryo-bag, then dunked it under the tap. It mightn't prove enough for the entire trip, but I was damned if I was going to let that get in the way of the present mission.

Having grabbed my last remaining insulin, I joined my team in the VIP lounge at Khartoum airport. Unfortunately, I plonked down one of my bags a little too heavily, and inside it was a bottle of whisky. By now I'd mastered the art of ordering wine, beer and spirits from a specialist company that supplied the diplomatic community in Khartoum. Entertaining dignitaries was an important part of my role as UN chief, and having a decent supply of alcohol was an absolute must.

The Scotch in my flight bag was supposed to be a gift for the few UN staff we had stationed out in Darfur. I'd been planning to invite them to my room for a morale-boosting snifter behind locked doors, only now the whisky was leaking out and pooling at my feet. Even for internationals, alcohol was only ever permitted at home. I didn't have a clue what to do, especially as two very officious-looking airport types were bearing down on me.

'We'll deal with that, sir,' one of them announced.

The other whisked up the offending bag, and they promptly disappeared. A few moments later, the bag was returned, minus the cracked bottle, and not another word was said about it. I was fairly sure they'd managed to decant the remaining contents and would be raising a glass to the UN chief that evening.

We loaded up our Beechcraft light aircraft for the flight into El Fasher, one of the main urban centres in Darfur. Four hours and one refuelling stop later, we descended into the airport. As we did so, I could make out the unmistakable shapes of a couple of fat helicopter gunships squatted on the runway. They were a glistening reptilian green, and from the air they looked like bright Meccano kits fresh out of the box – almost toy-like and unreal.

We touched down and taxied across the runway, and I got a closer look at the gunships. They didn't seem so toy-like any more. Sprouting under the stub-wings were the unmistakable forms of missiles and rocket pods. I am no military man, but up close they looked decidedly lethal. Beside the gunships sat the dull, camouflage-painted form of an Antonov, a Russian-made heavy transport aircraft that the Sudanese Air Force had converted into a bomber.

This airport, El Fasher, was the one that the Darfuri rebels had attacked back in April – so alerting us to the situation in Darfur. I couldn't very well comment on the presence of those warplanes, for I had Sulaf sat at my shoulder, and I knew I wasn't supposed to notice such things. But I had read Daniel Christensen's reports in which the locals had described helicopters strafing their villages, and it was ominous to find those gunships here on the runway.

We had precious little time in El Fasher. We would need to get out before nightfall so as to make the next destination on our agenda, which was another major population centre in Darfur. In the few hours that we had on the ground, I wanted to visit the IDP camps, plus the hospital, and get time to talk to the wounded.

We were whisked away from the airport to the office of the governor of north Darfur. A large group of officials had gathered to receive us. Protocol dictated that we had to meet and greet them all. Tea, cakes and pleasantries followed, and as the minutes ticked by I felt my frustration levels rising.

Finally, I steered the conversation around to the situation in the area. We had heard reports of more and more IDPs arriving in El Fasher, I explained, following attacks on their villages. I asked the governor to tell me what was happening.

He was a small man dressed in a jalabiya topped off with an enormous turban. We were speaking via an interpreter, and the answer he gave me was a familiar one: there had been a bad drought resulting in a terrible harvest. The fighting was over access to food, water and fodder for animals. The authorities were doing their best to re-establish security, he assured me, so people could return to their villages.

I didn't give much credence to what he was saying, but I knew I had to be seen to be engaging with the officials, hugely frustrating though that might prove. Of more concern was the sense I was getting that the governor was trying to stonewall us. I asked if we might move on, so we could get to see the hospital and IDP camps. In response, the governor told me 'all in good time' and called for more tea and cakes.

I was starting to feel as if our mission had been hijacked. Finally, with our hour of departure fast approaching, I got to my feet and announced that we were going to visit the hospital come what may. The governor could barely hide his irritation as we got back into our vehicles and drove out of his compound.

The driver was dawdling along as if we had all the time in the world, and a voice was screaming inside my head for him to go faster. By the time we reached the hospital, all that was possible was a quick, whistle-stop tour with no time to speak to the patients. Even so, with the help of my medical background I was able to determine a number of crucial factors.

One, you'd normally expect to see a full spectrum of injuries and illnesses at a provincial hospital such as this. Instead, the wards were cram-full of those exhibiting almost exclusively gunshot injuries. Two, there were scores of children, and it is highly unusual for children to make up the bulk of the casualties of war. Three, there were no wounded military personnel as far as I could see, though for sure some kind of major gun battle had taken place to cause such horrible injuries.

By the end of our whirlwind tour it was abundantly clear that the hospital was jam-packed with injured civilians, the majority of whom were far too young to be combatants. I asked one of the local doctors the obvious question: *where are the injured children's parents?* He was nervous and edgy as he replied – somewhat obliquely – that the children 'had been found wandering in the bush, but their parents were still missing and not around'.

We exited the hospital with no time to make for the IDP camps, so the governor's efforts to frustrate us had partially succeeded. On the drive to the airport, I asked him exactly how many people had been displaced by the fighting, and how many gunshot injuries they had in total at the hospital. Such figures would help us extrapolate the scale of the unrest across the whole of Darfur.

The governor shrugged. 'There are not so many displaced,' he announced, staring out of the window. 'And in fact there are few if any serious injuries.'

As we pulled up at our waiting aircraft, one thing was for sure: if it hadn't been for our last-minute dash to the hospital, our visit here would have been a complete waste of time. A whitewash. Another thing was also becoming clear to me: Tom Vraalsen was far from proving the great ally that I had hoped for. I'd expected him to pry, dig and probe, and to push hard for us to be given the access we sought. But he'd done nothing of the sort.

As we took off for our next destination – Nyala – I could hardly confront Tom over this, which was what I was tempted to do. It wouldn't look good if Sulaf and the other government minders saw two such senior UN officials arguing. Yet I was damned if I was going to leave El Fasher with nothing being said.

'Well, that was largely a waste of time, wasn't it?' I

remarked. 'We won't be able to say much, other than that the authorities tried to stop us from seeing anything. There's nothing for it – we'll have to send more people.'

Tom looked distinctly uncomfortable. 'Well, Mukesh, you know, we do have to try to build relations with the authorities. We have to trust them and be patient. This is how these things are done.'

On one level, Tom was right. That was the way in which international affairs were conducted. That was the way in which diplomacy progressed and relations between nations were built. I was now very much part of a system wherein unspoken rules and norms applied. You moved slowly, built up confidence and won trust, and you didn't embarrass and cause waves. But right now I suspected that we didn't have time for all of this.

After all, what norms applied when you knew that your host government was planning a *'final solution'* for its own people? Here we were flying out of El Fasher with scores of shot-up children lying in hospital, and we'd been barred from visiting the IDP camps. We could see the state-of-the-art machines of death squatting on the runway. After what we had heard already about Darfur, it didn't take a genius to work out what was likely going on here. Yet we were apparently supposed to act as if everything was normal and the visit going well.

As the Beechcraft climbed to altitude, I felt as if there was this enormous elephant sitting here alongside us, one that everyone was supposed to ignore. But this really wasn't me. If the emperor has no clothes, I'm the kind of person who points out that he's naked. Yet here I was feeling trapped within the prison of my own position.

As the aircraft droned onwards, I felt a growing sense of personal failure. I should have tried harder. Pushed harder. Cajoled. Demanded. Protested. Yet I had done nothing of the sort.

We'd taken it to the limit in terms of time spent on the ground in El Fasher, and we touched down in Nyala just a few minutes before nightfall. The Beechcraft did a quick about-turn and was gone. It was deemed too much of a security risk for it to overnight here, so it would fly to the nearest airport with landing lights and security.

The governor of south Darfur received us, and we set off in convoy for his residence. Upon arrival, we were treated to a banquet, complete with dancing and music, which allowed us little chance to talk. The show was dominated by men brandishing sticks and swords, and it was distinctly martial. It was accompanied by a lot of Arabic chanting, and I noticed that the performers all had Arabic features. In a region of mixed black African and Arab tribes, it struck me as being somewhat sinister. Where were the other ethnic groups one might have expected? I was relieved to get away from the 'show' and into the governor's guesthouse, where we were billeted. My room was cavernous, and it came complete with noisy plumbing, bare bulbs and smelly drainage. Before retiring to bed, I grabbed Roger for a 'security briefing'. In reality, I was desperate to unload my frustration onto someone, and Roger was the only person I felt I could trust.

'Well, today was a bloody waste of time,' I announced, once we were in the privacy of my room.

'Yes, sir,' Roger remarked, a little tiredly.

I couldn't get Roger to refrain from the 'sir' bit. I figured it was due to the years of military training.

'You saw those gunships and the Antonov parked up at the airstrip?' 'Yes, sir.'

'Well, more than a "yes, sir", how about volunteering what you thought about it? After all the reports we've had of them using helicopters and Antonovs to bomb villages, and now we see...'

'Well, sir, as you know it isn't my job to think about such things,' Roger interjected, 'not unless they impact upon the security of UN personnel...'

'And then we get a ten-minute bloody whistle-stop tour of the hospital,' I ranted on, 'and we don't even get to see the IDP camps. I mean, hours of tea and bloody biscuits and lies, and then we're shovelled back onto the Beechcraft and we're gone. A complete waste of time, wasn't it, Roger?'

'Sir, I can only give you my security opinion. I would need to drink several beers with you to remark on other matters, and unless I'm mistaken you dropped the whisky at the airport, so we don't have a drop between us.'

I bade Roger goodnight, vowing that, come hell or high water, here in Nyala we'd get to see what we'd come for.

EIGHT

The world is a dangerous place to live, not because of the people who are evil but because of the people who don't do anything about it.
Albert Einstein

FOR WHATEVER REASON, THE NEXT MORNING'S ITINERARY went more smoothly – or at least it did at first. After the obligatory meet-and-greet with officials, we were taken directly to an IDP camp. Set in the dust-dry desert bush on the city limits, it consisted of little more than a sea of makeshift hovels thrown together from sheets of blue plastic, acacia scrub and the odd bit of cardboard.

Our convoy pulled to a halt in the centre of the camp, and a group of onlookers gathered. One thing struck me immediately: compared to the Arab-looking martial troupe of the night before, everyone here had noticeably black African features. The adults were dressed in dirty and torn clothing, the children in whatever scraps of cloth they could find. The sea of faces that surrounded our vehicles looked lost, worried and confused, and very, very frightened.

Via my interpreter, I introduced myself to those nearest and told them that I wanted to hear exactly what had happened to them and why they were here. I reassured them they could speak freely, for I represented the UN and the international community. For the benefit of our minders, I told them that our mission was to assess their humanitarian needs – so food, water, shelter and security – and to do that I needed to understand the crisis.

What ensued was a kind of community story-telling in which men and women from all around the group threw in comments and often competed to be heard. From the desperation in their voices, and the anger and frustration on their faces, I could tell that these people were dying for someone to hear and give witness to their stories.

'One day early in the morning, the village was attacked...' 'People rode in on horseback to burn the village...'

'They carried torches and set fire to the huts...'

'We ran for our lives as the thatch of our homes burned...' 'The horse riders chased after us as we ran into the bush...' 'Some didn't make it…'

'Some fell before they could escape...' 'I lost one of my children…'

'I don't know who is left alive...'

It was now that I heard the first chilling intimations of rape. *They took the young women to the bush; they held them prisoner; they did what they wanted with them…*

I had heard the rumours, but these were the first direct reports of rape, muted and elliptical though they were. The people being attacked here were Muslim, as were their attackers, and in Sudanese Muslim culture rape is a horrific shame. It is seen as a stain on the victim and the family of the victim that lasts a lifetime. Even to talk about it openly is shameful, hence the coded references that I was now hearing.

I waved a hand for silence. 'Thank you for telling me all this. But I also need to know why your village was attacked and who exactly were the people that attacked you.'

One of the more vocal of the young men threw a defiant glance at Sulaf: 'These were the horsemen, the Arab horsemen.'

'But where did they come from and who sent them?' I probed.

I could feel Sulaf shifting uncomfortably at my shoulder. I heard a few sharp words rasped out in Arabic. I glanced at my interpreter, expecting him to translate what Sulaf had said, but his mouth remained firmly closed.

The same young man flicked his eyes about nervously. 'Just horsemen. Arab horsemen. That's all,' he muttered. 'Those people come on horses with guns and attack and burn the villages.' Then, in a quiet, beaten-down, defeated voice: 'They came to attack us because the rains had failed and there was fighting over food.'

I could see the fear in his eyes, and in those of the others who'd been talking. It was as if a common message had flashed amongst them: *say any more and we're finished.* I'd pushed it as far as I could.

In any case, I didn't need them to tell me more. I could read enough in their body language. On the faces of the women there was real, animal dread. And in the eyes of the men there was the sullen, downtrodden submissiveness of once proud husbands, brothers and warriors whose very means of resistance had been destroyed.

I thanked them for speaking so frankly, and in not pushing any further I was seeking to protect them. I turned instead to their humanitarian needs, none of which were being met in any meaningful way. People kept telling me that they were frightened, even here in the IDP camp, but they were equally fearful to move. They felt unsafe everywhere. *Unsafe from what, from whom?* That was the unspoken question, but I knew that I couldn't ask it. Here, this was the elephant in the room.

We'd been at the camp for a good 40 minutes by the time the governor declared it was time to leave. There was a meeting organised for us in central Nyala at which we could speak to the community elders. They were best placed to answer any outstanding questions, the governor suggested. We retraced our route and pulled up at a town-hall-like building. Seventy-odd people were inside, seated on rows of wooden benches.

Tom Vraalsen and I were ushered to the front, along with Sulaf. For a while we listened to a succession of speakers – mostly Arab- looking males in their later years – talking about drought, crop failure and the need for water and food aid. It was the well-rehearsed government line, and the 'meeting' felt wholly stage-managed. Tom and I were informally chairing it, and I was scanning the crowd for someone who might have something genuinely meaningful to contribute when I noticed a woman get to her feet at the back of the room.

It was remarkable enough to see a woman presenting herself to speak, for 90 per cent of those in the room were males. More to the point, this woman was most definitely black African, and she was dressed in a bright, multicoloured robe. She looked to be no older than her early 30s, and she had the air of a mother about her. I could sense the urgency with which she wanted to speak crying out of her.

I pointed in her direction. 'Please, let's hear from the lady at the back.'

The interpreter looked for the governor, as if to double-check, but he must have stepped out of the room, as he was nowhere to be seen. That meant that Vraalsen and I were more or less in charge here. The interpreter made some remark in Arabic to the woman, and she began to speak.

'Everyone here has talked about drought and crop failure,' she said, her voice quiet and calm, 'but this is not what happened in my village or to me. In the middle of the night, the raiders came. People were rounded up and marched out of their huts, which were set on fire. The raiders lashed us with their whips and beat us with sticks, and drove us out of the village. We hid in the bush and they set fire to everything: our huts, our animal enclosures, even our food stores.'

The woman paused to catch her breath, and it was as if the room was holding its breath with her.

'We hid all night in the desert, beneath small clumps of trees. In the morning, we went back into the village. Everything was burned and looted, and we were too afraid to stay. So we came here to Nyala to try to find safety. But the worst thing is that some of the young women from the village are missing...'

A man jumped to his feet. He waved his stick in her direction, angrily. 'Shut up and sit down!' he cried.

'Stop spreading your lies!' another yelled.

All around the room men were yelling at her to 'shut up' and to 'sit down'. The translator was doing his best to convey all that was being said, but I didn't really need him to. The threat in the words and the gestures required no translating.

'Let the woman speak!' I declared. 'Let her finish telling her story.

We are here to hear from everyone, from all sides.'

'We searched for the missing, but we couldn't find them anywhere,' the woman continued. The hostility in the room was palpable, and her voice was shaking with uncertainty. 'They are still missing, and we fear very much what is happening to those women and girls. Some of them are very young, just children. We fear they have been taken, and we want the authorities to help us find them.'

The entire room seemed to be on its feet now, waving sticks and yelling threats. The woman stopped talking and sat down. As soon as she did so, the meeting was declared over, and the officials went to usher Vraalsen and I out. This was the most compelling eyewitness testimony that we had heard, and the woman's courage had struck me powerfully. She had given the most disturbing account of women taken away to be raped, and I feared for her safety.

For a moment, I tried to resist the hands that were bundling Tom and me out of the door. For an instant, I glanced over in her direction, and I could see a group of sinister-looking men in plain clothes and sunglasses closing in around her. That was my last glimpse before I was hustled out of the building and bundled into the waiting car.

Within moments we were under way and making for the airport, and I could hear the governor urging the driver to make all speed. I sat in the rear of the vehicle feeling frozen. Doubtless, that woman had seen us driving around town with our UN flags. She'd know that we were outsiders with authority, if not that we were the United Nations. She had spoken with such clarity and dignity, and she had done so with amazing restraint. Had she been angry or raised her voice, I felt certain she would have been stopped much earlier.

To have spoken out like that was the ultimate in courage,

and what had we done for her? We had listened to her brave words, speaking truth to power; we had heard the threats being made against her, and, at the end, what had we done? We had abandoned her to her fate. I had little doubt who it was that had surrounded her: it would be the local Mukhabarat goons.

As we thundered towards the airstrip, I felt overcome by a sense of my own cowardice. We – *I* – had failed her, and I felt a crushing sense of shame. I was almost in shock as I was bundled onto the waiting Beechcraft. The pilot got us airborne, and I stared out at the city as it dwindled into the distance. But all I could see in my mind's eye were those sinister plain-clothes figures surrounding the woman who had spoken, and I had every fear for what they might do to her now.

I had no idea what retribution might be visited upon her exactly, but this was a regime that had vowed to unleash a 'final solution' against an entire people. What mercy could one brave individual expect? I vowed to do the one thing that I could to try to protect her. I'd get Roger to speak to his contacts and warn them that the eyes of the UN were upon that woman. But what, in reality, could we do? I hadn't even managed to get her name.

I sat on that flight consumed by a sense of my own failure. If I had failed to protect one individual, how could I ever begin to safeguard a whole people?

The final destination on our agenda was El Geneina, but it proved less than eventful. We touched down on a dirt airstrip in a small town consisting mostly of mud huts. El Geneina is situated in the far west of Darfur, and the troubles hadn't reached it yet. There were few reports of fighting, which meant there was little point in tarrying. With evening fast approaching, we took to the skies again, heading back to Khartoum.

During that long flight, I had time enough to reflect upon what had happened. Perhaps because I am a man and rape is a crime perpetrated by men, it was that woman's intimations of rape that had really hit me, plus the way that she had stressed how young were the victims. Any rape is a horrific crime, but the rape of a child is an abomination, one that sadly I had encountered all too often in the darkest places of the world.

During the 1994 Rwanda genocide, I'd flown into that country to spearhead the British government's aid effort. Upon hearing of the mass exodus of Hutus, I'd headed for Goma, a town on the border with Rwanda, along with my colleague, Peter Troy.

Upon reaching Goma, we'd discovered a sea of people like something out of biblical times. The Hutu exodus from Rwanda was the fastest relocation of a mass of people since Partition in India, wherein my grandmother and my teenage father had fled Lahore by train. A total of a million Hutus or more – many of whom had led the genocide against the Tutsis in Rwanda – had flooded into neighbouring Zaire. As news broke of the exodus, emergency aid flooded into Goma, but by then people were dying in their tens of thousands from cholera. Peter and I concentrated on getting water purification systems in, to try to fight the disease, but still there were people dropping dead by the roadside. We knew these were mostly the same people as had perpetrated the genocide, but a humanitarian disaster is still a humanitarian disaster, and for sure the children bore no culpability or guilt.

In amongst the Hutus there was the odd Tutsi refugee, ones that had fled the mass killings and were the first into Zaire. I went to visit a field hospital set up by Médecins Sans Frontières, to see how we might help. A local Zairian nurse showed me around, and I noticed there was one corner of the hospital kept isolated from the rest. I asked what it was for. The nurse told me that was where they kept the rape victims, and she offered to show me.

We entered the tent. There were rows of beds down either side. Each was filled with a woman, many of whom had children or babies with them. I was struck most powerfully by the woman and child lying directly in front of me. I was drawn to them as if by an irresistible force. I halted by the foot of their bed. The woman was tall, elegant and striking, in spite of the setting, and I knew immediately that she had to be a Tutsi, for only they had such a look.

The girl beside her appeared to be no more than four or five years old. The nurse explained that they had fled Rwanda during the early stages of the genocide and were some of the first to arrive in Goma. No one knew exactly what had happened to them, because mother and child had both been stuck dumb. They hadn't spoken a single word in the days that they had been here.

'What we do know is this woman and her daughter were raped,' the nurse continued. 'And raped with shocking violence and brutality. But, as I say, neither have spoken a word since their arrival…'

'Then how do you know?' I asked.

'We examined them,' the nurse explained. 'It is quite obvious from that examination...'

My mind filtered out the rest of the words, blanking them into a white noise. My brain couldn't cope with the horror, and especially not when it had been visited on this dignified woman and her innocent little girl. The nurse finished speaking and for a moment the woman glanced at me. She had these extraordinarily arresting eyes. But I couldn't hold her gaze – not knowing what had been done to her, and that it was my gender that was responsible.

She lowered her gaze and her hand went to caress the hair of the child in her lap. The mother was dressed in a loose, light-green hospital smock, but her daughter was still wearing a child's T-shirt with some cartoon images printed upon it. For an instant, an image flashed into my mind of what had been done to them both, and I felt violently, physically sick. For a moment, I thought of my daughters back home, and I couldn't imagine how I would feel were this to happen to them. I tried to hold it together for long enough to get out of there, but I left in a state of raw shock. I had never known anything like this – a woman and child so destroyed by unimaginable brutality and trauma. I understood then how devastating rape was as a weapon of war: it was of such malevolent power that a mother and child had been struck dumb by what had been done to them.

I left that Goma hospital feeling angry, humiliated and shamed that my gender – the male – was capable of such evil. And now, as our light aircraft thundered away from Darfur towards Khartoum, I felt a similar sense of anger and guilt about the woman who had spoken out.

To my eternal shame, I had done not one thing to try to protect her.

NINE

The purpose of our life is to be happy.
The Dalai Lama

IT WAS NEARING MIDNIGHT BY THE TIME WE TOUCHED DOWN in Khartoum. I was met by Omer and driven home. I'd invited Isabelle, the French OCHA worker who'd accompanied Tom Vraalsen on the trip, to billet herself in one of the spare rooms. Laid out in the kitchen was Ahmed's signature dish – an oily mess of baba ganoush. Rashly, Isabelle declared that this was her favourite meal, and so I left her with a beaming Ahmed and sneaked off to bed.

I woke in the early hours feeling awful. I was soaked in sweat and my pulse was racing. I felt dizzy and was trembling uncontrollably. I figured I was having a hypoglycaemic attack, with my blood-sugar level crashing dangerously low. It would hardly be surprising. I'd been flying back-to-back with my meals all over the place and not getting to test myself or inject insulin regularly.

My mind felt groggy and fuzzy, like it was wrapped in bales of cotton wool. I couldn't think straight, let alone move. I was feeling finished, and I was really scared. Acting on autopilot my hand reached out to the bedside table and made contact with my testing kit. I checked my blood sugar via a finger prick. It was at level 2. Normal is 4.5–7. It was dangerously low.

Thanks to Roger's security system, I was double locked into my bedroom. I knew I didn't have the energy to unfasten the door and make it downstairs to find some sugar. But still I had to try. As I moved towards the door, I fell with a loud crash.

Next thing I knew there was a loud banging on the door. 'Mukesh! Mukesh! Are you all right?'

Isabelle had heard the crash and rushed over. I crawled

to the door and somehow got the bolts undone. I could barely manage a whisper: 'Get me sugar... there's chocolate in the fridge.'

Tripping over her nightgown, she rushed off and was back an instant later to force a crumbly KitKat into my mouth. A mug of sweet tea followed, and I felt myself returning to something like normal. For now at least, the crisis seemed to be over.

I smiled weakly. 'I supposed if I'd eaten Ahmed's awful baba ganoush none of this would have happened. Was it truly horrible?'

'It was... so-so,' Isabelle smiled. 'But, Mukesh, you must be more careful.'

'I will, I promise. But please don't tell anyone about this. Otherwise, everyone worries and fusses so.'

I woke in the morning feeling reasonably well rested, all things considered. I had Omer drive me into the office, whereupon I called a meeting of my UN agency heads. Inside, I was seething over what had taken place in Darfur, but I forced myself to speak in even, measured tones as I laid out the findings of our mission. Having dealt with the specifics, I rounded off with this.

'Our response to the crisis in Darfur must be twofold. First, we have to draw attention to exactly what is happening more widely within the aid and diplomatic community, and more forcefully here in Khartoum. Second, we, the UN, need to launch a major humanitarian operation on the ground to help the victims. At this stage we are being told that this is Arab gunmen on horseback, at times supported by aircraft. Clearly, the government is not doing enough to safeguard and protect its own people, which is their key responsibility.'

I ended by asking for any questions or specific proposals as to how we, the UN, should react. The response was lacklustre and muted. No one seemed to want to state the obvious – *this has to be the Sudanese government's doing* – because the truth was far too uncomfortable to contemplate. As to my specific proposal to boost our presence in Darfur, it could hardly have met with more resistance. 'Well, you know, it's really very simple – we haven't got the staff,' announced one of the UNICEF people in the room. 'And moreover we have to get clearance, and is this really our priority? We have many things going on in many parts of the country, and we do not want to get blocked by the government in those areas.'

By rights, UNICEF should have been dealing with everything other than food aid in Darfur – so, health, water and sanitation. Without them, I had limited capacity to get a major humanitarian mission underway. I knew I couldn't order them in, but I could create the circumstances wherein they would be forced to act. I left the meeting convinced that only a large bomb under their backsides would move most of them.

But before planting that bomb I first needed to see Roger, and urgently. I'd asked him to follow up with his contacts, to try to and out what had happened to the woman who had spoken. I was desperate for some positive news, yet as soon as Roger walked into my office I could tell that all was not well.

'My sources confirm that woman was picked up by the local secret police,' Roger told me. 'They threw her in the cells and gave her a savage beating by all accounts. They claim to have released her, after which the trail has, unfortunately, gone cold.'

I cursed under my breath. 'But, Roger, that's a bloody nightmare. We could have done so much more on the ground. We should at least have said, "Please, do not harm that woman – we are watching." She risked everything to speak to us, and we didn't even say "thank you" or say anything to those goons.'

'Sir, we have to look after ourselves,' Roger remarked. 'The safety of our staff is paramount.'

Roger's job was to ensure the security and safety of UN personnel. He was paid to safeguard my fellow UN staff and me, and he was a realist. He had no responsibility for the security of those who spoke to the UN – often at great risk – for that lay outside his remit. But knowing that did little to assuage my anger.

'That's as may be,' I countered, 'but still we could and should have done more. We could have passed a message to the governor. We could have said, "We met this woman and she told us very useful things and please ensure she is looked after. The UN will be watching." Instead, we did nothing.'

I felt a cold rage taking hold of me. I had an image in my mind of that brave, dignified black African woman standing to speak, and all around her those Arab men yelling threats and abuse. She had had the courage to speak, and we the UN had done nothing. Worse, by not intervening to help we had more or less signalled to the governor and his cronies: *get on with the job, boys.*

I asked Roger what else we could do to try to protect that woman. He told me that if he pushed it any further, it might only make matters worse for her. If he kept pushing for answers, it might simply give them all the more reason to make her 'disappear'. He counselled that it was best to let it lie.

In short, that woman's brave words had been met with an abject lack of action on our part to protect her. In light of our failure, I felt like a total fraud.

Abuse because of one's skin colour hits me doubly hard, for I have been a victim of it myself. Having suffered it at school in England, I knew how soul-destroying it could prove, and my experience had only ever amounted to verbal abuse and bullying.

As a 16 year old fresh out of India, my first impressions of Wellington College were fine ones. It is built of a warm red brick with an elegant symmetry and approached via a long drive fringed with flaming rhododendrons. But as I gathered in the quadrangle beside the porter's lodge with the rest of the 'new boys', I couldn't help but notice that everyone else was white.

Prior to coming to England, I'd read a book called *Nigger at Eton*. It is the true story of a black African boy who ended up getting educated at Eton in the 1960s. It was both amusing and shocking as it related how he tried to adapt to the abuse. But in reality, Wellington College in the early 1970s was only marginally more enlightened, and by the end of my time there I would be tempted to pen my own schooldays memoir – 'Wog at Wellington'.

That first day at Wellington, Peter Waghorn, my housemaster, and his wife, Rosemary, invited me for dinner. In the warm surrounds of their family home, I began to feel a little more welcome, but the trouble was that I had never eaten with a knife and fork before. In India, most people eat with their hands, and it is considered polite and proper to do so. The project to 'get the boy to England' hadn't seen to teaching me how use cutlery.

Rosemary had cooked roast chicken, which requires real skill to get the flesh off the bones without picking them up and gnawing them. I sat next to her and wherever she cut, I cut, and that way I pretty much got away with it. The dessert was chocolate pudding, which was delicious, but the main meal had been tasteless and bland compared to Indian food. The Waghorns had four young children below the age of ten, and I sensed that they might become my family away from home, which was heartening.

But once dinner was done, I had to retire to the school dorm. Inside a vast and echoing hall were set rows of wooden cubicles each like a large wardrobe but with no roof. It was one cubicle per boy, inside of which was an iron bedstead, a wooden desk and a door that was not lockable. After the summer heat of Chandigarh, I found it cold. On the first night, a group of boys bundled into my cubicle and yanked off my blanket in an effort to see if I was 'brown all over'. I was wearing pyjamas, and I managed to yank the blanket back before the boys charged off, banging the door and laughing uproariously.

Early the following morning, I headed for the bathroom. It was a big, open place with four washtubs set against one wall and a line of sinks on the other. The system for bathing was that seniors went first, juniors next, and lastly the new boys like me. Coming from a strict Hindu family, I had always been taught that cleanliness brought one closer to God. I had washed every day at home, and this system of bathing in someone else's grey-brown water really didn't appeal.

For a moment, I considered using the sink for a stand-up wash, but then I noticed a boy scrubbing his testicles under one of the taps. He had cleaned his teeth and washed his face in the sink, and now he was doing the same to his manly bits. I was an Indian boy on my second day at an English public school, and I stood there wondering if testicle scrubbing was some kind of esteemed English tradition. Was I expected to do the same, and would not doing so only serve to further single me out as the brown oddball from India?

I decided that from now on I would get up very early and wash before anyone was awake. There was no heating in the school as far as I could tell, and I started to have these cold baths alone in the echoing washroom. That was fine for the first month or so, but the English winter of 1971 turned out to be unusually cold. By November, the water was frozen, and there was frost on the inside of the windowpanes.

In India, bathing had been a daily ritual. You would wash to purify yourself before prayer. Usually I'd take a bucket of water from the tap, soap up, and pour it over my head with a cup. The water never needed heating. There was a general belief that Westerners didn't bathe regularly. Grandma had warned me about this. 'I suppose you know that *vilayatis* – foreigners – are dirty people who don't bathe properly. They use a lot of perfume to cover up their smell.'

At Wellington College, I began to worry that maybe Grandma was right. I'd been introduced to the rituals of testicular ablutions and shared bathing, and I concluded that I had landed in a country of philistines. I couldn't understand how the people of England could be so 'unclean' and yet at the same time treat me as if I was somehow inferior simply due to my skin colour. It didn't make any sense.

Wellington College had been founded in 1856 as tribute from a grateful nation to the Duke of Wellington, one of Britain's foremost military commanders. Its purpose was to educate boys orphaned by war, and as a result it had a very strong martial tradition. I had joined Lynedoch House, which had been named after another great Napoleonic commander. It was a very physical school, while also striving for intellectual excellence.

Fairly quickly it became clear to the other pupils that my brown skin didn't in fact make me stupid, as they had mostly thought. Few could compete with me in my best subjects – biology, chemistry and maths. My fellow pupils appeared to find this baffling: I was this odd-looking brown boy from India who actually appeared to be smart. They resorted to teasing me for being a 'swot', in addition to mocking me for being a 'wog' and a 'nigger'.

My real problems weren't academic: it was what to do in terms of sport. Rugby was the big thing at Wellington. I managed to get out of that by claiming that I couldn't see without my glasses. I was soft and podgy for my size, but I knew I'd have to take up some kind of sport or I would suffer. One day I spotted a notice about 'fencing', and without having a clue what it was I signed up for it. As luck would have it, I would prove to be a natural swordsman.

I took up foil, sabre and epée. Each employed a distinctive kind of sword requiring a different way to stab, slash or cut. It was a one-on-one sport, which suited me, and it was very, very fast. I became the fencing club secretary and won my colours, which meant that I could represent the school. More importantly, I was no longer just the pudgy brown-skinned swot. I was also something of a fencing champ, which was a martial sport of real standing.

But still the bullying continued. My greatest tormentors were two boys called Holden MacShane and Freddy DeWitt. They led the teasing mercilessly. At the end of the second term, I decided that I'd have to face them down, or it would only get worse. I challenged Freddy DeWitt to the 'Big

Kingsley' – a ten-mile cross-country run around the Wellington estate – to prove I was his equal.

Holden MacShane, my other chief tormentor, reacted in the strangest of ways to the challenge. He became my coach. He seemed determined to get me to a level of fitness wherein I'd beat DeWitt.

He got me out running daily. 'Come on, you bastard, you nigger, you wog!' he'd yell. 'Faster! Faster! You're going to win this one if it kills me!'

Gambling was a big thing at the school, and it turned out that MacShane had taken out a giant bet that I would beat DeWitt. DeWitt was a keen rugby player and I was only a sissy 'wog' fencer, so there was no need to guess who people were putting their money on. DeWitt didn't even bother to practise, he was so confident of winning. By contrast, MacShane had me out in all weathers slogging through the mud, his abuse ringing in my ears.

In India, I was used to hot and dry weather. I was used to cycling to the library in Chandigarh for a day's relaxing reading. Here in England I found myself struggling through the dark, dripping, muddy forest with cries of 'wog' and 'nigger' ringing in my ears. A part of me was incensed, but there was also a part of me that was almost flattered that MacShane had taken on this role. Yet mostly I was determined to win for myself and to shame them all.

The great day dawned. The start point was Grubbies, the tuck shop. The entire year seemed to have assembled to see us off. Many had come to laugh and jeer, and to lay their final bets. MacShane would be running ahead of me as my pace setter and to ensure that I didn't lose the way. We set off, DeWitt immediately opening up a strong lead. I fell further behind, and by the mid-point DeWitt was ahead of me by a good mile or so.

But as we entered the last lap DeWitt began to slacken. In my slow, plodding, tortoise-like way, I managed to lessen DeWitt's lead. Imperceptibly, I began to overhaul him. On the approach to Grubbies, I finally overtook him. I crossed the line a good half of a football pitch ahead, and I'd done it.

I'd beaten DeWitt in front of the entire school year.

MacShane was dancing about ecstatically. 'You bastard! You bastard! You did it! You did it!' No doubt he was already savouring his winnings.

Freddy and I shook hands like proper English gentlemen, but like most of the other pupils he was in shock. Against all expectations, the swotty wog from India had beaten DeWitt, the white rugby-playing Englishman. From then on the bullying stopped. I didn't exactly become popular overnight, but I was left in peace to get on with my studies.

I never ran another cross-country race in my life, but that experience taught me a crucial lesson. When faced with bullies and racists, the only response was to fight back. If you didn't, they would come for you in the middle of the night and make your life a living hell. I'd learned that lesson at age 17 the hard way, and I'd never forgotten it.

And I held it in my mind's eye now, as I contemplated my next move to combat the horror that was unfolding in the far western deserts of Sudan.

TEN

All truth passes through three stages. First, it is ridiculed. Second, it is violently opposed. Third, it is accepted as being self-evident.

Arthur Schopenhauer

FIRST OFF, I CALLED TOGETHER THE DIPLOMATIC COMMUNITY in order to brief them. We gathered in my office, the key ambassadors and chargés being keen to hear what we had discovered in Darfur. Tom Vraalsen was still with us, and as Kofi Annan's special envoy he was senior to me, meaning that by rights he had to lead things.

He proceeded to give a short briefing in very low-key terms. There was no mention of the scale of the unfolding violence, of the causation of that violence, or of the woman who had spoken out about the abductions and rapes. By the time he was done, I was seething. Shortly after the briefing, he had to head for the airport to return to Oslo, but before he left I challenged him.

'Why were you not more forthright?' I demanded. 'After all we saw and heard, could you not have been a good deal more blunt with the ambassadors?'

Tom hesitated before replying, 'I didn't feel I could do so without first discussing it with New York.'

In other words, he'd have to check with Kofi Annan, his boss in UN headquarters, before saying anything more forceful on Darfur. This was hardly encouraging. From my experience, New York was a giant black hole into which everything disappeared and nothing ever emerged. Moreover, UN headquarters didn't even seem to want to know, let alone be bothered, about Darfur. Their attention was focused laser-like on the north–south peace talks, with everything else being ignored.

That evening, I paid a visit to the British ambassador,

William Patey, at his residence. He was a good, plain-talking type, and he didn't take long to get to the point.

'What the hell was that about earlier today, Mukesh? Why is the UN being so mealy-mouthed about the whole thing?'

While Patey and his fellow diplomats hadn't been to Darfur, they had access to their own sources of information about what was happening there. They had been hoping for full disclosure from us, the UN, so as to enable them to stiffen their public resolve. Sadly, they'd got nothing of the sort.

'I've no idea,' I told him, 'especially since the full picture from Darfur is hugely worrying. There are violent raids being visited on rural villages, and it's that which is driving people into the camps. Those villages are largely black African, the raiders Arab horsemen. The Sudan government is very much implicated in supporting, if not driving, the violence. We've just seen glimpses of what's going on, and it's probably far worse and likely to get worse still.'

Patey shook his head, grimly. 'So it's as bad as we feared. We suspected terrible things were going on. We didn't know it all, but we had our suspicions. It's a real wasted opportunity for the UN to take the lead.'

'The question is, what to do?' I asked. I was hugely disappointed that Vraalsen had not been more forthright.

Patey shrugged. 'I'll report to London on all that you've told me, and we'll see what happens. But right now that's about all we can do, Mukesh.'

'Perhaps there is one other thing,' I volunteered.

If I had a confidante in Sudan, William Patey was as near as I got to it. More importantly, if the idea that was coalescing in my mind was to get anywhere, I'd need his full support and that of his fellow diplomats.

'What do you have in mind?' William asked.

'The conflict in Darfur is generating enormous humanitarian needs. That's clear. We need to massively expand our presence there, and all of that will cost money. I'm planning to launch a Special Fund for Darfur. Based on our assessments, we'll need $22.8 million for food, water, medical supplies and logistics. I'm going to appeal to all major world governments to contribute. Once we get access, we can get international staff in to track, document and report what is really happening, which is of course my real agenda here.'

William smiled knowingly. 'Kind of a "stalking horse" as we Brits might call it.'

'Exactly. It's my stalking horse. The more internationals visit and see for themselves, and the more eyes we have on the ground, the more voices I hope will be raised in the wider sense, so blowing the whistle.'

I left William's place late and feeling more positive about things generally. He had assured me he would fight my corner with the international diplomatic community, which was key to getting the money flowing. Without funds, all of this was going nowhere.

The following morning I set in train my still barely nascent plan. If I was to get millions of dollars of aid flowing into Darfur, I'd need a solid framework within which to do so. First off, I gave it an identity: 'The Greater Darfur Special Initiative'. I put Daniel Christensen in overall charge of the GDSI, with the remit to spend two weeks of every month on the ground in Darfur. I also got an old colleague of mine, Rob Holden, pulled out of DFID and sent on secondment to me in Khartoum.

Rob and I went back a long way. He was a rough-and-ready north of England lad whom I'd once all but sacked from DFID because he couldn't seem to get the hang of writing like a proper civil servant. Rob had pleaded to be given a second chance, to show what a committed and heartfelt humanitarian he was. He'd gone on to be my chief operations officer during the troubles in Kosovo, East Timor and Sierra Leone. I knew I could count on him to manage ramping up a massive aid effort into Darfur.

I'd put Daniel at the tip of the spear, prioritising actions on the ground, and I'd have Rob getting our teams in, while I oversaw it all from Khartoum. I needed an extra element to make the GDSI complete: we needed to understand the ethnic make-up of the tribes that populated Darfur. All evidence pointed to this being a racially driven conflict, but we needed to be able to differentiate between regular, seasonal infighting over resources and what was happening now.

Accordingly, I recruited Marianne Nolte, a Dutchwoman working with UNDP, to the team. Marianne was a sociologist and a political historian who'd been around Sudan for years. She had an in-depth understanding of what 'normally' happened year-on-year in Darfur. Normally, nomadic Arab tribes came south during the dry season, seeking grazing for their livestock. This brought them into conflict with the settled black African farmers. There would be skirmishing, and then the tribal elders would sit together and reach agreement on when and where the nomads could graze.

Arab and black Africans alike shared Islam as their common religion, and there would be intermarriage, to build alliances and dampen down the potential for conflict. Most importantly, none of this seasonal infighting would lead to the kind of mass horror or fleeing populations that we were seeing now in Darfur.

Marianne figured that the traditional system of conflict resolution had broken down and that racial identities were being manipulated to fuel enmities between tribes. She'd heard reports that Arabs were now using the term '*zurka*' – crudely translated as 'black bastards' – to describe their black African neighbours in Darfur. I asked her to research and document this exhaustively, so we would know exactly what we were talking about here.

My next priority was to raise the cash we needed. There was only one sure-fire way to secure $22.8 million: it was to travel to the capitals of the main donor nations and to make an appeal in person to those who held the purse strings. That was what I planned to do. It would also be an opportunity to see my family and to pick up some much-needed prescription supplies of insulin.

But before going global, I had one more mission to

undertake within Sudan: I needed to see John Garang, the rebel leader, again. I needed to secure from him a strong and unequivocal message on Darfur. I needed him to tell me categorically that because of Darfur he couldn't sign any peace deal with Khartoum. Then, I could take that message to the international community, and that would be my golden bullet in terms of getting world governments to act.

I flew south to see Garang armed with an agreement between the UN and the SPLM to establish an UNDP office in the south of the country. This was what Garang had asked of me at our first meeting: *honour the UN's original agreement with us*. It was largely a symbolic gesture, for I would be relocating just the one staff member from Khartoum to this UNDP office in the south, but still there was great significance and meaning embodied within that symbolism.

Garang had asked me to overnight at his base in the bush, and I figured this was some kind of breakthrough. In spite of the fact that I represented an organisation – the UN – that had badly let him down in the past, we seemed to have made a connection. Perhaps he had heard about the shake-up that I'd caused within the UN in Khartoum and concluded that I was my own man.

The rebel leader greeted me at the airstrip with a flashing smile. There was the firm, crushing handshake followed by the beginnings of a tentative bear hug. He took me directly to see the site that he'd set aside for the UNDP office, and from there we moved out to his base beneath the trees, for the document signing. This was a hugely meaningful act, and as I passed him the papers I could tell that the importance wasn't lost on him.

Over tea, we had a discussion about developments since the last time we had met. The Naivasha peace process appeared to be crawling towards some kind of resolution, and we talked about how we could build a new nation united in peace. We talked about road building, healthcare, education, agriculture and mine clearance, plus demilitarising child soldiers, as some of the key priorities.

But it was then that Garang started to voice concerns that ultimately led back to Darfur.

'I believe a good Naivasha agreement is the best chance of Sudan remaining one united country. But the team that is negotiating from the north is dominated by extremists in Omar Al Bashir's government, and that excludes the opposition and the marginalised groups. So, I am concerned that I am doing a deal with a party that doesn't fully represent the north.'

Garang paused, and I let the silence lie between us. 'If I, John Garang de Mabior, do a deal with Al Bashir, then it must not be at the cost of other groups in the north. If we sell them down the river the rebels on the eastern front, or those in Darfur – that will be a betrayal and a disaster for our country. And bear in mind the Khartoum team has no one on it from Darfur.'

'So without the Darfuris peace is untenable?' I probed.

He glanced off into the distance, then back to me. 'I am not going to sign for peace until the picture in Darfur is clear. In signing, I will become the vice-president of Sudan, and at that moment I will have to take responsibility over Darfur. I am not stupid. Whatever form the planned government of national unity may take, the real power will remain with the military, and, more importantly, the Mukhabarat. Thus the new government of Sudan will be powerless to change the tactics in Darfur.'

Garang took a sip of his tea, as he let what he'd said sink in. 'I've fought long and hard to stop the human-rights abuses that took place against my people, here in the south, but how can I control what the military and the Mukhabarat do in Darfur? I cannot. And then I will get blamed for not stopping all this nastiness, and I will lose my reputation as a humanitarian defender.'

'So what next?' I probed. 'What will you do about it, and is there anything I can do to help?'

He fixed me with this very direct look. 'Dr Kapila, I will delay signing the Naivasha agreement for as long as it takes so that Darfur can be solved.'

'Is there anything I can do to help?' I repeated.

He laughed. It was a deep booming laugh, as if my question truly had amused him. I figured that the whole conversation had been leading up to this moment. It was as if he had wanted to solicit my help from the start but had been probing and testing the ground, somewhat unsure how to proceed.

'Go take this message to your friends and make them understand what I am saying. Tell them that I will not sign Naivasha while Darfur is in flames. Tell them what I cannot tell them, stuck here in the bush as I am. Make them understand.'

He didn't specify who 'my friends' were, but he didn't need to. I had already told him that I was about to embark upon my tour of world capitals, to raise funds. He wanted his message to go direct to the seats of power, and for me to be its bearer. I told him that I understood and would be happy to have those conversations.

Garang had every reason to guard his moral authority. He had fought for decades to win dignity and rights for the people of the south, and he needed that to be set within the context of equal rights for all peoples in Sudan. Who could argue with that? The movement in the south had never been as united as it was now, under him. He had underpinned all of this by building confidence and trust in himself as an icon and as a moral figure – the Nelson Mandela of Sudan, almost.

Mandela had been a fighting man before he went to prison, whereupon he refined his ideology. Garang had been in his own prison, trapped in the bush as he was. The only way that Garang could remain in power in the long run was to be seen as a champion of all oppressed people in Sudan. If he had his credentials stained by the blood of Darfur, he would be finished, and he knew it.

The logic of his position was clear and coherent. He was a clever guy playing the long game. And what struck me most powerfully was his total conviction over Darfur. It was like a lightning bolt of insight: *of course, a man such as this cannot sign for peace while Darfur is in flames.*

That evening, a couple of crates of Ethiopian beer were produced, ones that had been smuggled in across the border. We sat in the shadows around the fire, the air around us alive with chirruping cicadas. At some stage a troupe of dancing girls formed up, and they shimmied and shook as powerful drumming pulsed through the night-dark bush. This was a very black African show, as opposed to the governor of Nyala's martial troupe that I had seen during my visit to Darfur.

I wished Garang good night with a warm feeling of contentment. I'd been billeted in a simple mud hut, one furnished with a bed made of a wooden frame strung with rope. It was set against the hut's one window. From the angle of the bed it offered a view of the brilliant, starlit heavens. There was no electric lighting – no electricity full stop – across almost the entire south of the country, and so no urban lighting polluted the sky. The view was like nothing I had seen before, except perhaps during magical childhood nights in India.

On summer evenings, Grandma used to drag the charpoys – low beds not dissimilar to the one that I was now lying on – onto the flat roof of our Chandigarh house. It was cooler up there, and my cousins and I would gather to hear her stories. More often than not she'd tell us a tale from the Bhagavad Gita, one with a strong message about good and evil. We'd sit there wide-eyed in wonder, and we'd always beg for another once the first was finished, then fall asleep before that was done.

Occasionally Grandma would choose to tell us a real-life story, more often than not one anchored in our family history. The tale about Grandpa Narsing Lal Kapila – our rebel grandpa – was a favourite. Grandpa Narsing Lal was my father's father, and he was the founder of the Sanatan Dharam High School, in Lahore, a fine establishment set in the heart of the Muslim Punjab.

At that time, Lahore was a renowned centre of high

culture wherein the Mughal kings did much to nurture poetry, literature and fine architecture. Education was well respected in that society, and my grandfather was seen as a strict and disciplined educationalist and a pillar of the community. He firmly believed that everyone could improve themselves via education, although he was never one to suffer fools gladly.

In time, Grandpa had answered Mahatma Gandhi's call to liberate the nation and free it from British colonial rule. He wasn't a freedom fighter as such, but he became one of the intellectuals who formed part of the non-violent, civil-disobedience movement that made the case for why an educated, historic country like India should throw off the yoke of British control.

My father in turn was very heavily influenced by Grandpa Narsing Lal's life and work. He took from him an unyielding belief in the ability of education to empower the individual, and of the individual's ability to transform a nation.

I drifted off to sleep reflecting upon all of this, and the strong affinity I felt for this African rebel leader, Garang, and for his life's mission. The following morning, I awoke with the dawn, and we grabbed a quick breakfast, for I would need to be off early to make my scheduled flight back to Khartoum. That done, Garang took me to one side to have a final, private chat beneath the spreading acacia trees. The sun wasn't up yet, and the bush was cool and quiet.

'There is one more thing that I think you need to know.' He was speaking very deliberately. 'You should know that the Khartoum regime are in alliance with a vicious Arab militia called the *Janjaweed* – a name which means the "devil horsemen". They are raising this militia and arming it to wage a proxy war against the rebels in Darfur. When those refugees refer to "Arab horsemen", they mean the Janjaweed. And believe me, as long as the Janjaweed are armed and let loose in Darfur, there will never be an end to the violence and the bloodshed.'

I thanked him for this final piece of vital information,

and we said a warm farewell. The bear hug was reassuringly powerful this time, and I assured the rebel leader that I would take his message to the world. As my aircraft took off from the dirt airstrip, I realised how much this visit had been a turning point for me. I now knew that in truth the Naivasha peace talks were going absolutely nowhere if they continued in isolation from Darfur.

I also knew the identity of the mysterious 'Arab horsemen' that so many victims had spoken of. *The Devil Horsemen*. It was a horribly chilling name, one that boded ill for the future of the people of Darfur. Garang had been absolutely clear about one thing: as long as the Janjaweed were on the rampage there was no possibility of a peace deal being signed between him and Khartoum.

When I had accepted the offer of the post of UN chief in Sudan, I had done so in the belief that we were on the brink of a major peace deal being agreed. It was early August by now, so some five months into my posting, and I knew the reality. In truth, there could be no successful outcome from the peace talks unless the horror in Darfur was stopped. It was a very different reality from what I had anticipated, and few if any involved in the peace negotiations seemed to know it. On several occasions, I had been to attend the peace talks. They were taking place in Naivasha, a lakeside town set in Kenya's Rift Valley. Publicly, both sides appeared optimistic of a deal being reached, as had General Sumbeiywo, the Kenyan in charge of brokering the talks. Most of my UN agency heads appeared to be equally hopeful. But privately General Sumbeiywo had admitted that things were grinding along painfully slowly, with endless wrangling over the key issues as most saw them – money, oil and power.

But after this heartfelt meeting with Garang, I knew there was another, major obstacle standing in the way of peace. My talks with the rebel leader had been wide ranging and enlightening, and I respected him hugely. And, crucially, he had given me the ammunition I needed to lobby world governments on the issue that lay closest to my heart – Khartoum's 'final solution' in Darfur.

As to my relations with those at the heart of power in the north of the country, they felt increasingly hollow. It was as if I existed in some kind of a weird bubble in Khartoum. On the surface, I'd got acquainted with various government people, but I had no relations with them socially. The nearest I'd come to knowing anyone was Sulaf – my contact at HAC – but our 'gentlemanly' liaisons were largely a facade.

It was all very different from my earlier time as a young medical student in Khartoum, when I had made good friends and felt a real connection. Now, over everything was cast the dark shadow of the Mukhabarat, the real power in the north. They listened in on and watched what we were up to, just as they monitored more or less every aspect of people's lives.

Trying to work with the regime in the north was like hammering on a concrete wall through which you could neither pass nor see. You could get to the outer door – the government people – but what went on beyond that, at the real heart of power, was inaccessible.

Even with the government people I felt I had little understanding of what they really cared for. There wasn't even any extremist Islamist rhetoric with which to grapple. There was no heart or soul. There was nothing. In the north there was a secret state within a state, and that remained completely hidden.

But the time was soon coming when it would reveal itself to me - all-powerful and red in tooth and claw.

ELEVEN

Mutual denials settle nothing.
The Sage Kapila

I WAS AT MY HOUSE, PACKING TO LEAVE FOR MY TRIP OVERSEAS, when there was a call on my mobile phone.

I went onto the veranda to answer it. 'Hello, this is Mukesh.' 'It's Nadia. Have you heard?'

I could tell immediately that something was wrong. 'Heard what?' 'About Sergio. There's been a bombing in Baghdad, and he's either seriously injured or dead.'

Sergio Vieira de Mello was the chief of the UN in Iraq, and a very close friend. I was so utterly shocked I was speechless. I rushed into my room, grabbed my radio and switched on the BBC World Service. From their live coverage, I learned what had happened. Al Qaeda in Iraq had bombed the UN, and Sergio and several of his staff were feared dead.

I listened to the news reports throughout the night as the rescue operation unfolded. From those I learned that Sergio had indeed died, and one by one the names of the UN team who had perished alongside him were announced, including two other close friends.

This was a dark and sobering moment. My mind was filled with memories of the time that Sergio and I had spent together in Kosovo, East Timor and elsewhere. He had been a true inspiration and a very good friend. Classically handsome and full *of joie de vivre* as only a Brazilian can be, Sergio had been hugely stimulating to work with and fun to be around. He was a totally committed humanitarian with a very big heart.

At the same time that I was offered my posting to Sudan, Sergio had asked me to join him with the UN in Iraq. I had opted for Sudan, and had I gone to Iraq I'd probably be lying in the rubble alongside him.

The first thing I did when I got in to our office the following morning was to open a condolences book. 'The flame that warmed us and showed us the way has gone,' I wrote. 'I've learned so much from you and we will miss you forever.'

I left the book in the meeting room and sent out word that everyone was welcome to add their thoughts. Over the following day, scores of people from the UN, the diplomatic corps and aid agencies came to sign, but not one representative from the Sudanese government did. In the closely controlled Khartoum media, there wasn't a mention of Sergio's death or the barest expression of sympathy with the wider UN.

I found this outrageous. Sergio may have been serving in Iraq – an intervention that the Sudanese government didn't support – but he was doing so in the name of peace and on behalf of all world governments that made up the UN. For me, the Khartoum regime's silence signalled that his death didn't matter to them. I was saddened by their behaviour, not to mention appalled.

At our office, we flew the light-blue UN flag alongside that of the Sudan. I wanted to bring both to half-mast, as a sign of our sympathy and respect for Sergio and the others who had died. However, with the government expressing not the slightest sympathy, I didn't feel I could bring their flag to half-mast. But equally I couldn't lower the UN flag alone. So I opted to bring down both flags completely and for the office to have bare flagpoles for the week following the tragedy. I steeled myself for the Sudanese government's reaction, but strangely there was none. What did happen, however, was the start of a massive security upgrade both at the UN office and at my residence. Roger pointed out that Sergio was my opposite number in Iraq, and if he could be hit there, so I could be hit here. He set in train a programme to beef up entry and exit security, to fit shatterproof film on all windows and to erect CCTV covering strategic points. And he used the opportunity presented by my going overseas to book Omer, my driver, on a course to learn defensive driving skills.

I left Khartoum on a flight routed to Oslo so I could meet first with Hilde Johnson, Norway's minister for international development. Hilde was a real child of Africa. She was born there, spoke Swahili - the native language of East Africa – and I knew her well from my time in DFID. I had come to admire her commitment to the poor, as well as her blunt and direct manner. Along with the USA and the UK, Norway was part of the troika of nations pushing forward the Naivasha peace talks – all of which made Hilde a good port of call to kick off my fundraising.

I had written out a number of bullet points, clarifying the key reasons for backing my Darfur initiative. A picture was emerging that terrible things were happening, but ours remained a half-formed, patchy understanding. Even so, the lessons from Rwanda and Srebrenica were that action taken early enough could prevent genocide, as opposed to trying to pick up the pieces afterwards. I figured that was where we were at now, and that early intervention could prevent the 'final solution' from becoming a reality in Darfur. Moreover, I needed to warn the key players that there would be no peace in Sudan unless the killer elements in Darfur were brought under control, just as Garang had told me.

Hilde received me warmly in the modern glass-and-steel building that housed her Oslo ministry. She listened carefully to all that I had to say on Darfur. She seemed shocked by what I told her, and she was happy to pledge funds to my Greater Darfur Special Initiative. But she seemed reluctant to do anything that might threaten to derail the Naivasha peace process.

'We are aware of Darfur, and we're concerned about it,' she reassured me, 'but we think getting a good north–south peace deal will solve that problem, as it will all problems in Sudan.'

'How long do you think that will take?' I asked.

'It's imminent,' she told me. 'In two to three months, we

figure we'll have a historic agreement that will set a whole new precedent for Sudan.'

It was then that I told her about the message that Garang had given me – that he would sign no peace deal without Darfur first being addressed. Hilde seemed a little shaken, but her advice to me was to hold out for the peace deal being signed. She also pointed out that Norway was a small player on the world stage, and if I wanted real action to be taken it would need to be led by Norway's partners in the troika, Britain and the US.

From Oslo, I flew on to Stockholm, Copenhagen, Amsterdam, Rome, Paris and from there to London. Along the way, I raised several million dollars towards my $22.8 million funding target, but at each juncture I was told to take my wider concerns over Darfur to those who wielded real influence – the British and the Americans. I knew therefore that my London meetings were going to be critical.

I headed first to DFID, to argue for funds, and from there to the Foreign and Commonwealth Office (FCO) – those who set foreign policy within the British government. Although I was serving as the UN chief in Sudan, I was actually on secondment to the UN from DFID, which meant that I was still a British government employee. Due to the senior posts that I'd held at DFID over the years, I retained my security clearance up to the highest level within the British government – Beyond Top Secret – and I had requested as full a briefing as possible over Darfur.

During my career, I'd spent a good deal of time at the FCO's grand building in Whitehall. I felt strangely at home within its white-pillared splendour with cool marbled floors and giant, golden-framed oil paintings of great figures from Britain's colonial past staring sternly from the walls. In the calm hush of one of the FCO's fine conference rooms, I met with the Foreign Office and Secret Intelligence Service people who covered Sudan.

A series of satellite photos were laid out on the conference table, scattered amongst half a dozen buff folders encoded with their security level classifications. The briefer explained how this was our most up-to-date surveillance and intelligence from Darfur. Each image showed a progressive worsening of the 'scorched-earth' policy being pursued in the region.

As he flicked through the photos and talked me around each one, a pattern of destruction emerged that was more extensive than I had ever imagined and which was clearly targeted at specific villages, leaving others untouched. Over time, the destruction reached out from the three state capitals – El Fasher, Nyala and El Geneina – like ripples spreading from a stone thrown into a pond.

'For a number of reasons, we suspect the Sudan government is responsible,' the briefer told me. 'The only aircraft in the conflict are theirs, and we have plenty of evidence of Antonovs bombing villages. We also know that a fleet of brand-new helicopter gunships has been acquired from the Ukraine, complete with foreign pilots and maintenance crews. It's what we call a "turn-key operation" – you simply turn the key and they're ready to go.'

My mind flashed back to the Antonov and the pair of glistening gunships that I'd seen armed for war at El Fasher airport. I remarked that I'd seen such military hardware in the field in Darfur and what they were showing me here confirmed my worst suspicions of what it was being used for.

'There is a marked similarity between the tactics being employed in Darfur and how they went about their scorched-earth policy in south Sudan,' the briefer continued. 'Crude but effective petrol bombs are rolled off the rear of the Antonovs to firebomb villages, and troops with militia in support lead the attacks on the ground.

'The pattern is clear: Antonovs bomb a target identified by military intelligence; once the village is burning, the Janjaweed move in. They kill the men, loot the houses and disappear into the bush.' The briefer paused. 'In truth, it's obvious who's organised all of this. What's not clear at this stage is whether the Janjaweed are acting under government orders or if they're exceeding those orders. But in a sense that is a moot point, as the government's fingerprints are all over it.'

I'd heard the rumours in Khartoum; I'd read the patchy reports filtering into our office; I'd listened to the IDPs and the woman who had spoken out tell their horrific stories of what had happened on the ground. But here were the hard facts and the irrefutable evidence. The meeting was being chaired by the FCO person leading on Sudan. The briefing done, I turned to him to ask the obvious question.

'So, if we know exactly what's going on and who is responsible, what are we doing about it?'

'Well, Mukesh, old chap, Naivasha is obviously the key,' he replied. 'It's vital that nothing derails the north–south talks, which will help settle Darfur. If we, or you, put too much pressure on Khartoum, it may well make matters worse. If you really hammer Khartoum, they may go and do something even more extreme, as they don't like being told. So softly-softly is the way to deal with this. In the meantime, how much money do you need for your Darfur fund?'

I explained that I was looking for $22.8 million, and that DFID had pledged a good amount of that. But then I brought things back to the issue at hand.

'A few days ago, I met with John Garang. He told me categorically that he won't sign a peace deal while Darfur is suffering. He was very, very clear that he doesn't want to have their blood on his hands. He said, "Tell your people I am committed to the north–south agreement, but I can't sign while Darfur is in flames."'

The FCO mandarin gave an almost imperceptible shrug. 'Well, that's certainly interesting, but it doesn't change our position. The main game is Naivasha, and we can't get distracted from that. We must be patient. It's best not to rock the boat, Mukesh, old boy, or risk pushing anyone into a corner, for that will only serve to make matters worse.' I saw him glance ostentatiously at his watch. 'Now, I do have a pressing luncheon to attend, so if that's all...'

Our meeting done, he escorted me along the polished

corridors, all the while chatting amiably about individuals that we had in common and about how I was dealing with the heat in Khartoum. I barely heard his words and replied on autopilot. I was shocked and deeply disturbed by what I had seen and heard during our meeting, and on several different levels.

I had come here intending to alert the British government to the darkness spreading across Darfur. Instead, I now knew that they were fully aware of it, and on a level far more detailed than my own. Another thing was crystal clear, having seen those satellite images. A campaign of destruction was being orchestrated across three provinces, one that required enormous effort, planning and resources.

I left with a mixture of conflicting thoughts whirling through my mind. I had expected the British authorities to learn from my observations over Darfur, and I had hoped that might change things in terms of policy. Instead, I had discovered that they knew already, and in far greater depth than I did. Indeed, I suspected that they knew Garang's position well but had opted to play a game of brinkmanship, trading off the suffering in Darfur against a peace deal.

Yet on one level I was almost relieved that my own government knew so much. After all, they were the masters at international politics and power games. Perhaps I should allow myself to be guided by the experts – those with the political, security and intelligence expertise that I lacked. I was a humanitarian, and perhaps that was what I should concentrate on – relieving the human suffering.

On the long flight to New York, I had ample time to ponder all of this. But the more I tried to convince myself to leave it to those who knew, the more I felt like a fraud. Their advice to me had been: *don't rock the boat, or you'll push Khartoum into a corner and make it worse*. But in a situation where a regime had pledged to effect a 'final solution', how could it get any worse? How could my action push the regime into a corner any darker than that?

If the 'final solution' was to crush the Darfuri rebels, that alone was bad enough. But I feared that phrase also referred to crushing the people, or – to paraphrase Mao – the water within which the fish, the rebels, could swim. In fact, I couldn't see how they could have their 'final solution' without murdering countless civilians, for the rebel army was peopled from the villages all across Darfur.

In order for Khartoum to achieve its 'final solution', it had to define and isolate the enemy. It had done so by making them 'the other' – the black African rebels and the natural enemies of the Arab-dominated north. It had raised an 'Arab' militia – the Janjaweed – to unleash a terror operation and hit the rebels where it hurt most, in their home villages. Race had become a defining element of the horror, and while their 'final solution' was still in its early stages, it was gathering momentum.

The barbarity would have to be targeted against civilians if they were going to achieve their aims. Surely, then, the West had to send a powerful message to force Khartoum to back off. I had been present in the immediate aftermath of the Rwanda and Srebrenica genocides, but I hadn't been at the centre of things or at the heart of world power. Now, in Sudan, I felt as if I was. I was the UN resident chief, and that gave me real influence, not to mention the responsibility to act.

I thought back over what I'd told myself so many times before: *not on my watch will they...* I needed to be true to myself. I needed to ensure that I would not be – *I would never be* – one of those few good men who did nothing. I had never seen things so clearly as I did on that flight to New York, and it was in part thanks to the intelligence that the FCO had shared with me.

As I reflected upon all of this, I knew that I couldn't toe the line over Darfur, as that FCO mandarin had suggested. If nothing else, I had to continue to press for the UN to take action. On that long and sleepless flight, I rediscovered my mission, and I was determined to galvanise international action to prevent the 'final solution' from taking hold in Darfur.

My first duty upon reaching New York was to visit UNDP. As UN resident chief in Sudan, I was an UNDP appointee, and, effectively, my direct boss was the head of UNDP, Mark Malloch Brown. Malloch Brown was a fellow Brit with a distinguished World Bank and UN career, and a man that I both admired and from whom I expected great things.

At first he and I talked through my battles against corruption and graft within the UN system in Sudan. I was surprised when he pointed out to me that my efforts had caused 'considerable upset'. I knew they had. I didn't need him to tell me this. The point was, regardless of the upset, it was the right thing to do. We moved on to my meeting with Garang and opening up the UNDP office in the south. This, he told me had 'compromised' UNDP's relations with the Khartoum regime.

He went on to warn me that if I carried on in such a 'maverick' spirit, he foresaw serious trouble ahead. I left his office with nothing resolved after a strained and dispiriting meeting. I felt as if I had little or no backing from my own boss in New York. It was hugely disheartening, and I felt badly let down by Malloch Brown, a man who up until then I had truly respected.

I headed over to the UN headquarters building, a massive 38-floor concrete and glass edifice along New York's East River. I always felt reverential whenever I entered the place. Its bulk rose above me, with the flags of all member nations encircling it, making me feel so small. But at the same time this was the place where, in the words of the UN Charter, 'we the peoples' of the world gathered together and somehow managed to get along.

This was the site of the UN general assembly, the security council chamber and the trusteeship council room where so many countries – including my native India – had been formally decolonised. It was a place steeped in history, one where small countries and big were supposedly equal. For believers like me, this was the mecca.

I was here to see Jan Egeland, the Norwegian head of

OCHA and my boss in my capacity as the UN humanitarian coordinator in Sudan. Jan, I suspected, was as concerned as I over Darfur. I used the intelligence that I had gleaned in London and from Garang in south Sudan to put him more fully in the picture.

'You know, Jan, we're only seeing the tip of the iceberg,' I warned him. 'Underneath, this is a very organised operation, and we'd better be prepared for refugee numbers mushrooming in the weeks ahead.' Jan looked worried. 'This is all very disturbing. On a regional level, the Central African Republic and Chad can take more refugees. We'll need the UN country heads from those nations to ready their host governments to receive them, plus we'll need to discuss and plan carefully how we might coordinate all of this.'

As he and I sat there discussing how to plan for the coming crisis, it struck me as being utterly bizarre what we were doing. We knew – *we knew* – that this storm was approaching, and yet no one seemed to be doing anything to try to stop it. We were preparing for a man-made humanitarian crisis of terrible proportions, when what was really needed was action to stop the storm before it could break.

'Look, Jan, the thing is the great powers know all about this,' I told him. 'They know what is coming; they know who is behind it. So someone needs to say something about this, to fire a warning shot across the bows. Could we, the UN, not go to the security council, to get them to raise such concerns?'

'I agree – we must act,' said Jan. 'I've expressed my concern at a senior level and with Kofi Annan direct. But you need to speak to Kieran Prendergast. We need him on side, for Kofi Annan will turn to his political advisor to gauge his response on Darfur, and that's Prendergast. Prendergast is British, of course, so he should have the same interests and influences as you. Go talk to Prendergast. Maybe he'll be influenced by the man on the ground. Brief him and get him on side.'

As the floors get higher in the UN headquarters building, so the position of the occupant is higher up the UN chain. Ergo, Kofi Annan's office occupied the uppermost, 38th floor. Sir Kieran Prendergast's office was on floor 36, and as head of the UN's Department of Political Affairs (DPA), he would advise Annan on all matters political. Intervening in Darfur would be a political act, albeit one driven by humanitarian imperatives, and that's why we needed Prendergast on side.

I was looking forward to seeing Prendergast, someone I knew well from my DFID days. He was the former British high commissioner to Kenya, with the reputation of being a specialist in African affairs. I had gathered evidence of the darkness descending upon Darfur, and now I was trying to muster the political will to shine a light into that darkness. This meeting was critical to that process, and I had enormous respect for the man I was going to see.

Prendergast was a large, avuncular figure, with a wispy beard, a balding, jowly face and a slight stoop. He tended to dominate a room, as he did now, greeting me with an affable air.

'Mukesh, good to see you, old chap. How is it going in Sudan?'

He offered me coffee and we made the usual small talk. He had his back to the window, which had a fantastic view over the New York skyline. From here, you really might feel as if you were ruling the world. Oddly, I was finding it difficult to get to the point with him. Each time I tried to raise the issue of Darfur, he seemed to steer me in another direction.

Finally, I grasped the nettle. 'Look, Kieran, we really need to speak about Darfur. The north–south peace talks are making painful progress, and there is hugely divided opinion over their prospects. I'm hearing from the Norwegians and Brits that things will be quick, but from my talks with John Garang I fear it'll take far longer. In fact, Garang is adamant that he won't sign unless the troubles in Darfur – which are fast escalating – are addressed. I presume you've seen my reports on the Darfur situation? I've come here for your advice.'

'To be honest, Mukesh, I'm not sure if I'm in a position to advise.' He shrugged. 'You're the man on the ground, after all.'

'Well, leaving aside the peace process, what do we do about Darfur?' I pressed. 'Let's not underestimate this. We're seeing more and more displaced reaching even as far as Khartoum, plus refugees are spilling over into neighbouring Chad. There are serious reports of terrible violence, of burning villages and even mass rape, all of which appears very organised. And the raids are being supported by the use of aircraft, so no doubt Khartoum is involved.'

Prendergast spread his hands. 'Mukesh, these people have been fighting each other for a very long time, so what's new in all of this? It escalates, it de-escalates, and eventually they will fight each other to a standstill.'

I couldn't believe what I was hearing. I tried a different tack. 'Sudan hasn't been taken to the UN security council for a long time. Surely there should be a discussion in New York between concerned states to take political action to dampen the fighting and protect the innocent, and to relieve the suffering on a humanitarian level. The right place to do that is the security council.'

He gave a faint flick of his hand. 'I've been around that part of the world for a long time, as you know. Trust me, there's very little you can do about it. You'll see. And in any case, the UN has its own priorities right now – Iraq and all that – and we can't waste our political capital on Darfur.'

Prendergast rose to his feet to signal that the meeting was over. 'Anyhow, it's been very nice to see you, old chap. Pop around next time you're in New York.'

I was speechless. I felt as if I had been dismissed out of hand. Any hope of calling a halt to the horrors in Darfur lay in political action, not humanitarian plaster sticking. But the UN clearly wasn't intending to get involved, and that was that. I left the building feeling deeply let down by those I had until now respected so much.

And I didn't have a clue where I could turn next.

TWELVE

To be faithful in little things is a big thing.
St Augustine

FOR WANT OF ANY BETTER OPTION, I WENT TO SEE ISABELLE Balot, the Frenchwoman who had accompanied Vraalsen on our visit to Darfur and whose swift action had saved me during my diabetic attack. I sensed that she shared my concerns over Darfur, and I knew that she was used to reporting pretty much directly to Kofi Annan, so I wondered if she might be able to offer some kind of help.

As we talked, Isabelle mentioned that she'd be interested in getting more hands-on experience in Sudan. Nadia's six-month term as my special assistant was almost up, and I needed to find a replacement. Isabelle, I figured, would be perfect. Not only did she know the country well, but she also knew how to navigate the labyrinthine corridors of power here in New York.

I went to see Isabelle's boss and secured an agreement to have her seconded to me for six months. Even so, when I left New York on the shuttle flight to Washington DC, my overriding feeling was one of failure. Apart from Jan Egeland's moral support and recruiting Isabelle, I had achieved nothing.

I felt badly let down by senior UN colleagues who seemed to be blocking any action on Darfur. I was also starting to lose my respect for Kofi Annan himself. I knew that the issue of Darfur had been raised with him repeatedly. I had done so in numerous reports from the field and Jan Egeland had done so directly in New York, but so far, for whatever reason, it appeared that he had opted to do absolutely nothing.

There are two possible routes to access the UN security council. A nation state that is a member of the security council can ask it to investigate an issue. In London, I had pressed for Britain to raise Darfur as an issue and got absolutely nowhere. The second route is via the UN itself. The UN secretary-general has the right to raise an issue directly with the security council if it is of grave importance. This was what I had hoped I might catalyse in New York. Instead I had been told: *no, thank you, this is one mess we don't want the UN dragged into.*

As my plane descended into Washington DC's Ronald Reagan National airport, I was struck by an unsettling realization. I had just been with a number of Brits who were close to the apex of power at the United Nations, yet they were frustrating action being taken over Darfur, and seemingly London was equally disinclined to act. For a moment, I felt ashamed to be British myself, and my time in Washington would only serve to accentuate that sense of national shame.

I held long meetings with both the US State Department and the National Security Council, at which it soon became clear that the US government knew as much as the British about what was happening in Darfur. Their level of satellite imagery and intelligence gathering was equally sophisticated, and the State Department people seemed genuinely concerned. I decided to raise the vital issue with them: could the US not take the issue of Darfur to the UN security council?

'You know what, we'd really like to,' an assistant secretary of state told me, with disarming honesty. 'Trouble is, we can't do anything without the Brits being on board. We're dependent on their political support right now in Iraq. The Brits are supposed to be the experts on Sudan, so we need them to take the lead.'

'Well, the British have extensive information on what's happening in Darfur,' I told him, 'and they share your concerns. But right now it seems they're not willing to go to the security council either.'

The official shrugged. 'That's too bad, 'cause it means we can't. But we agree we should, and we're outraged by what is going on in Darfur.'

He went on to explain that their outrage was driven in part by the powerful lobby of US civil society and religious groups working on Sudan. They were under constant pressure from charities and churches to do the right thing.

'Britain is your country, Dr Kapila,' he remarked, fixing me with a direct look. 'Why don't you go persuade them?'

I shook my head despondently. 'Sadly, I've just come from London, and I don't think we're going to get much joy there.'

I felt that the US government genuinely shared my fears over Darfur and wanted to take action. But with the Iraq war ongoing, they figured they needed the support of the British more than they needed to take action over Darfur. That was the realpolitik here. In short, there seemed to be no clear route through to action, not with the UN blocked from within and the US blocked by Britain.

I left America feeling torn. On the one hand I'd managed to raise – or had I been bribed to stay quiet? – several million dollars for my Greater Darfur Special Initiative. Now, at last, we had a fighting fund with which to get things going on the ground. But on the wider political level, I had achieved absolutely zero.

It is an age-old given that in war – and I felt as if I was preparing for a war now – you should choose your battles carefully. I had already decided that I would fight the battle over Darfur, whatever form that might take. It is also said that you should get to know your adversaries: I now had a better idea of who my enemies might be.

As I flew back to Khartoum, I felt a growing sense of isolation. Apart from Jan Egeland, I had little or no backing within the organisation that had hired me. Quite the contrary: the more I pushed and agitated, the more I felt an inexorable deterioration in relations. It was as if key people were already trying to distance themselves from me, sensing that I was refusing to play the game. In my mind, I was being faithful to the noble ideals of the UN and doing what was right over Darfur, but in their eyes I was a loose cannon and a rebel.

Darfur felt to me like a typical chicken-and-egg scenario. No one seemed willing to take the lead, which meant that no one ever would – and that included the UN. I returned to Khartoum feeling very isolated indeed. I had no one to talk this through with, no confessor or soulmate with whom to test my thinking and dry-run my plans. I sensed that from now on my decisions would be very much mine alone.

My main preoccupation now was gathering facts – securing hard evidence and documented testimony. The seriousness of the war that I was going to fight meant that I needed incontrovertible proof. I needed to muster that information before I could act. I didn't know exactly what form that action would take, but I knew that if I went forward on insufficient evidence, my enemies would use that to discredit and defeat me.

I have two documents hung upon the wall of my study at home in Cambridgeshire. One is a copy of the British Official Secrets Act, which I had to sign to gain my top-level security clearances (I hung it there partly in jest, *lest I forget,* but in practice have always taken it seriously). The other is a poster that has faded much over the years but has become a part of me. It shows a photo of a little girl helping a kitten through a cat flap, beneath a line from St Augustine: 'To be faithful in little things is a big thing'.

If I have a motto in life, perhaps that is it. I strive to be consistent, constant and faithful, and I speak up for those who are down and for the underdog. Invariably, this motto has come to mind whenever I've needed to make any monumental decisions in life. This is the filter that I use – *am I being faithful in the small things?* – and I don't tend to think of the consequences.

If you are faithful in small things in life, then you are even more bound to be faithful in the big things. Thus, I couldn't *not* act on Darfur. I needed to gather all the evidence, and I feared I would be forced to make a stand alone, which meant that trouble was coming for me personally. But if I was to be faithful to that line from St Augustine, no other option was open to me.

Things felt different now in Khartoum. Post Sergio de Mello's killing, it had all become somehow more sinister. When Omer met me at the airport, he had this peculiar, manic look in his eyes. Instead of pootling through the Khartoum streets as usual, he drove me home like a bat out of hell. He went via a network of back streets and at breakneck speed. Apparently, this was how those running the defensive driving course had taught him to drive.

Shortly after my return to Khartoum, Isabelle Balot flew out from New York to join me. Nadia was loath to be replaced, but I sensed that if she remained close to me for any longer – and with Darfur demanding ever more rigorous and spirited action on my part – that relationship would destroy her. She would be seen as my ally and accomplice, and she would fall with me. I tried explaining all of this to her, but Darfur in particular had got under her skin.

Nadia returned to her previous UN post – a necessary move but one made reluctantly on her part. In her place, Isabelle brought a very different range of skill-sets. Nadia was a humanitarian first and foremost. Isabelle had an international political background, and she knew well the machinations of New York. She was a cosmopolitan Parisienne, with the dress sense to match, but more importantly she had direct lines into Kofi Annan's office. I hoped that together we might raise the alarm over Darfur at UN headquarters.

From early on, I'd sensed with Isabelle that here was a very rare thing within the UN – a person who knew how to work the system, yet felt instinctively the rights and wrongs of a situation. Sure enough, beneath Isabelle's worldly exterior there proved to be someone with a warm and emotional heart. She wrote poetry in her spare time, and she had an independent and feisty nature.

Her bosses in New York would expect her to be above all else a UN bureaucrat. They would expect her to guard the interests of the UN, as indeed they did me. But as time would prove, Isabelle would take a stand independently on what was right, regardless of the consequences. She didn't much care if doing the right thing ethically was the 'wrong' thing as far as the UN hierarchy saw it. And it would be Isabelle who would put steel in my soul when the time came for me to break the conspiracy of silence over Darfur.

In keeping with his new security consciousness, Omer decided to swap around where I sat in the vehicle. No longer did he hold the right-hand door open for me. That, he explained, was where any self-respecting assassin would expect the 'principal' – as he now referred to me – to sit. Now, it was the left door, and Omer made Isabelle sit as a kind of decoy in the right-side seat.

'*C'est la place du mort*,' she joked – the dead man's seat.

Yet even with his new obsession, Omer couldn't help but mention what was happening in Darfur. One morning we were driving to a meeting and he threw in some elliptical comment about the terrible things that were happening in such and such location. I realised that he was trying to alert me to the horrors of Darfur. It was an odd thing for him to do, especially since he doubled as a Mukhabarat spy. But that was Omer: in spite of his double agent role I couldn't help but like my driver and somehow trust him.

There was one part of war-ravaged Sudan where we did have an international peacekeeping force on the ground – the kind of thing that was needed in Darfur. That force had largely put an end to the fighting in the Nuba Mountains, a remote area situated in the very centre of Sudan. There were many similarities with the situation in Darfur. The Nuba are a black African people who had raised their own rebel army. They had been targeted by government forces and allied militias in a war of extermination. And, as with Darfur, the Nuba Mountains were remote and inaccessible: the only way in was a long flight by light aircraft.

A few days after my return from my global tour, Isabelle and I flew to the Nuba area to see how the peacekeeping force there was operating and to check if here was a model of how we might solve the troubles in Darfur. As we came in to land, the sharp peaks of the Nuba Mountains reared out of the baking desert like the teeth of some ancient dragon that had been turned to stone. We landed at Kadugli, the capital of the region, where we were met by the peacekeepers.

The first thing that struck me was this sense of distinctiveness. Slopes were green and vegetated, and here lived a people quite different from those of the north or the south. I was also struck by how incredibly basic everything was. We travelled on rough dirt tracks navigable only by 4x4s, and everywhere we went we saw straw and mud-hut villages, and the most rudimentary forms of agriculture. Here, people still farmed using sharpened sticks, so even the introduction of an iron hoe was an agricultural revolution.

The peacekeepers – the Nuba Mountains Monitoring Force – seemed to be doing a fine job. This was an UN-mandated force, one consisting of a good number of internationals who were mostly ex-military. Those internationals were the eyes and ears of the world community here, and it struck me that this was exactly what was needed in Darfur. I visited several of the peacekeeping outposts, and from those stationed there I learned how the operation was managed.

But I also learned something new and unexpected about the conflict in Darfur. The Nuba area was an important point of access into southern Darfur. Almost in passing, I asked if the peacekeepers had seen anything of significance in terms of the troubles there. They told me that they had. Any vehicle passing through the Nuba Mountains had to be checked, as part of the process of monitoring the ceasefire. Recently, they had stopped numerous trucks carrying arms, but because the weapons weren't destined for Nuba territory the peacekeepers had to allow them through. The key point was this: *those arms shipments were destined for Darfur*. These weren't Sudanese military vehicles, and the convoys weren't manned by soldiers. Instead, both the trucks and those driving them were ostensibly civilian, but at the same time the convoys had clearance from the very top of the Sudanese government.

The convoys had begun a few weeks back, and they were increasing in frequency. In short, this appeared to be some kind of undercover or covert operation being run from Khartoum. In the opinion of the peacekeepers, those arms shipments could only be serving one purpose: weapons were being sent by the Khartoum regime to arm the Darfur militia – the Janjaweed.

I'd come here seeking to explore a possible model of how to bring peace to Darfur, but in doing so I'd discovered another piece of the jigsaw puzzle of how the 'final solution' was going to be implemented there. It was chilling. The fact that these arms shipments were ongoing suggested that Khartoum was gearing up to unleash the full extent of the planned horror. Knowing that only fuelled the urgency I felt to do something to stop them.

Upon my return to Khartoum, I decided to raise the stakes by organising a delegation of UN and aid agency people to fly into Darfur. Médecins Sans Frontières was one of the key agencies trying to get access, and I had huge respect for them. If I could get MSF in on the ground in numbers, they would be able to operate far more decisively than the UN and with more freedom to speak.

So began yet another frustrating game of cat-and-mouse with the ministry for humanitarian affairs (HAC). Publicly, HAC claimed they were desperate to get humanitarian workers into Darfur, but when it came to securing clearances I was being blocked at every level. Regardless, I went ahead and assembled the team that I wanted to fly into Darfur, and I berated Sulaf until finally he granted us clearance. That team consisted of Isabelle, Daniel Christensen, Roger and a collection of the key people from MSF and other agencies. Tom Vraalsen was in Sudan, and he also chose to join us. We took off in the Beechcraft, heading for Nyala, the largest city in the region, which was also the main place from where Daniel was picking up reports of fighting and displacement.

I opted to take the seat up front alongside the pilot. He

was a Ukrainian, and he was dressed in the smart white uniform of the UN's flight service, complete with shiny peaked pilot's cap adorned with gold braid. As we pushed onwards towards Darfur, I yelled a request at him above the roar of the aircraft's turbines.

'Can you fly a long loop around Nyala as we approach? I want to pass over some of the rural areas.'

'Sure can, sir,' he replied.

I turned to speak to Daniel and Isabelle, in the seat behind me. 'I've asked him to fly an aerial recce as we approach Nyala, so keep your eyes peeled.'

I felt the aircraft banking around as the pilot put us on a new bearing. I gazed out of the front and side windows at the featureless brown expanse that stretched below us. For several minutes, there was nothing. Then, on the distant horizon, I caught what looked like smoke from a barbecue rising into the hot air. But at this distance, that smoke cloud had to be a good half-kilometre wide at its base.

As the aircraft drew closer, I could make out the distinctive orange glow of a fire raging at the base of that column of smoke. We flew nearer still, by which time I could see a ring of fire almost directly below us, the pillar of smoke rising before our tiny aircraft like a dark and impenetrable wall. Circles of glowing coals lit up the smoke, and as I gazed downwards I could see that each was a village hut in flames. We were flying at 10,000 feet, but even at this altitude I could almost feel the heat from the fires scorching my eyeballs.

We passed that first village and continued for a few kilometres before coming across one that appeared to be completely unharmed. Then, five minutes later, we flew over another village that was being consumed by the inferno. The pattern repeated itself as we flew across maybe half a dozen villages that had been put to the torch and a similar number that were completely unharmed.

I found myself thinking: *here it is, the evidence, right now; these are fresh fires burning as we pass; this is highly selective.* The killers had been sent to some places, skirting around others. I knew from all our research that villages here were either Arab or black African. You didn't get mixed settlements. Here then I was seeing the targeted destruction that I'd been told about in all its stark horror.

'We should start our approach to Nyala, sir,' the Ukrainian pilot remarked. 'We filed a flight plan taking us in on the airport approach flight-path... There's only so far I can veer away.'

I told the pilot that I understood. I'd seen enough already to make my blood run cold. I felt the pilot bring the aircraft around, and some 20 minutes later we touched down at Nyala airport. Nyala was the city at which the woman had spoken out to us about the rapes during our first visit to Darfur, and in my mind at least that woman had never been forgotten.

Our main priority now was to get to see Intifada Camp – an IDP camp on the outskirts of town. We only had two hours on the ground, and this time I was determined not to fall into the governor's clutches. We had UN vehicles awaiting us at the aircraft steps, and after a quick round of diplomatic handshakes we headed directly for the camp.

As we drove, one of our local UN workers briefed us: the destruction of the rural villages was escalating, and much of the countryside was in flames. IDPs were flooding into Nyala, but even here attempts were being made to drive them out again. There were precious few aid agencies working on the ground and those that were here were unable to cope.

Intifada Camp was a sprawling expanse of makeshift shelters and tents set in the baking hot scrub. It was three months since we had last visited Nyala, and now the scale of the dispossessed and the suffering was infinitely greater. There were thousands – probably tens of thousands – of displaced people, and all were noticeably black African. The black tribes of Darfur are the Zaghawa, the Fur, the Masalit and others. All here hailed from those ethnic groups.

The local authorities refused to let the people of Intifada Camp be counted, and they were continuously trying to force them to move. As a result, the population was in a permanent state of flux. It struck me that these were the escapees from stage one of Khartoum's 'final solution', so it was hardly surprising that they couldn't find sanctuary here – in one of the places from which that 'final solution' was being orchestrated.

But worse still were the governor of Nyala's plans to bulldoze Intifada Camp and shift it some 30 kilometres into the open desert. I could guess at the hidden agenda behind such plans. It was hugely inconvenient to have the camp sitting on the city's periphery, for here was the proof of the sheer scale of the brutality being visited on the black African tribes of Darfur.

Having been alerted to the plans to move the camp, I raised my objections right there and then. I pointed out to the governor that the UN had serious problems serving the camp's needs as it was. If it was pushed into the remote bush, the challenges would be insurmountable. No doubt this was the aim in relocating the camp: to remove it from international access and view. But I made it clear that this was unacceptable, especially when the camp's occupants didn't want to go.

Having made my objections, and with our allotted time in Nyala done, we took off for El Fasher, the next stop on our itinerary. Once we were airborne, and a safe distance from prying eyes, I asked the pilot to drop down to the lowest altitude possible as we flew northwards across Darfur. It wasn't long before the first burning villages came into view.

This time the pilot managed to fly at a few hundred feet as we swept over. I could make it out in heart-stopping detail: here, a grain- store flaming fiercely, the dried sorghum burning with a furnace-like heat; there, decapitated heads of men and livestock hanging on a thorn hedge and about to be consumed by the flames; and every now and then the smoking skeleton of a wooden bed lying beside a hut wall. Nowhere in those burning settlements was there a soul to be seen. They were lifeless ghost towns.

We were an hour into the flight when a storm of dust rose up ahead of us. I pointed it out to the pilot and asked him if we could take a closer look. And so we flew in low over a force of galloping horsemen streaming as one across the desert. As soon as the pilot realised what this force of riders was, he pulled back on the controls and climbed to gain altitude.

I glanced across and his eyes met mine. 'If we fly over too low, we may be shot down,' he yelled in explanation. He waved a hand around at the Beechcraft's interior. 'Even small-arms fire can damage such an aeroplane.'

We passed over the galloping column at too high an altitude to make out the individual features of the horsemen or the weapons I knew that they were carrying. But one glance at the horizon all around us testified to their macabre power: there were plumes of smoke all around us.

Some were blacker and more solid, indicating a recent attack on a village. Others were fainter stains amongst the shimmering heat, meaning that the fires were already dying down.

Here, then, all around us was the work of the dreaded Janjaweed.

THIRTEEN

Pain can lead only to pain, not to liberation from it.
The Sage Kapila

WE PUSHED ONWARDS, THE ATMOSPHERE ON THE
AIRCRAFT one of a stunned and shocked silence. We had
heard about villages being burned, but none of us could
have conceived of the scale of the devastation. To the rear
of the aircraft was our HAC minder, a diminutive man
called Abdul Karim. Sulaf had been unavailable for this
trip, and in theory Abdul Karim was his deputy. In practice,
Abdul was a full-time Mukhabarat apparatchik, and Sulaf
his front man.

Abdul Karim possessed none of Sulaf's urbane bonhomie
and charm. He was a silent, closed character, but I sensed
that his eyes were always watching. He professed to speak
little or no English, though we guessed he had more than
he let on. He sat there stonily with his eyes front, as if by
his not seeing the devastation we might be persuaded that it
wasn't happening. His very presence meant that our
ability to voice our alarm was hugely constrained.

We touched down at El Fasher and were driven direct to
the governor's residence. At the airport, I'd noticed a
heavy military presence, and everywhere were men in
military uniforms. We arrived at the governor's place, and
the diplomatic niceties were rapidly dispensed with. I
described to the governor exactly what we'd seen during
our flight and asked him to explain what was happening.

The governor replied that it was 'lawless elements'
running amok. He told us he was doing all in his power to
bring those 'bandits and brigands' under control. I pressed
for an explanation as to who it was exactly that was
burning the villages, but the governor stuck doggedly to
his 'lawless elements' line. He never once intimated that
his own government might be driving the devastation.

It was only once our meeting was done that cracks started to show in the party line. One of the governor's assistants accompanied us to the airport. En route, it became clear that this man was deeply troubled. He confessed to being appalled at what was being done in his government's name. He was terrified of the Janjaweed, as were many local officials. *'My God, what have we done? We have created a monster in the Janjaweed...'*

We boarded our aircraft, and I suggested that we cancel our planned visit to El Geneina. We had seen and heard enough. We had witnessed the scale of the devastation, and our time would be better served compiling an urgent report – one with which we could alert the UN community and key governments. The fact that the UN country chief – plus Tom Vraalsen, Kofi Annan's special humanitarian envoy – had personally borne witness to the destruction had to lend weight to our words.

On the flight back to Khartoum, the mood amongst MSF and the other aid agencies was clear. There was a burning sense of urgency to get their people into Darfur. But getting them in would prove the challenge, and I would need to play a dual role here. On the one hand, I would have to agitate with HAC to get them access. On the other, I needed to gear up the UN's response, by chivvying my own agency heads to ramp up food aid, water provision and healthcare capacities.

But even were such efforts to succeed, I kept wondering how I could have done things earlier and more effectively. So far, we had failed to halt the devastation, but perhaps there was still time? I'd seen snapshots of the destruction, but I had to presume that vast tracts of territory remained untouched. How could I prevent the horror from reaching those areas?

We were late back to Khartoum, and I was up early chafing at the bit. All that day, Isabelle and I worked on compiling our report on our visit. There was still a tiny part of me that doubted if our analysis was right: could it really be as bad as we now believed? But when I voiced my uncertainties to Isabelle, I was struck by the firmness of her response and her absolute clarity of mind.

Isabelle had seen and heard exactly what I had. There was no way to interpret the evidence other than how we were now doing. Isabelle was a mid-level professional from UN headquarters with a fine career ahead of her. I had expected her to be more diplomatic and circumspect, but not a bit of it. Instead, I was struck by the quiet strength of her anger and her sense of outrage. She knew exactly what had to be said, and she was damned if we weren't going to say it.

It was late in the evening and several drafts before the report was finally done. It would still be office hours in New York, which was some seven hours behind Khartoum time. We emailed it off to all the key players: Jan Egeland at OCHA, Mark Malloch Brown at UNDP, Kieran Prendergast in the DPA, and to Kofi Annan's office direct. I also did a round of emails to the diplomatic community, alerting them to the 'urgent Darfur report' that was attached.

That done, I felt some relief from the withering sense of failure that had taken hold. I had done my duty: I had sent out an urgent alert to all with the power and the means to act on Darfur. Yet still I felt restive and unsettled. In the back of my mind, I feared that our actions would change nothing, and that tomorrow it would be business as usual on the world stage while Darfur burned.

I stayed late in the office, my light burning on my desk. I went over to my glass-fronted bookshelf and ran my hand over the tomes lying there. My mind was searching for something – idly, unfocused, unconsciously even. My hand came to rest on the reports from Rwanda and Srebrenica, those that I had for some unknowable reason decided to bring with me when I'd flown out to Khartoum to take up my post.

While Isabelle sat in the office next door tapping away on her computer, I began to re-read those documents. They outlined in unequivocal terms how the UN had failed to provide alerts to member states, to enable those nations to take action. The UN leadership had failed to use their right of initiative to prevent the mass murder by briefing and alerting the world community. Instead, their approach had been typified by a quiet timidity, which had in turn allowed member states to hide behind the UN's silence.

Kofi Annan had commissioned the very reports that I was reading. After their publication, he had apologised publicly for the UN's high- level failures. But what did that matter? What difference did an apology make, if the modus operandi remained unchanged? Words are cheap. Actions are all that matter. And right now it struck me that the UN could once again be guilty of a collective and unconscionable failure to speak out over Darfur.

It wasn't as if the UN didn't know. No one in New York could hide behind the cloak of ignorance. Repeatedly, alerts had winged their way from my office to the key players, with yet another today. I had even been to New York in person to argue for action – with zero effect as far as I could tell. So, what exactly had the UN learned since the Rwanda and Srebrenica genocides?

As I flicked through those reports, it struck me how chillingly reminiscent were the events now unfolding in Darfur to those of Rwanda in particular. Repeatedly, phrases jumped out at me that could have been written right now, about Darfur. I kept reading and re-reading those words. It was somehow of totemic value just to hold those reports and to repeat those phrases in my mind, as if they were a touchstone from which I could derive much needed strength.

As I read and re-read, I felt a growing sense of clarity. The first jolt of insight struck me like a bolt of lightning: the reports concluded that crimes against humanity were a level of evil generated by specific will and intent. They required an overarching mastermind to conceive of such atrocities, and a command and control centre to perpetrate them. As such, this was not a case of 'nasty people doing nasty things to each other in nasty places', which was what the cynics at senior levels of the international community seemed to want to believe. Crimes against humanity were a specific and deliberate act – a game-changer – and always had been.

The second jolt of insight was even more powerful: when a person suspected that crimes against humanity were being perpetrated, then the responsibility to prevent and to protect was a resolutely personal one. In other words, if I was privy to the fact then it was my personal responsibility to act on that knowledge. That responsibility was far greater the higher the position of the individual. So, if the office cleaner found a scrap of paper in the trash that revealed such crimes were being committed, she discharged her duty by bringing it to the attention of her boss. But when you were in a high position, your personal responsibility to act was magnified a hundredfold.

I was struck by this vivid realisation: whatever I had done to report the horrors of Darfur, I still had not discharged my duty. Because of the absolute totality of the evil, it was my personal responsibility to do my utmost to prevent and protect. In other words, I had an inalienable duty to do whatever it took to stop the evil. That duty was not discharged simply by reporting to headquarters in New York. Alone in my Khartoum office late into the night, I had an absolute eureka moment, a 10,000-volt revelation. With absolute clarity, I understood what I had to do: *I had to act in every way possible to prevent this evil*. Upon realising the overarching responsibility that I bore, I felt totally liberated. Regardless of what abuse I might have to take from the UN, I had a personal responsibility to act, guided purely by my own sense of right and wrong.

I could be true to myself.

I had an absolute duty to be so.

Nothing else mattered.

Moulded as I was by my early life, and guided by my own personal witness in Rwanda, this freedom to act was of utmost importance to me. When news had begun to filter out of the 1994 Rwanda genocide, the then British government's aid agency had asked for volunteers to lead a relief effort into the country. And so it was that myself and Peter Troy, our

Rwanda desk officer, had set out for the stricken country to see what might be done.

We flew to Kampala, in neighbouring Uganda, where we were loaned two Land Rovers by the British High Commission, together with their Ugandan drivers. One vehicle carried Peter and myself, and the other was piled high with tents, food, water and fuel. As we set out, we knew that the Tutsi-dominated rebel army, the Rwandan Patriotic Front (RPF), was poised to rout the extremist Hutu regime – the one that had engineered whatever horrors had taken place.

We followed in the wake of the advancing RPF troops until we were some sixty kilometres and two days into Rwanda. We reached the RPF position in Byumba, where the rebel commander advised us in no uncertain terms to go no further than his front line. His soldiers appeared to be disciplined and well armed, and to me they looked like a professional African army, not your archetypical 'rebels'.

We inched forwards with the RPF units and eventually we reached a forested area. With the sun sinking fast, the place took on an altogether more sinister feel. We crested the brow of a hill, and all of a sudden the city of Kigali was laid out before us. All we could see were faint flickering pinpricks of light where campfires and oil lanterns had been lit, but otherwise the city was a sea of darkness. We wondered whether to camp where we were or to descend, but eventually we chose to continue.

We entered Kigali proper, and with no maps and not a clue where to go we simply drove towards the centre of the city. The thing that struck me most was the absolute stillness of the place: the eerie, brooding quiet interspersed with the occasional howl of a dog as it devoured a dead body. The absence of all human noise – voices calling, cars honking, engines grunting; the very heartbeat of a city – carried with it a dark menace. It was a moonless night, and even the cicadas had stopped their rhythmic chirruping.

We came to an area of relatively smart housing and noticed a group of Save the Children vehicles. We went in and asked if we could stay the night with them, and together the dozen of us camped out on the floor in our sleeping bags. They had arrived shortly before us, and no one had a clue what was going on or what would happen next. The following morning, Peter and I went out to recce the area. The city appeared to be devoid of all life. Eventually, we came across a tiny little sign that announced 'The Orphanage of the Missionaries of Charity'. This, I knew, was the order of Mother Teresa of Calcutta (now Kolkata), the revered Albanian-Indian nun and charity worker now sadly deceased, and for some reason I found myself compelled to enter.

The orphanage turned out to be a small encampment of tin-roofed huts set at the roadside. I stepped down from the tarmac into a tiny reception area, beyond which was an expanse of about half an acre, the entire space jam-packed with children. Few seemed to be older than eight or nine years old, and some were just babies, and I couldn't imagine how any more could be crammed into that small area.

The diminutive sisters were dressed in white and blue habits. I asked them what had happened here. They told us how Tutsi parents had flocked to the orphanage and begged the sisters to take their children, knowing that they faced all but certain death at the hands of the Hutu mob. The sisters had taken in one and all. Not a single child had been turned away.

As the mass killing had gathered pace, so the foreign aid workers had left, and even the UN peacekeepers had abandoned the country. Yet this handful of Indian sisters had chosen to stay to provide a safe haven, while all around them the slaughter continued.

'When the Hutu soldiers and militias heard what was happening, they came here,' the head sister who could not have been more than 5 ft tall told me. 'We stood in the entrance and blocked their way. We told them, "You cannot come in – this is a sacred place of God." And you know, those militias and the soldiers – they turned and went away.'

Those were the most moving words that I had ever heard. The sisters had managed the seemingly impossible with a modesty and bravery that defied all comprehension.

'Yours is a story of the most extraordinary courage,' I told her. I had tears in my eyes. 'You have made me believe again that there has to be a God, even in the midst of this horror and this bloodshed.'

I asked them what help they required. They had a little milk powder and maize flour, but only enough to last a few days. As we went around noting down their most urgent needs, I was stuck by the quiet serenity of the place. There was a sense of calm and peace there that was humbling.

One or two of the little ones ran up to me, their eyes alight with mischief. As I grasped tiny hands and tried to fathom what they had lived through, the sisters trundled this way and that, administering to all. They picked up those who had tumbled over, kissed a child who had hurt his knee, settled squabbles between those playing games, and removed the smallest so they didn't get trampled upon.

Peter and I compiled a list of all that the sisters needed. We left the place with a sense of wonder that those Indian women had somehow endured – thousands of miles from their homes in Calcutta and with nothing but their strong conviction and frail bodies between them and a rampaging, blood-crazed militia. Peter and I managed to get the supplies they needed flown in, and we persuaded the Royal Marines to come in and install a desperately needed electricity generator for pumping water from a nearby well.

During the darkest days, there had been next to no international presence in Kigali, apart from a few beleaguered members of the International Committee of the Red Cross. In perhaps its most shameful moment ever, the United Nations had pulled out its peacekeeping forces even as the genocide gathered pace. The UN force was commanded by a very capable Canadian general, Roméo Dallaire. Dallaire had realised what the Hutu militias were planning and requested clearance from UN headquarters to go in and disarm them. That clearance had been denied by the UN through its then head of peacekeeping, Kofi Annan.

The Hutu militias had proceeded to turn their weapons on the peacekeepers. They set upon an isolated contingent of Belgian soldiers, tied their hands behind their backs and murdered them. In the aftermath of those killings, the UN terminated its mission. But Dallaire repeatedly refused orders from UN headquarters to pull out, and with just a few hundred troops he saved many more lives. He finally left when he could hand over to a successor mission, but even so Dallaire's epic struggle in Rwanda would haunt him for the rest of his days.

After getting our supplies to the orphanage, Peter and I ventured out to assess the needs in the rural areas. Once we left the city, the forest closed in, the air alive with the chirruping of birds. We drove southwards for forty-five minutes, ending up at a place called Ntarama. As we hit the village, all birdsong abruptly ceased. There was absolute stillness all around us, as if we had reached this spot on the road where all life suddenly came to an end.

We pulled up in the centre of the village, and it was then that we heard the horrible, spine-chilling howling of dogs. In the midst of a sunlit opening was a tiny redbrick church. We had stopped perhaps a hundred yards short of it, but even from this distance the stench was overpowering. It was the sickly-sweet smell of death, something that was becoming horribly familiar to us after days in Kigali.

We were drawn to that church as if moths to a flame. The closer we got, the more overpowering the stench became. As we walked up the path towards the door, I saw scrawny dogs gnawing on things – human limbs. We stopped at the open door and peered over the threshold. The first thing I noticed was the pulpit and the hymn numbers on the board on the wall. Beneath that was a tangled heap of bodies – men, women, old people, kids, babies even.

I saw women with naked tops and their breasts hacked off. I saw a little baby clutched to his dead mother's breast, but with its legs hacked away. The place looked as if it would normally hold a congregation of around 200, but the corpses of at least 1,000 people were piled in there. We couldn't go further than the open door due to the heaps of bodies.

All around the church the windows were splintered where the Hutu mob had smashed their way in. There were even severed hands still clutching the bibles with which those in the church had been praying. Peter and I turned and left with not a word having been said between us. There were no words for this. No human speech was capable of articulating such horror.

We drove directly to Kigali, and all the way the silence sat heavy between us. It was as if we had been struck dumb by what we had seen. During that journey, one thought crystallised in my mind, and with a clarity like no other. The abject failure of the UN to back General Dallaire and his peacekeepers had allowed all of this. And yet that handful of Indian sisters had stood firm in their Kigali orphanage, when they had nothing but their faith to protect them.

I hoped I knew where I would have stood had I been on the ground as the storm clouds gathered over Rwanda. I hoped to God I would have stood with those Indian sisters and not with those in UN headquarters and in powerful world capitals who had abandoned the Rwandan people to a horrific fate.

I told myself then: *Mukesh, if you are ever in a position to help stop the slaughter, you will not be one of those supposedly good men who choose to do nothing, and in so doing allow evil to triumph.* It was on the drive back from Ntarama church that I first pledged to myself – *not on my watch*.

As I closed the door to my midnight office in Khartoum, I found myself renewing that pledge – *not on my watch will they triumph*. Whatever it took, I would stand against those who would allow the killers to prevail in Darfur. I would stand against those who had called for a 'final solution', regardless of the cost. This was my personal responsibility, and it would not be shirked.

I left my office with my mind made up. I would do what I had to do. I would leave no stone unturned, and I would damn them all if need be.

FOURTEEN

God doesn't require us to succeed, he only requires that you try.
Mother Teresa

THE FOLLOWING DAY I ARRIVED LATE AT THE OFFICE, BUT people noticed immediately that I had a spring in my step.

'Good to see you looking so well today, Mukesh,' Mona, my secretary, remarked.

It had taken a long and concerted campaign to get Mona to stop calling me 'sir', but eventually I had succeeded. She was right – I felt more alive than I had in many a day. I felt as if a burden had been lifted off my shoulders and that I had a sense of purpose again. But, at the same time, there was a part of me that felt daunted. The path that I had chosen would not be easy, and I had a premonition of what it would cost me. But this wasn't about me any more: it was about doing whatever it took to stop this terrible evil.

My fear was mostly about whether I would last the course, however long it might be. Of course, I still had my normal duties to fulfil as UN resident chief, ones that were distinct from Darfur: progressing the Naivasha peace talks, battling HAC to get clearance for UN and other agencies, as well as all the normal diplomatic and government niceties. But none of that mattered to me very much any more. Now, I would focus on one priority: Darfur.

My first action was to plant a small bomb under the Khartoum diplomatic community. I sent a copy of the Rwanda and Srebrenica reports to all diplomatic missions, with a note explaining my interpretation of the law and how that might apply to the situation now unfolding in Darfur. On the surface, it would be a polite invitation to dialogue over the issue. Underneath, I was acting as an agent provocateur. In effect, I was saying: *take note – this is your personal responsibility, too.*

My second action was to escalate my campaign to get aid workers onto the ground. I wanted to flood the area. To that end, I needed to recruit half a dozen extra security officers of Roger's ilk. Instead of running security from Khartoum, I would send them directly into the field. Our people would be getting into situations of real danger, and I needed security there to assess the threat and determine if and when we needed to pull individuals out.

But it was my third course of action that was by far the most controversial and risky. If I were to call a spade a spade, I would need to get as much proof as possible that this was 'ethnic cleansing' and 'genocide'. As UN resident chief, I was in a position where people would listen to me, but they wouldn't do so if I made accusations that I couldn't substantiate. What I needed was someone from outside the UN system to go deep into Darfur – to the forbidden areas – to seek out the facts, and I had just such a man in mind.

Tim Mansfield was very smart and widely experienced in politically sensitive humanitarian operations. He worked for a ground-breaking conflict-resolution group that I knew well. In Aceh, it had established contact between the rebels and the Indonesian government in an effort to broker peace. More recently, when the Taliban were preparing to dynamite the Bamiyan Buddhas, I had asked the group to go in on behalf of the British government and strike some kind of deal to prevent it (though sadly they had been too late to stop that mindless act of cultural vandalism).

I got Tim to fly out from his European office so I could brief him. I knew I had to be watchful here, and to tread very carefully. I had given myself carte blanche to do whatever it might take regarding Darfur, but I was acutely aware of what was at stake. In commissioning my own clandestine investigation, I was deliberately stepping outside the UN system, to do what we could not. I was also moving into very sensitive territory as far as the Sudanese government was concerned. Knowing how comprehensively my office and residence were likely to be bugged, I took Tim to a venue where I hoped we could talk in confidence. There was a particular Indian restaurant in Khartoum that served up a very fine speciality – or 'Special Tea' as they preferred to call it. You could go in and order some spicy dishes, plus Special Teas all around, and you'd be given a set of glasses wrapped in brown paper. You could then remove the beer or wine you had hidden in your bag and serve, keeping the bottle hidden under the table. Drinking alcohol in public was forbidden in Khartoum, and that Special Tea system was the answer.

Over our brown-paper-wrapped glasses of beer, I explained to Tim that I needed him to go into the closed areas of Darfur, to link up with the rebels. I needed him to do two things while there: one, to document the violence and horror now unfolding in the worst-hit areas; two, to find out what the rebel leaders were fighting for, so we could examine options for peace talks.

'We need to know what exactly the rebels are fighting for and who is in command,' I explained. 'We know what the rebels in the south fought for and what Garang's vision is, but the rebels in Darfur remain a mystery. So I need you to go in, contact them and find out what they want.'

'I figure I could get in from the Chad side,' Tim remarked. 'What's your ideal timescale?'

'There's no time to lose. As soon as you're able to go.'

I explained to Tim that by sending him in I was deliberately operating in a grey area where no one had the power to stop me. As Khartoum would never issue him a travel permit, he'd be on a covert and illegal mission. It would be a massive scandal if it leaked out that the UN resident chief had commissioned someone to enter the country in such a manner, so I needed him to do this without my fingerprints being all over it.

Tim set out on his secret mission in late September 2003. Neither he nor I knew how long it would take, whether he would be successful or what the results might be. His was a hugely risky undertaking, and I decided that only those who needed to know about it would know, and that was only myself and Isabelle. Isabelle thought it a fantastic idea and just what the situation called for.

It is at its centre that a storm is most calm, and that was how I felt now. I knew the storm was beginning, and if I was to ride it out I'd have to remain at its calm heart and with a clear mind. And in spite of the risks, I felt comfortable with Tim's mission. From past experience, I'd learned to think outside the box and never discount the truly radical ideas that one might have.

In 1999, in Sierra Leone, the West African peacekeeping force (ECOMOG) was about to be overrun by the murderous Revolutionary United Front (RUF). If ECOMOG were routed, it would spell disaster in a civil war of unrivalled horror and brutality. The peacekeepers were in dire need of trucks so they could move around and outmanoeuvre the rebels. No one seemed able or willing to provide those vehicles, when I suddenly remembered that my then employers, DFID, had a warehouse full of trucks left over from the Balkans conflict.

They were old but serviceable, and we were spending half a million British taxpayer pounds a year to do nothing with them other than to keep them in working order. DFID had no mandate to intervene in a security issue – providing transport to peacekeepers. That was the ministry of defence's (MOD) domain, but they had no budget to make it happen. The solution I hit upon was to sell the trucks to the MOD for one pound, whereupon they could airlift them to Sierra Leone.

That is exactly what happened, and the ECOMOG peacekeeping operation was saved. It was only then that my bureaucratic colleagues woke up to what I had done. They got very upset and demanded an explanation. I outlined how I had saved DFID £500,000 a year, and by so doing had also advanced the interests of peace, security and development in Sierra Leone, a key British ally.

Sir John Vereker, my ultimate civil service boss at DFID, who was later to become the governor of Bermuda, was obliged to rap me on my knuckles, but my audacity brought a twinkle to his eye. He defended me with gusto when we were summoned before the powerful Public Accounts Committee of the British Parliament to explain what I had done.

I learned from my Sierra Leone experiences that, if you were sure that you were doing the right thing, it was better to take the risk first and face the consequences later – as was the case now, with Tim Mansfield's secret mission into Darfur.

Shortly after Tim had set off, I received the oddest of text messages from my driver. Omer would often text me to coordinate pick-up times: 'Sir, I am waiting for you outside.' But this time his message read: 'Sir, don't say: "Oh my God, what big trouble I'm in." Say instead: "Oh trouble, what a big God I have."'

It was bizarre. I could only imagine that Omer was trying to warn me about some comment that I had made where I could be overheard. Whatever his relationship to the Mukhabarat, as far as I was concerned Omer did his job as driver and minder well. All the same, knowing that those orchestrating the 'final solution' were able to so closely monitor those trying to fight it was sinister.

A few days after Tim's departure, my cell phone rang in the middle of the night. I kept it switched on at all times, for if there was an emergency with any of our people it would be my call as to how we would respond. I flailed around for the phone and checked the caller ID: *number unknown.* I checked my bedside clock: 2 a.m.

I pressed the answer key: 'Hello, this is Dr Kapila.' A voice responded: 'This is Hassan.'

'Hassan who?' I asked.

'Hassan calling from Darfur. I am speaking for the SLA.'

I sat up in bed, suddenly very much more alert. The SLA was the Sudan Liberation Army, one of the main rebel groups in Darfur.

'Oh, Hassan. Well, this is nice...' I really didn't know what to say. And in the back of my mind I was aware that the Mukhabarat would be listening in.

'How are you, my brother?' Hassan asked.

'Well, I'm just fine. More importantly, how are you and the SLA?' 'We in the SLA are fine. But you know, my brother, the government is killing our people all across Darfur. We, the SLA, are trying to fight back and defend them, but we are facing many challenges. You know, we would like the United Nations to do something really to help us.'

'Help in what way exactly?'

'Tell the world leaders what is happening in Darfur. Tell them about the terrible things the government is doing. And you can help our people directly by bringing aid.'

'Yes, well, we are a humanitarian organisation, and we do bring aid to all sides.' I was wording my replies very carefully, aware of who was listening. 'Our problem is we can't get access to large parts of Darfur. How can we cross the front lines to get to your side to bring help? Can you think of a way?'

At that moment, the connection was lost, or perhaps we'd been cut off. It had sounded as if he was speaking on a satellite phone, due to the peculiar metallic echoes on the line. I'd just have to wait for him to phone again. I lay down under my thin cotton sheet to digest what had happened. I wondered if this meant that Tim had made it through and passed my number to the rebel leader, for how else could he have got it?

Either way, this felt to me like a very significant breakthrough. Finally, I had a direct line of communication to the Darfuri rebels, and as far as I knew this was the only one the international community had right now. I lay there wondering how best to use it. If we could just get the two sides talking, and at a venue public enough to give it some profile, surely Khartoum would have to abandon their plans for a 'final solution' and cut some kind of deal.

I wondered whether I should say anything to UN headquarters about Hassan having been in touch. My instinct told me not to. For now at least I'd keep this as a me-and-Hassan thing only – albeit with the Mukhabarat listening in.

The following night, he called again. Again, it was 2 a.m., and again we did the 'how are you, my brother' thing for a while.

'I want to thank you for all you are doing for me and my people,' Hassan continued. 'But, my brother, we respect the UN and we rely on the UN, and we feel we are being forgotten here in Darfur and we need your help.'

'Hassan, I'd like to do much more to help,' I assured him. 'But to be able to do so I need more information. What exactly is happening there right now in terms of attacks against you and your people?'

'Well, you know, my brother, we have to keep moving.' For the first time, I detected a faint hint of vulnerability in his voice. 'Government aircraft keep bombing us, and we have to keep on the move. As to our villages, they are being hit by the Janjaweed and they are also being bombed from the air. We rebels can keep hidden in the bush, but for the villagers this is not easy... Still, we are very confident we will overcome and throw the government forces out of Darfur.'

'I'd like to broker a ceasefire,' I suggested. 'Between you and Khartoum. Would you be willing to talk? You can fight each other to a standstill, as they did in the south, or you can negotiate. The more fighting there is, the more innocent civilians will die.'

'Yes, my brother, we know this. But we don't trust the government. Does a snake change its spots? No, my brother. We don't trust them to keep their promises, and so we must keep fighting.'

'But a ceasefire could be monitored by the world community. By the UN. There could be peacekeepers, as there are in the Nuba Mountains. That way, all sides have to be seen to abide by the rules.' 'A snake never changes its spots,' Hassan repeated. 'So we are not keen on a ceasefire, at least not yet. We need to control Darfur first, and then we will talk about peace.'

'OK, so when you are ready to talk, what is it exactly

that you want? What are you asking of Khartoum? What are your demands? You need to know what you want before you can start talking.'

Hassan went into a long diatribe about how Darfur was neglected, how there was no development and how the region failed to get a fair share of national income. But underneath all the anger and the angst, I could tell that there was no coherent set of demands. I figured that the rebels were unclear in their philosophy, just as Garang had suggested.

Somewhere towards the end of Hassan's rant, the connection was lost. I'd failed to ask the rebel leader for his number. It struck me that the Mukhabarat might have the facility to block his calls. More worrying, I figured they might have the ability to track them and pinpoint the whereabouts of the satphone. I wondered how much danger Hassan was putting himself in by calling me.

There had been a hint of vulnerability in Hassan's voice, and it surprised me. Rather like Garang, I had expected the Darfuri rebel leadership to be confident of victory in the lands occupied by their people. I wondered what it must be like trying to fight a war on the ground when the enemy had total control of the skies. Basically, an attack could come at any time, and there was nothing the rebels – less still the Darfuri villagers – could do about it.

What would that feel like – to be hunted like an animal? What would it feel like, knowing that you were a mouse to your hunter's bird of prey? What would it feel like to cower in the bush as the bombs tumbled from the sky? As it happened, I was just about to find out – for the victims were even now fleeing such attacks and washing up like unwanted flotsam in Khartoum.

Clustered around Khartoum were a series of massive IDP camps. They had formed during the decades of civil war, and they were full of black Africans fleeing the conflict in the south. Whole generations had been born and died in those camps, but it was now that we started to receive worrying reports of people being forced out of those camps and of possible mass disappearances.

The camps were magnets for new arrivals from Darfur – those fleeing the kinds of attacks that Hassan had described to me. Only the toughest could make it the 1,000 kilometres or more to Khartoum, and I could see why the government might want to 'disappear' them. Having angry and bitter Darfuris on their doorstep was a real security issue. These people were eyewitnesses to the horror the regime was visiting upon them, and they were far more accessible here than in Darfur.

Having heard reports of these mass disappearances, I figured that a visit to one of the camps was vital. I was determined to make the visit without any HAC minders, for that was the only way to ensure that people could speak openly and freely. I decided I wouldn't seek Khartoum's clearance, for if I sought permission it was bound to be delayed, if not outright refused.

I checked with Roger over any security implications. If we were going in without permission, he was adamant that we shouldn't stay for long. Khartoum might have agents in the crowd, and they might try to arrange it so that we were attacked or even taken hostage. I told Roger that we'd need to balance security concerns with our need to hear people out, and it was in that spirit that the visit went ahead.

We would act first and face whatever were the consequences.

FIFTEEN

There are three kinds of evidence: perception, recognition of signs and testimony.
The Sage Kapila

OMER DROVE ME TOWARDS THE OUTSKIRTS OF KHARTOUM, together with Naqib, one of Roger's security staff. The IDP camp turned out to be nothing more substantial than a sea of raggedy tents set upon a dusty field. We pulled to a halt in the midst of a parched semi-desert setting. In the near distance, the city rose above the camp, forming a glittering backdrop to the poverty and hopelessness.

I got down from the vehicle, and for the first time ever I was able to mingle freely with the victims of whatever was unfolding in Darfur. There wasn't a single minder in sight, and it was truly liberating. A massive crowd gathered, drawn to us by our foreign appearance and the UN flag fluttering from the vehicle.

I didn't have a translator, so the first thing I did was ask for anyone who spoke English. A young man dressed in a stained and raggedy jalabiya stepped forwards. One of his eyes was half-turned in on itself, as if from a recent injury. He introduced himself as being Idris, one of the 'leaders' of the camp. He struck me as being immensely young to be a community leader. Normally, they were the elders. But one glance around me showed that just about everyone here was young. Young men, young women and a scattering of children: there were no elders present.

I explained to Idris that we were from the UN, and I asked him the first question that came into my mind: *where are all the old people?*

'Many were killed – those too old and too slow to run away,' Idris explained. 'Those who did survive, we had to leave behind. We are the fit ones who managed to walk and get lifts on trucks. It's taken us three months to get here.'

'Please, start at the beginning,' I asked. 'Tell me how you were attacked and by whom, and what happened afterwards.'

'The first thing when they attack the village is they set it on fire,' a woman volunteered, 'by dropping bombs from the air. When they hit the earth, they burst and throw out fire everywhere.' The woman was dressed in a bright orange robe with a rainbow-coloured scarf draped around her head and shoulders, but what struck me most was the burning anger in her dark eyes. 'When you run from your hut because of the fire, they shoot you with their guns, otherwise you get burned alive inside your hut.'

'That's what they always do,' a second woman remarked. 'They set the fire and when you come out they shoot you down.'

'Sometimes they come in the night, and you just have to run,' said a third woman. 'But if you have so many children you cannot run with them all, and that's what has caused us to lose our children...' 'The old people cannot run, so they just kill them,' the woman in the rainbow headscarf added. 'They cannot run fast enough, so they are shot. They don't have the energy to run and to hide themselves.'

'All of the people here – no one has all of their family,' Idris remarked. 'Everyone has lost someone.' He turned to a woman beside him. 'This lady has lost three boys, and also her mother and her father were killed in front of her.'

I could sense the tension in the crowd. No one was in tears, in spite of the horrific stories they were relating. I sensed how easily trouble could flare here, as these victims hungered for a way to vent their anger and wreak their vengeance.

'With the children, the raiders used a rope to tie them onto their horses, and pulled them away,' the woman with the rainbow headscarf remarked. 'As they dragged them, they beat them on their backs with sticks.'

'Where did they take these children?' I asked.

A series of angry voices cut in. 'No one knows!' 'There is no answer to this one!'

'No one knows where they take them!'

'Sometimes they take them to look after their animals,' Idris added. 'They stole cows and sheep from us, so they took them to look after the animals. So they make them like their cow-boys...'

'But some they take to their houses to be like – how do you say? – like slaves. And some maybe they just kill them, but their families never know this because they've lost them, so they suffer even more.' 'They come with their aircraft and also the Janjaweed with their horses,' the rainbow-scarfed woman explained, 'dropping their bombs on our villages and driving us out and stealing our animals. Two people on one horse, with one riding and the other one is shooting the gun. But none of us had the guns to defend ourselves...'

'If they caught a pregnant woman, they cut open her stomach,' Idris added. 'They cut it open and if it is a baby boy they throw him onto the fire. Can you imagine – *onto the fire*! And if it is a baby girl, they just leave her there to die.'

The crowd started telling me about the females that were captured. Girls as young as six or seven had been raped. Some were raped in front of their mothers. Husbands were forced to watch as their wives were beaten and raped repeatedly. In many cases, women were abducted by the raiders and taken to their camps. Some would return after several days, but others simply disappeared.

As I listened to these stories I felt physically sick. Some 90 per cent of the women in Darfur had been subjected to female genital mutilation, or FGM. In FGM, a pre-pubescent girl's genitalia are sliced off and what remains is sewn up, in part so as to prove that she is a virgin upon marriage. I had practiced gynaecology myself, and I could envisage how their genitalia would be ripped open during rape, the violence leaving wounds that might never heal.

As Rwanda had demonstrated so powerfully, sexual violence is a cheap and easy way of waging war against civilians and of spreading terror. It is also a simple way to wipe out entire cultures and societies, by destroying people's dignity, self-respect and their sense of self-worth. If these Darfuri men weren't able to protect their wives and daughters, what kind of men were they, they would ask themselves.

I felt a hand on my shoulder. 'Sir, I think we need to go.' It was Naqib, my security guy, and his expression was tense. 'The crowd is getting restive...'

'Just a few more minutes,' I interjected. I glanced at my watch. 'We've been here for 30 minutes, and the government are bound to find out about this visit anyway. Give me 15 minutes more and we'll leave.'

'Well, sir, OK – 15 minutes. But no longer.'

I turned to Idris. 'And what about race?' I asked. 'I see all here are black Africans – I presume Zaghawa, Masalit, Fur...'

'Of course, race is the thing!' Idris replied angrily. 'The Arab raiders call us abusive names. *Zurka. Abeed.* This means like "nigger" and "slave". It is hugely insulting.'

'And with the women, they say, "We'll give you slaves Arab babies!"' the rainbow-scarfed woman added. '"We'll rid this land of you niggers!"'

'What do you want us, the UN, to do most?' I asked.

'Well, you are a big man,' Idris answered. 'You are the UN's man in Sudan. But we saw no one from the UN in Darfur, and we met no one from the UN on the way here. So, you should do more to help. But mostly we want to be given the means to deal with this ourselves, to make amends for what has been done.'

I felt the hand on my shoulder again. 'Sir, we need to go. Your 15 minutes is up plus a good deal more.'

Naqib was right. It was time to leave. But before departing, I promised Idris that I would do two things. One, I would raise their plight directly with the government, and in particular the threats to move them from this camp. And two, I would ensure that we, the UN, put more staff into these camps, to keep a closer eye.

Omer fired up the Land Cruiser and we pulled away from the camp. How many more IDPs were there like this all around Khartoum, I wondered. By anyone's reckoning, there had to be tens of thousands. If the government did try forcibly to move them, these people were not in the mood to go quietly, and I left Idris's camp with a sick, ominous feeling in the pit of my stomach.

Once back at my office, I kicked into gear a number of immediate actions. I pulled UN staff off their office duties and had them moved out to the key IDP camps. They would be there to oversee aid deliveries and to be my eyes and ears. That done, I made my representations to the government. I made it clear that the IDPs around Khartoum were fully on our radar screen and that the authorities needed to document their presence and safeguard them. I warned them that the UN was watching.

But, once again, Khartoum simply laughed in the face of such threats. The government's response was swift and brutal. Barely hours after I'd issued my warnings, they sent in a convoy of Mukhabarat people to investigate my 'unsanctioned' visit to the camp. They singled out the individuals that I had spoken to – Idris, the camp leader, amongst them – and took them away 'for questioning'. And there was worse to come.

That night, the entire camp simply disappeared, some 10,000 people being spirited away. One day we'd had our people there, overseeing aid and watching. The following morning, they returned to find the camp gone. Just as soon as I was alerted, I telephoned my contacts at HAC. I made it clear that we, the UN, had been providing aid and assistance and we needed to know as a matter of urgency where that camp had gone.

The response I got was chilling. I was called to a meeting at HAC, but not with my regular contact, Sulaf. Instead, I was taken to see an official with whom I'd had few if any dealings. This, I suspected, was one of the top Mukhabarat people operating at the heart of the HAC. He told me that they could not have Darfuris 'wandering freely around Khartoum'. Instead, HAC had moved them to an area where 'we can properly give aid and control them'.

I asked where exactly those people had been moved to, so we, the UN, could provide assistance.

He fixed me with this frosty look. 'Dr Kapila, we, the government of Sudan, are coping just fine. We do not need your help. If we needed it, we would have asked for it. These people are none of your concern.' Once back at my office, I resorted to the only option left open to me. I asked Roger to investigate, and I got Isabelle to draft an urgent report to UN headquarters, alerting them to the 'disappearance' of 10,000 IDPs. I also sent the most vigorous objections in writing to the Sudanese government. I received not the slightest hint of a response. I had expected nothing more from Khartoum, but the silence from New York was deafening.

It was Roger who got me the first solid information as to what had happened. He came to my office and shut the door somewhat heavily.

'Sir, I've been able to confirm some of the details,' he sighed. 'As you surmised, the camp inhabitants were rounded up in the night. They were put on buses and driven into the desert, to where exactly I'm still not sure. There are suggestions that the men have been taken into secret detention centres – the so-called "ghost houses" – for interrogation and maybe worse. That's as much as I have for you right now.'

I shook my head in despair. I'd suspected as much. But it was another thing entirely having it confirmed.

'My God, but this is terrible...' I muttered. 'Roger, it's a repeat of what happened to that woman who spoke to us in Nyala. But then it was only one person. Here, it's 10,000 who have been disappeared. It's a bloody nightmare.'

'Sir, I agree it doesn't look so good,' Roger remarked, with his signature understatement. 'But until I learn more we can't know for sure...'

'But we can extrapolate, can't we, Roger?' I cut in. 'Khartoum is now so organised in terms of its powers of oppression it can disappear 10,000 people overnight. Fact. They've been trucked away to a secret location where we, the UN, cannot reach them. Fact. Now, Roger, I have images in my mind of a deep desert death camp, complete with torture cells and more. And I have images of mass graves bulldozed over in a matter of hours. And do we have any reason to think that all of this may not be true?'

Roger sighed. 'No, sir, we have no information to confirm or deny that scenario. I will do my best to get that information, of that you can rest assured.'

'I know you will, Roger, and I'm thankful for it. But of one thing I also am certain: wherever those people have been taken, hundreds will not be coming back.'

Roger scraped back his chair and got to his feet. 'Best I get going, sir. I'll find out what I can.'

He left me alone with my dark thoughts. Had my actions in going to visit that camp so backfired that 10,000 people had been disappeared? Had I brought down the wrath of Khartoum upon them, with all the consequent effects? Or had it just accelerated the process of their disappearance, which was more or less inevitable? I just didn't know. But either way, I felt the crushing burden of failure weighing heavily upon me again.

For a moment, I wondered what could have happened to the noble and honourable Sudanese Arab culture, the one that I had so fallen in love with as a young medical student during my first visit to Khartoum. How had that been reduced to this – to the dark machinations of some fascistic regime perpetrating their version of the 'final solution'?

I knew in my heart that these weren't the actions of the wider Sudanese people. A small group of mass murderers were hell-bent on betraying their great culture and history, and bringing disgrace upon a fine and honourable way of life. And that in turn meant that anything that could be done to bring that power-crazed minority under control had to be done.

The day after the IDP camp disappearance, Hassan, the rebel leader, called me. It was late at night, and we spoke for a while about the ongoing attacks against villages in Darfur before he mentioned the numbers of refugees fleeing across the border into Chad. I told him that the UN was already working to set up Chadian refugee camps, my counterparts doing good things there.

'You have heard about the Black Book, my brother?' Hassan ventured. 'It is a very important piece of work, a rallying cry for us all.'

'I've heard of it, yes,' I told him.

Copies of a so-called Black Book were being circulated

around Khartoum. It was a kind of grass-roots development and activist manual, cataloguing some of the Khartoum regime's worst human- rights abuses and presenting a vision of a new Sudan free of prejudice in terms of race, colour or creed. It was authored anonymously but was clearly the product of the underground movement, and it called for a democratic revolution against the current regime.

'The Black Book outlines much of what we want, my brother,' Hassan continued. 'If we are to talk peace, then the Black Book must lie at the core of that peace. No more women getting raped because they have the black skin. No more boys getting carried off to be cow-boys because they are black...'

There was a burst of static and the line went dead. Hassan had just been getting into his stride about this Black Book. I figured I needed to get hold of an English translation – if such a thing existed – so I might get a sense of what peace talks might be based around, should I ever get both sides sitting at the same table.

The following morning I told Isabelle that Hassan had been in touch again. 'Oh, good. How exciting!' she remarked. 'What did he say?'

I outlined our conversation, and Isabelle agreed that it was vital to keep the lines of communication open, but she also figured I should brief New York. I asked her to draft a simple memo detailing the ongoing contact, one that I hoped might lead to some kind of peace negotiations. The memo was sent, but again there was a deafening silence from UN headquarters.

Faced with this wall of silence, I felt as if I had been excommunicated. I felt as if I had become the nuisance that just wouldn't go away. I had become the kind of inconvenient trouble that no one wanted to deal with in New York.

I also briefed Roger on my contact with Hassan. I figured it was best that he knew, just in case anything did happen to me. If 10,000 IDPs could be 'disappeared' from Khartoum overnight, in theory anything was possible.

'How long has this contact been going on, sir?' he

queried.

'Oh, just a few weeks. I don't have his number, you see, so it's only ever when he calls me, which always seems to be around two o'clock in the morning. Most inconvenient when one's trying to get a good night's sleep.'

'I'm sure it is, sir. The trouble is it may not be very good for your relations with the government, either. How do you know this Hassan guy is for real? He could be a government agent posing as a rebel leader and trying to set you up. If they've recorded you saying anything out of hand, or if you've strayed out of your remit... Well, sir, they could use material like that to discredit you.'

'Yes, they could,' I replied. 'But don't worry, I'm being very careful.' 'Do you want me to ask around about this Hassan? Make some enquiries?'

'Roger, I've not said anything stupid. Nothing that can get me into water that's any hotter than I'm in already. I am a symbol of the UN here, and I need to be available for people to talk to. I expect people to approach me – it's what I'm here for. So, no, Roger, no need to start an investigation.'

Roger warned me to be doubly careful in my dealing with Hassan, and more generally, but he agreed to let the issue lie. That was a relief, for the last thing I wanted was Roger to launch a security investigation into Hassan. If he did, it might lead him to Tim Mansfield's secret mission in Darfur.

And it was vital to keep that quiet, at least until Tim could get back to me with his findings.

SIXTEEN

This is a war of the unknown warriors, but let us all strive without failing in faith or in duty.
Winston Churchill

THERE WERE LAYERS OF SECURITY AROUND MY UN OFFICE now, and we had a strict routine for coming and going from the compound. One morning, Omer drove me out of the gated inner sanctum, after which we passed under the raised barrier that was manned by an outer cordon of guards. But just as he went to turn onto the main road I realised that I'd forgotten something. The file of flights for which I needed to seek clearance was lying on my office desk.

'Omer, hold up a second,' I remarked. 'I've forgotten something.

I'll just be a minute.'

Before he could stop me I'd opened my door and was stepping into the road. I noticed a flash of movement out of the corner of my eye, and I turned to see a figure lunging for me. At the same moment the security guards leapt into action. While one dived on the figure and wrestled it to the ground, another shoved me out of the way. I landed in a dusty heap, and before I could say a word I was picked up and bundled into the car.

There was a squeal of tyres and Omer tore away from the scene. He was hunched over the wheel, 100 per cent concentrated on his driving. I sat in the back of the speeding vehicle feeling shocked and shaken. There was no way that I could misinterpret what had happened. Someone had attacked me. The question was, who was it and why?

I didn't feel as if I could raise it with Omer during the remainder of that manic journey. I was feeling more than a little guilty that I'd broken rule number one of our routine: *never get out of the vehicle in an unsecured area.* My meeting with HAC went ahead, although it was an unusually pointless affair, deprived of my flight files as I was.

En route back to the office, I asked Omer if he had any idea what had happened earlier.

'No, not really, sir,' he replied, eyeing me in the driver's mirror. 'But we need to stick with the security procedures, wouldn't you agree?'

I told him that I did.

As soon as I was back at the office, Roger was there to see me. 'So, Roger, I guess you've heard about the funny events that happened at the front gate?' I ventured. 'Most peculiar.'

'There's nothing overly funny about it, sir,' Roger replied. 'At least not from the perspective of the UN security officer there isn't.' He paused. 'Word from my people is it was an attempt to assassinate you.'

'*A what?* But why on earth...'

'My sources tell me it was a woman who attacked you. I've been led to believe she's crazy – a madwoman. But that's only what certain people are telling me, sir, and from certain sources I never take anything at face value.'

'So who or what do you think it really was?'

'Usual answer, sir. I'll work my security sources and try to find out more. In the meantime, we'll double our vigilance. And, sir, please stick rigidly to the security procedures.'

I was seven months into my posting by now and, whatever the truth here, this was worrying. The attack had only been possible because I had decided on a whim to stop the vehicle and dismount, so it was more than likely a chance happening. Unless of course someone had been ordered to wait outside the gates for as long as it took to get the opportunity to strike.

For now, there was just no way of telling. In any case, concerns over my own security were soon to be overshadowed by threats to the security of our entire operation in Darfur.

It was the end of the first week of December when Roger raised a point of urgent concern during our early-morning briefing.

'Sir, I've heard through my channels that there's going to be a major attack by SLA rebels on El Geneina, the most vulnerable urban outpost in Darfur. I don't know when exactly, but I'm told it's imminent.'

'And how do we react to this?' I asked.

'Sir, we have to take this seriously. I'd suggest you consider evacuating all UN staff from El Geneina, at least until the trouble blows over.'

'Roger, are you sure? That would be a very serious move. I'm desperately trying to get people into Darfur to deliver aid, and to be our eyes and ears on the ground. I seem to be fighting HAC daily to try to get flights in. If we pull out of El Geneina, that'll send entirely the wrong message, don't you think?'

'Sir, I'll remind you of your primary duty, which is the security of the UN staff. If there is an imminent threat, then action has to be taken.'

'I'll need some time to consider this. Let's keep the situation under review. Meanwhile, gather more information to convince me we need to withdraw.'

Somewhat reluctantly, Roger agreed to what I wanted.

Two things vexed me greatly about Roger's suggestion that we pull out of El Geneina. First, I was aware that my predecessor, Mike Sackett, had done something similar, and it had been used as an excuse to get him thrown out of the country. He'd received reports of a threatened attack on Juba, the capital of south Sudan, and he had decided to evacuate all UN staff. The Khartoum regime hadn't liked it because it sent a signal that they couldn't guarantee the security of the UN.

Mike had stuck to his guns, and a month later he was asked to leave the country. Likewise, if I pulled our staff out of El Geneina – one of the three state capitals in Darfur – I might well suffer similar consequences. In effect, we would be saying that we had no confidence in the government to safeguard us from rebel attacks in Darfur.

But I was also reluctant to evacuate because of the

damage it would do to our standing as humanitarians. Over the years, the UN had earned a global reputation of always being the first to withdraw at the slightest hint of trouble. As a result, many tended to view the UN as lacking in backbone. We needed to have a stronger, more robust presence in Darfur if we were to be taken seriously and demonstrate that we were committed to building peace in Sudan.

By now we had four internationals on the ground in El Geneina, plus seventy local UN staff. There were also the handful of non-UN aid agencies for which I'd recently secured access, and for whom I also had a security responsibility. I had urged them to go into Darfur alongside us, and if we were even to think of withdrawing I would need to advise them to do likewise.

Over the next few days, Roger became ever more insistent that we pull out. 'Sir, I'm getting serious reports about rebels congregating around El Geneina and the government reinforcing its garrison. Sooner or later there's going to be trouble, and we'll get caught in the crossfire. We need to get our people out while we can.'

I decided to speak to Sulaf, for if we were to consider pulling out we'd need flight clearances to do so.

'Sulaf, I'm being advised by my security chief to pull the UN out of El Geneina,' I told him. 'In fact, he's putting me under some pressure to do so.'

'But why would you want to do that?' he asked. He seemed genuinely surprised at what I was suggesting.

'I'm told the rebels are poised to attack the town, and that our people are in danger. Can you guarantee our safety if there's fighting?' 'Yes, yes, of course I can. After all, we are there to protect you.

And if you needed to withdraw, of course I would be the first to warn you.'

I reported back to Roger what Sulaf had said. I knew Sulaf was a front, and that behind him sat the Mukhabarat, but when all was said and done he was one of the few people I almost trusted at HAC. Roger shrugged off Sulaf's reassurances. 'Sir, that's what he has to say in public, but privately he knows they can't guarantee our safety. My security network is mostly people in HAC, and those people are very, very worried. So this is like the two faces of the same beast, the public and the private one.'

'So, your advice is still that we withdraw?' 'It is. As soon as possible.'

'What happens if I ignore your advice?' I asked.

In response to my question, Roger drew himself up to his full height. 'Well, sir, you're the boss... But it'd be foolish if you didn't listen to my advice.'

'But what if I don't listen?' I persisted, smiling. 'Well, sir, eventually I'd have to inform New York.'

I laughed. 'Yes, I figured so. Don't worry, Roger, I will listen to your advice. But see if you can't bear with me for just a few more days.'

Roger agreed to hold off for now. But sooner or later he'd be forced to issue me an ultimatum: either I took action or he'd have no option but to alert the head of UN security to my failure to heed his advice. It was fair enough, really, for mostly I was playing for time here.

I'd just got word from Tim Mansfield to meet me in Nairobi, for his trip into Darfur was done. From him, I could discover what was happening in the closed areas, those regions barred to outsiders – and that included the majority of Darfur. And having that information had to have a bearing on whether we withdrew from El Geneina, one of our key operational centres in the region.

I flew south to Nairobi and checked into the Serena Hotel. As the name suggests, the Serena is an island of manicured tranquillity amongst the chaotic noise and bustle of Kenya's capital city. It was one of the few places where I felt we could meet in complete privacy and without any danger of being watched or overheard.

Tim's arrival was phoned through to my room from hotel reception. I hovered by the door, and just as soon as I heard a faint knock I flung it open. I was hugely relieved to see him. I had encouraged him to risk his life, and the dangers he had faced had weighed heavily upon me. He stood there with a somewhat exhausted-looking smile on his face, but otherwise he seemed to be fine.

For a moment I was tempted to give him a bear hug, but the English public schoolboy within me held me back. Instead, we shook hands and I ushered him inside. I had a quick glance up and down the corridor, but there was no one else to be seen. I told myself not to be so paranoid. It would have taken a real James Bond type to trail Tim from the depths of war-torn Darfur to my bedroom here in the Serena Hotel.

'Tim, it is so good to see you!' I declared, once I'd firmly closed the door. 'And you're looking so well. The trip wasn't too draining?' Tim shrugged. 'It was a bit of an epic, but I'm fine. Really, Mukesh,

I'm fine. Most importantly, I got what you asked for.'

He delved into his rucksack and pulled out a laptop. He gestured at it. 'So, where d'you want to do this? Here?'

'I think just here is nice and private, don't you? I can offer you drinks from the cabinet. You probably need something strong, after what you've just been through?'

'Just some mineral water's fine.'

I served the drinks, and Tim fired up his laptop. He gestured at the first image that he'd pulled up on the screen. It showed a group of rebel soldiers clustered around a 'technical'-type vehicle – a battered Toyota Land Cruiser with some kind of heavy machine gun mounted on the rear. It was one of the first pictures that I'd seen of the SLA rebels, and they struck me as being visibly less well resourced or armed than Garang's fighters.

'I spent some time moving around with these guys,' Tim remarked. He pointed at a figure on the screen. 'That guy there, that's Hassan, the one who's been calling you.'

'Aha,' I smiled. 'Now at last I can put a face to the voice. But tell me, why does he always insist on calling me at two o'clock in the morning?'

'He figures Khartoum may be less alert then, so he'll get more time. Plus, it's very, very dark by then in the bush, so less chance of being spotted from the air. It takes a while to set up the satphone and find satellites, so he doesn't want to do all that when he's likely to be seen by any warplanes.'

'Tell me, what's the risk of that happening or maybe the call getting traced?' I asked. 'It's something that worries me. I mean, I want him to keep calling, so we can maintain a dialogue and explore options for talks, but...'

'Hassan figures Khartoum doesn't have access to that level of technology. I'm not so sure. In any case, he's a rebel leader and risk goes with the territory, I guess. For example,' he pressed a key and the next image flipped up on the screen, 'they were hit from the air several times while I was with them.'

The photo showed a smoking bomb crater in the midst of fire- blackened bush. 'Correction,' I said, '*you* and they were bombed several times.'

'Yeah, me as well, but more importantly,' there was a click as he moved to another image, 'I also saw warplanes bombing villages. I saw how they rolled these crude firebombs off the rear ramp of the aircraft. They're little more than a drum of fuel with some kind of explosive charge attached, but when they drop them at low altitude they're highly effective at setting villages on fire.'

The image on the screen changed to one of a circular mud hut, its grass-thatch roof a sheet of orange flame. Image after image followed, those of burning huts mixed with rings of smoke-blackened earth – all that remained of huts after the fire had done its work. As Tim flipped through those photos and talked, my mind was back in the UN aircraft as I flew over Darfur, seeing scores of villages burning from the air. This, then, was the grim reality on the ground.

'I've seen the planes attack, and those attacks are followed by the helicopter gunships,' Tim continued. 'The gunships are followed in turn by army vehicles, and they come in support of the shock troops – the Janjaweed. So, it's not just men on horses: these are combined operations between the Janjaweed, the Sudanese military, and with the Air Force flying in support.'

Tim paused and glanced up from the screen. There was a haunted look in his eyes. 'Mukesh, there is no other way to describe what I've seen: this is an orchestrated, organised, targeted military campaign of extermination.' He wiped a tired hand across his features. 'You mentioned their use of the phrase "the final solution". This is what I believe we're now seeing in Darfur.'

Of course, this is what he and I had both suspected. We had both feared as much. And now, thanks to Tim's mission, we had the eyewitness evidence to prove it.

'But, Mukesh, there's worse.' Tim turned back to his laptop and opened a new file. 'In fact, it's worse than anything you spoke about when first you asked me to go and investigate.'

He flipped up a new image. It showed what looked like the ruins of some mud walls.

'Dynamited well,' Tim announced, softly. 'Deliberately blown up so that it's rendered useless, which deprives the people in that village of their water supply. That's if the survivors ever try to return.'

He flicked up a new image. His finger hovered over the screen. 'Bodies thrown into a well.' His voice had an edge now, betraying a cold but heartfelt anger. 'I guess they'd run out of dynamite by the time they reached this village. But bodies thrown into a well renders it pretty much useless as a source of drinking water, obviously.'

Click. A new image. 'Dynamited irrigation ditch. Darfur, as you know, is a semi-arid region. With water, the fields are fertile – very. Without water, nothing grows. Mukesh, they're destroying the people's very means of survival – their irrigation systems.'

His finger clicked several more times, revealing further images of blown-up and ruined irrigation ditches. 'You see. Look at this one. And this one,' he continued. 'This evidences the exact nature of the conflict. This destruction of their means of livelihood means that the villages become uninhabitable and the people can never return...'

'And that equates to ethnic cleansing,' I finished the

sentence for him. 'This is evidence of a deliberate, planned strategy to wipe a race of people off the earth and to destroy by all means their ability to survive. They're leaving behind only scorched earth.'

He glanced at me. 'There's no other way to interpret what I've seen, and the images are here to prove it.'

He clicked again, and a horrific photograph appeared. It showed a heap of twisted bodies, many if not all of which showed signs of having been burned.

'The victims,' Tim announced. 'Some you can see are very young. One of the most horrific aspects of this conflict is how they're capturing young kids and even babies, and they're burning them alive...'

He went to flick onto another image, but I reached out a hand to stop him. 'Tim, I think I've seen enough. I understand exactly what you're telling me. Do I need to see more?'

He fixed me with this look. 'Yes, Mukesh, you need to see every last one of these images. Every last one.'

I flicked my gaze back to the screen. I told Tim to continue. I understood now: *he had to show me*. He had to unburden on someone all that he had witnessed, and who better than the person who had commissioned him to travel into the heart of this darkness.

I had sent him into the fires of hell: the very least I could do was bear witness to what he had found there.

SEVENTEEN

To perceive is to suffer.
Aristotle

AS FURTHER STILLS OF BURNED AND SMASHED BODIES, FIERY huts and wrecked wells flashed across Tim's screen, I reflected on all that he had discovered. For the tribes of Darfur, the land upon which they lived defined them. It was their homeland and it was central to their identity. Generations of their dead were buried there, as testament to the longevity of their line. If you took them away from the land and destroyed their means to return, you finished them.

But the impact of those macabre photographs was more than that alone. Those images also hit me so very heavily – each like a blow to the heart – because of who I was and my role in all of this. Of anyone, I had the highest responsibility to the people of Darfur to prevent and protect, and yet here I was confronted by the irrefutable proof of the secret horrors being perpetrated in those areas closed to us. I felt sick to death at it all.

One other thing struck me. The margin between life and death was so very slim in Darfur, where people eked out a harsh semi-desert existence. The ability to cope was that much more limited than it had been in, say, Rwanda, a relatively fertile tropical country. Consequently, the ability to destroy people's means of livelihood was that much greater. Rolling crude petrol bombs out of aircraft was so cheap and easy, as was dynamiting their wells and irrigation systems.

As to the use of mass rape – which Tim moved on to in his last set of photos – that was the cheapest means of waging terror of all. One of his final images flicked onto the screen. It showed a young girl of no more than eight or nine years old. She was dressed in a light pink cotton

177

robe, and one of her eyes was swollen and bruised. She had her gaze cast to the ground in bewilderment and in shame. I will never forget that look. It was empty, haunted – the gaze of a child whose life was no longer worth living.

'One of the child victims,' Tim announced, quietly. 'Generally, they tend to let them live, so as to destroy any sense of worth amongst their family and their village.'

He pressed a button and the screen went blank. There was silence for a long moment. In the background, the air-conditioning unit was whirring noisily, but over it I could hear the rasp of our laboured breathing. He and I both were fighting back the tears.

'Thank you, Tim, for all of that,' I finally managed to say. I wiped at the corner of my eyes with the back of my hand. 'Tim, I want you to know that I appreciate enormously what this has cost you, and what you risked to secure every one of those images. But tell me, what to do next? What do you advise?'

'Mukesh, we have to do something urgently to dampen the violence. We know now how terrible it is, and what the ultimate objective is, so we have to try to stop the fighting and allow the civilians some relief from these attacks.'

'So how do we go about doing this? Is the idea of peace talks at all possible?'

'I think it is. I've got to know the SLA leaders well. If we propose a ceasefire so that access can be provided to deliver aid, maybe we can stop the worst violence. I presume it needs to be us and not the UN, because this would be too potentially explosive for the UN to handle?'

'It does need to be you,' I confirmed. 'Even if I did get a green light from New York – which I figure is all but impossible – by the time I got it, the killing would be done.'

'OK, so we will take the lead. We'll suggest a meeting between the SLA and the Khartoum regime in Chad, at which a ceasefire can hopefully be agreed. If Khartoum refuses to negotiate, that gives you the ammunition you need to accuse them of being obstructive and trying to prolong the conflict.'

For the first time in what felt like an age, I smiled. 'Tim, that sounds like a plan to me. But tell me – what *don't* we know? What evidence are we lacking?'

I was forcing myself to think like a detective here, one who was gathering evidence and compiling the case for the prosecution. But it wasn't one person – one murderer – that I was trying to nail here. It was the architects of a system designed to deliver mass murder and to wipe an entire people off the face of the earth.

'With all the evidence you've gathered, are we missing anything?' I asked. 'What proof if any is lacking?'

Tim paused for a second. 'Well, we know the motive: ethnic cleansing on the basis of race. We know the means: aerial firebombing, followed by military and militia attacks on the ground. And we know the perpetrators: those at the helm of the Khartoum regime, and the Mukhabarat, together with the Janjaweed. But you know, Mukesh, there is one element we don't yet know – the full scale of the thing.' 'We can extrapolate, but we don't have the full proof, is that what you're saying?'

'More or less. Mukesh, I spent just days on the ground. I went to one tiny area. I was told by those I spoke to that the same tactics are being repeated across Darfur, but we don't have evidence of that, or proof. I guess it's just possible that the kind of scorched-earth tactics I've seen are isolated.'

'Agreed. I very much doubt it, but it's possible. Question is, what do we do about it?'

'You mean, how do we discover and document how extensive it is?' 'Yes, Tim. I guess we have to continue with what we've been trying – flooding the area with UN workers and other agencies. If we get on the ground across a wide enough area, we can relieve the suffering and gather evidence of the exact extent of the horror.'

'I can't think of a better way,' Tim confirmed. 'It's probably our only option. That's unless you want to send me back in to do it all on my own!'

I shook my head and laughed gently. 'No, no, no. I need

you to front-up the peace negotiations. We've got to explore urgently the scope for some kind of ceasefire. You'll come to Khartoum, to make the proposal direct to the regime?'

Tim told me that he would be there as soon as the relevant meetings could be arranged. And so, with a final heartfelt thank you to him for all that he had done, I checked out of the Serena and flew back to Khartoum.

Within 48 hours, I had got Tim his meetings. He walked into the lions' den, and somehow he persuaded Khartoum to send representatives to Abeche in Chad for face-to-face talks with the Sudan Liberation Movement (SLM), the political wing of the SLA. In a matter of days, a ceasefire had been signed, and Tim and I set about writing up the terms for opening up all areas to humanitarian access. Finally, we'd had a real breakthrough, one that I could barely have hoped for a few days ago. At the same time, I sent an urgent report to Jan Egeland and Kieran Prendergast in New York. It alerted them to the dire situation in Darfur and asked that the UN should 'press for an all-inclusive, internationally monitored ceasefire'. If we could build upon the SLM– Khartoum peace deal, perhaps we could bring about a permanent end to the conflict. Perhaps we could get the peacekeepers in, which for me would be like achieving an impossible dream.

I received no response whatsoever from New York, but by now this was only what I expected. The UN was this massive, immovable steel and concrete wall through which there was little or no communication possible. There was no point beating one's head against it. All I could do was try to understand its limitations and find ways to work around them. But still I felt let down. More importantly, I felt the UN was letting down the most vulnerable, voiceless people in Sudan by choosing to ignore Darfur.

Sadly, our joy in achieving that peace deal proved to be painfully short lived. Without significant international backing, the peace crumbled. Before the ceasefire had a chance to take hold, fighting sparked again, and within hours it was spiralling out of control. Reports came in that aircraft had continued to firebomb villages even as the peace was being signed. Hassan had repeatedly told me that a snake never changes its spots. True to form, Khartoum had used the ceasefire as a smokescreen behind which to further its aims.

Tim flew back to Europe, but neither he nor I had given up on exploring the options for peace. No doors would be closed, not when the stakes were as high as they were here. But neither of us was kidding ourselves that the prospects were good. We'd keep talking to the rebel leaders and keep lines open with Khartoum. But without the UN stepping up to the mark, any peace that we might broker lacked crucial international backing and support.

I felt such little reason for hope, and perhaps because of that I resolved to redouble my efforts as agent provocateur. In the days following the collapse of the ceasefire I issued a call for action. In a report to Jan Egeland – my one remaining ally in New York – I wrote the following. Crisis in Darfur, Sudan: Insecurity continues on an unprecedented scale, possibly emerging as the most serious emergency in Africa ... More than 600,000 people are internally displaced and an additional 70,000 are refugees in Chad. The violence is caused mainly by government- aligned militias. Any strategy to solve the problem should include strong international pressure on the government of Sudan (GOS) to control the militias as a prelude to disarmament...

I signed off the report asking for 'a high-level political initiative from the UN secretary-general' – in effect, a plea for Kofi Annan to intervene directly on Darfur. I also asked for the UN to explore the possibility of starting emergency airdrops of aid into Darfur cross-border from neighbouring Chad.

I emailed that report to New York on 1 December 2003. Jan Egeland responded quickly, pledging his support, but there was no hint of any meaningful response from the rest of the UN – those with the power to take action over Darfur. Of course, one of the most effective strategies when faced with unpalatable truths is to do nothing. *All it takes for evil to triumph is for a few good men to do nothing...*

The wall of silence didn't stop me from agitating: I simply shifted my targets. I decided to appeal directly to the few individuals within the UN system who I felt had backbone and principles. I asked Ruud Lubbers, the Dutch head of UNHCR (the United Nations High Commissioner for Refugees), to raise the issue of Darfur direct with Khartoum. I got Mohamed Sahnoun, a highly respected Algerian and special envoy to Kofi Annan, to fly out. I briefed him on the scale of the war crimes in Darfur and the Sudan government's culpability.

Sahnoun was a passionate advocate of post-conflict peace building, and I had learned a lot from him over the years. I hoped that Khartoum would listen to a fellow Arab and respect him. He duly went and spoke in very forthright terms to the government. But in spite of his and Ruud Lubbers' interventions, it was clear that the UN remained hopelessly divided. In fact, its most powerful players had opted to downplay the whole issue of Darfur.

As for me, I was largely emasculated by the inaction from UN headquarters, or at least I was on an international level. But within Sudan I was still the UN chief, and that gave me the mandate to act as I saw it. But even as I turned my mind to gathering the evidence we needed on the scale of the thing, the fates were conspiring otherwise.

Roger began issuing dire warnings about the urgent need to withdraw the UN from El Geneina. He insisted that the rebels were poised to attack and that our people were in mortal danger. In his view, there was no time to lose: the UN had to pull out. I wanted us to be in there until the very last moment, but, in the interim, I took the difficult decision of advising the other agencies to leave.

They duly got their people out of El Geneina on a flight that we provided, and all that remained now were the UN personnel. Two days later, I finally bowed to what Roger argued was inevitable. I hated doing this. It was the very opposite of what we needed to do. But I couldn't ignore Roger's advice any longer. He was on the verge of reporting my lack of action to New York, at which stage I could be overruled.

I needed clearance from HAC to get our evacuation flights in, and I filed my request with Sulaf in the normal way. But the response I got was far from expected. I was in my office when I took a call from Ibrahim Mohamed Hamid, the minister for humanitarian affairs. He and I had prior form, and ever since our first meeting we had done our best to avoid each other.

Early in my tenure, we'd met to discuss the root causes of the Darfur conflict. Hamid had proceeded to inform me that the Darfuris were 'ill-disciplined black savages that we have to bring under control'. At first I'd thought this was a language issue, and that he couldn't really mean what he'd said, especially as he'd spoken those words as if he expected me to agree with him.

I told him that I couldn't really tell a black African or an Arab Darfuri apart. 'Oh no,' he replied, 'it's very easy. They have very dirty habits and they are uncivilised. We are not.' It was then that I realised he meant exactly what he had said. His attitude bordered upon open hatred, and he simply presumed that I, as a relatively light-skinned Anglo-Indian, would concur. My response had been to do everything I could to minimise contact with the objectionable Mr Hamid.

But now he had phoned to speak with me direct, and it was the issue of our planned withdrawal from El Geneina that had prompted his call. He proceeded to inform me that withdrawing the UN would send all the wrong signals and that it was unacceptable to HAC. I told him that it was my call as the UN resident chief whether we withdrew our staff on security grounds.

'Dr Kapila, may I remind you of what happened to your predecessor,' the minister warned. 'After withdrawing the

UN from Juba, Mike Sackett lasted no time at all. Why are you so determined to follow in his footsteps? Withdrawing UN staff is a hostile act against the interests of my government. And again, I will remind you of the Sackett example.'

'Mr Hamid, we have repeatedly asked for action by your government to facilitate humanitarian relief and to stop the violence in Darfur, but it appears that your government is unwilling or unable to act. How can we trust your guarantees of security in El Geneina when you are unable to control the violence or give access? Clearly, such assurances can't be relied upon.'

There was a moment's silence. Then this: 'May I remind you, Dr Kapila, that the Mukhabarat can make life very difficult for you if you evacuate.' There was a clear edge of menace to his voice now. 'We have the power to do that, you know.'

I noted the 'we'. He was being quite blatant about HAC being a front for the Mukhabarat. This was the nearest that anyone had come to making a direct threat to me, and my indignation flared. I was on my feet now, marching back and forth across my office.

'Mr Hamid, it is you who are supposed to facilitate our work, not obstruct it! If need be, I will take up this issue with senior officials here in Khartoum and with their counterparts in the international community.'

'Again, I will remind you most forcefully of the Mike Sackett example...'

'Minister, our aircraft will be ready to take off at first light tomorrow,' I cut in. 'If the flight is not cleared, I will personally go onto the world's media and announce that your government is holding UN staff hostage...'

Suddenly he exploded. 'Who the bloody hell do you think you are?! This is our country! We control things here! We are in charge! Not your bloody UN! You will be kicked out of the Sudan...'

I am not in the habit of swearing, and certainly not to the ministers of my host country, but it was now that I saw red.

'So do your bloody worst!' I told him, before slamming down the phone.

An instant later I had the handset up again, and I punched the speed dial for Roger's mobile phone. As I waited for him to answer, I could feel my pulse pounding in my head. With Hamid openly making threats, I figured my days in Sudan had to be numbered. So be it. Relations had been rapidly souring. Finally a line had been crossed: they had started to menace me openly.

I didn't take kindly to being threatened or bullied. It was like a red rag to a bull, and for a moment I felt like I was back at Wellington College challenging Freddy DeWitt to the Big Kingsley.

Roger's laconic 'Sir, this is your security chief' pulled me back to the present.

I proceeded to issue my instructions. 'Roger, mobilise our aircraft and flight crews to evacuate our staff from El Geneina starting at first light tomorrow. And, Roger, that includes everyone – international and local staff, plus their families.'

'Yes, sir,' Roger responded. 'And not a moment too soon...'

Roger must have wondered what the hell was going on. I'd fought against this evacuation for weeks and here I was suddenly making an about turn.

At dawn the following morning, we had all available UN aircraft lined up on the runway with pilots awaiting clearance to get airborne. This had become a game of brinkmanship, and clearance was only granted for take-off at the last possible moment – as the aircraft spooled their engines up to speed.

It seemed as if I had won that battle, but I didn't kid myself for one moment that I had won the wider war.

EIGHTEEN

I felt despair. Though it seems to me now there's two kinds
of it: the sort that causes a person to surrender and then the
sort I had which made me take risks and make plans.
Erica Eisdorfer

THE COUNTER-ATTACK WASN'T LONG IN COMING.
IT WOULD take several days for us to evacuate all 80
or so of our staff, plus their families. On the second day
of our flights, Roger greeted me in a sombre mood. He'd
brought cuttings from the Sudanese newspapers, including
cartoons that showed 'the UN' running away from Darfur.
The cartoons came with headlines decrying what an insult
this was to the entire Sudanese nation. The UN 'needed to
be taught a lesson' was the tone of the articles. Roger and
I understood well how things worked in Khartoum. If the
government had a particularly unpalatable message to
deliver to one of their detractors, they would often choose
to do so via the government-controlled media. There
were several advantages in doing so.

One, it was deniable. The government could claim that
the media had said something but of course that was far
from being the official position. Two, it meant that we
couldn't complain about government harassment or
intimidation. And three, it was an altogether more sinister
way to deliver a message. There were any number of
Islamic extremists in Khartoum. Any one of them might
read the press reports and decide to take matters into their
own hands.

If I had any remaining doubts how furious our
withdrawal had made them, I was just about to have them
allayed. The regime's anger centred on the fact that we had
given the rebels credibility by suggesting that they had the
military capability to threaten a major urban centre in
Darfur. The more credibility the rebels had, the more

supporters they might attract and the more they might actually start to threaten the centre – the rule from Khartoum.

It was Sulaf who delivered news of Khartoum's counter-stroke. He appeared visibly shamefaced when he told me what HAC's 'considered reaction' was to our withdrawal. If the UN's security couldn't be guaranteed in El Geneina, there was no reason why other parts of Darfur should be any different. Ergo, security couldn't be guaranteed anywhere in Darfur. Ergo, we would have to withdraw all our staff.

We should evacuate the entire UN operation from Darfur.

Sulaf accepted that his government couldn't order us out. But if we didn't agree to go, they would withdraw permission for all flights into and out of the region. In fact, they had already done so. All pending flights had been cancelled. As a result, we could get no workers, food or equipment into or out of our operations. I had urgent requests pending for ballistic blankets to provide mine- protection to our vehicles and even these had been denied.

With a ban on all flights, this made our operations dangerously unworkable. I had no way to keep my staff on the ground. I couldn't even feed them. I knew at once that I had been outmanoeuvred. By agreeing to Roger's request that we withdraw from one area, I had effectively damned the entire UN operation in Darfur.

I did wonder whether Roger had been set up here. Perhaps he had been fed false information to force our withdrawal from one area as the excuse to kick the UN out wholesale. Either way, I felt hopelessly naive and as if I had been manipulated and used. When up against the machinations of the Mukhabarat, I was beginning to feel like a lamb to their lions.

By the end of the third week of December, we had been forced to withdraw all our staff. The other aid agencies had no option but to follow suit, for they too had been ordered out by Khartoum. With zero humanitarian presence, and the

Christmas shutdown all but upon us, Darfur had become completely cut off from the outside world. It was the worst of all possible outcomes. I had been comprehensively outsmarted by the authors of the 'final solution' in Darfur.

The night that our very last staff member was withdrawn, I sat alone in my concrete edifice of a house feeling absolutely useless and empty. How had I let things come to this? After all my remonstrations and fine words, I had been outwitted by those who were hell-bent on wiping out an entire people.

With all the experience that I carried with me of mass murder around the world, I seemed to have learned so very little. I had presided over the removal of the international community from the very ground over which a terrible darkness was spreading. It was a catastrophic failure by anyone's reckoning.

It was late into a sleepless night when I heard my mobile phone ring. I figured it could only be one person – Hassan. Hassan must have called me a dozen times by now, over the course of which he and I had built up a rapport. I appreciated the enormous risks that he was taking in calling me. It was a brave act, and I feared that one day it might prove a fatal one.

But right now I was going to have to break the news to him that all aid agencies had been forced out of Darfur and that the fault for this lay largely at my door. I felt broken, defeated and horribly ashamed, and for the first time I was tempted not to take his call.

I reached out a reluctant hand. 'Hassan, it's Mukesh.'

'There's been 14 wells destroyed in El Fasher,' Hassan's voice rang out, echoing down the line. 'And the villages with them. This thing is escalating, and there is more killing...'

There was a sudden, sharp burst of cracks in the background. 'What's that, Hassan? It sounds like gunfire?'

'There's fighting nearby,' came a terse reply. 'We have to keep moving. I don't know for how long we can talk. You have my number? If we get cut off, try to call.'

'Yes, yes, of course. But, Hassan, there's something you need to know. We, the UN, and all other agencies have been forced to pull out...'

There was a click and then an echoing silence. The line had been cut. Tim had given me Hassan's number when we met in Nairobi. I tried calling it several times that night with no joy. I lay awake wondering what had happened. I feared that Hassan had got into some kind of pattern with his calls and that they would be tracking his signal in an effort to nail him.

I felt an overwhelming sense of impotency. I thought back over all the risks that we had taken to establish this contact. Tim Mansfield's mission had been beset by dangers, and it had risked the UN's wrath on the one side and Khartoum's ire on the other. Over the weeks, I'd felt a growing affinity with Hassan, yet he was sounding more and more desperate with each call. We were both of us becoming increasingly isolated and hunted on all sides.

It was the night of 21 December when I took that call from Hassan. Two days later, I was on a flight routed via Frankfurt to London, and I had failed to raise the rebel leader in the interim. During the few days since the UN and other agencies had been forced out of Darfur, my confidence had imploded. I sat on the long flight heading home, feeling as if my tenure as UN chief – the zenith of my life's work – had been defined only by failure.

Tim's mission had failed to secure any meaningful peace settlement. Rather than flooding Darfur with humanitarians, I had succeeded only in getting them thrown out. Hassan, my rebel leader friend, was more than likely running from missiles homing in on his satphone signal. The UN was proving hopelessly impotent and closed to me. And as for Khartoum, it was turning openly hostile.

Eight months earlier, I had flown into Sudan feeling as if I were riding the winds of destiny, and with the prospect of a historic north– south peace accord in the offing. Now, I was flying out feeling hollow and defeated. A part of me had wanted to refuse taking Christmas leave. I'd wanted to don my sackcloth and ashes and do real penance for all my perceived failures.

It was Isabelle who had talked some sense into me. She pointed out that over the Christmas and New Year break the UN office was basically shutting down. There was nothing I could achieve by remaining in Khartoum. All that I would do was stew in my own very dark and desolate juices, which would do me no end of harm. She had reminded me that I was human and that I was close to burned out. I needed some time away. I needed to go home to see my family and recharge my batteries. She reminded me that Darfur needed me to do that so I could return to the battle with the energy and the will to fight. And thus she had convinced me to go.

I touched down at Heathrow airport and caught the train to Peterborough, where Helen was waiting with the family car. For a moment I found myself standing in my normal position, by the rear right-hand side of the vehicle.

Helen poked her head out of the driver's window 'Well? What are you standing there for?' she laughed. 'There's a free seat beside me. Aren't you going to get in?'

My mind was still in Khartoum, and I had been waiting for Omer to open my door for me.

Just as soon as we were home, my teenage daughters surrounded me with delighted hugs. Seconds later they were bombarding me with questions. What was it like in Sudan? What kinds of things was I doing there? How many people had I saved? This was the last thing that I wanted right now. I wanted to get away from all of that now that I was back with my family.

All I managed to say was something about it not being 'very pleasant'.

'Typical!' my oldest, Rachel, snorted. 'We'll learn more about what Dad is up to from watching the news!'

'It's just not been very nice, that's all,' I tried again. But I knew it sounded terribly lame.

After two decades of me working in the world's trouble

190

spots, my family had grown used to me telling them very little about what I had been up to. They didn't like it exactly. They would always try to find out more, especially my daughters. But they had grown accustomed to my reticence. The trouble was, I couldn't tell them. I really didn't want to bring all of that unspeakable horror into my home. This was the place where life was good. My sanctuary. The warmth and safety of home.

I glanced around our little cottage, searching for my dog, Megan. It was odd not to have her waiting by the door, the position she'd normally adopt a good quarter of an hour before I reached home.

'Where's Megan?' I asked.

'Well, we've had something horrid happen, too,' Rachel remarked. 'Best you sit down, Dad. Ruth, you'd better tell him...'

My youngest, Ruth, was always drafted in whenever there was some family business that needed extra-careful handling. I did as I was told, collapsing into one of the sofas. The girls bundled themselves on top of me.

'So, what's the bad news?' I asked. 'Someone not doing so well at school?'

'Dad, there really *is* some bad news,' Ruth began, her voice growing sombre. 'You know Megan's been ill? Well, she was up and down for the last few weeks, and, anyway, she's died. We didn't want to tell you when you were away, 'cause we guessed things were a bit tough for you out there.'

The girls took me into the garden to show me Megan's grave. They'd buried her at the base of the hedge that ran down one side of the house, so she could be close to the family even in her place of rest. It was a shady corner, and they'd planted some daffodils there, ones that would flower every spring.

'We're going to get a bird bath to go on top of the grave,' Ruth explained, 'in the space we've left clear of flowers.'

The girls left me alone for a few minutes. I had missed Megan enormously in Khartoum. I would have given anything to have her with me – a constant companion and uncomplicated friend. She would have been the perfect foil to the dark machinations that I had been dealing with.

Khartoum was officially a 'family posting', which meant that I could have taken Helen and the children with me. But there was no way I would have wanted to take the girls out of school or Helen away from her medical practice, only to drag them out to the hot, dusty – and, for me at least, increasingly menacing – streets of Khartoum. For a moment, I remembered the photo that I had of Megan on my bedside table in Khartoum. The thought brought a smile to my face, and especially when I remembered how I had come by it. The girls had got it a couple of years back for my Christmas present.

They'd taken Megan to the local photographic studio, groomed her and had a professional portrait done.

My mind wandered from that photo to another one – of my wife shortly after we were married. I'd met Helen when I was a teenage Oxford medical student. I'd gone to do some aid work back in my native India. By chance, Helen had volunteered to serve as a roving medic – a kind of 'barefoot doctor' – in one of the remotest parts of my home state, Bihar. I had been amazed when I'd come across this young, pretty, 20-something white English girl administering healthcare in the midst of the isolated bush.

The conditions Helen was working in were incredibly basic and challenging. On one occasion she had to deal with a local woman who had been in labour for so long that the baby inside her had died. The only way to save that woman's life was to cut the foetus up inside the womb and extract it, and that is exactly what Helen proceeded to do. She was a year out of medical college, and she was making life-and-death decisions with the most extraordinary courage. After three days walking from village to village – petrol was in far too short a supply to drive anywhere – we sat on the steps of a beautiful Hindu temple, watching the sun sink over the distant horizon. The moon came out and the fireflies were bright, and a light breeze gently cooled us. It was such a romantic setting, and I sensed the two of us were falling in love. We kissed there and then on those steps, and it was then that Helen proposed to me.

'Will you marry me?' she asked.

'I'll let you know tomorrow,' I told her. I was only 19 years old.

What did she expect? And in any case, I wanted another kiss.

The next day I said 'yes'. It was then that we had to break the news to my parents, who were plotting for me for me to marry a nice young Indian girl. They were more than a little shocked, but they didn't stand against the match. Helen was warm and homely, and able to it in just about anywhere. She was almost Indian in many ways.

Yet it was marrying Helen that would further my growing Englishness, and the birth of our children would cement that process. It was almost inevitable that in time I would give up my Indian citizenship and become British. And it was in taking up my British citizenship that I also took up many of the values of my adopted country – foremost amongst them those of providing aid and assistance to the developing world. And it was that which had taken me to so many of the world's more troubled regions and eventually to Darfur. I turned away from Megan's grave and started back towards the cottage. But as I did so, the image of my dog's last place of rest flipped into one of the images from Tim Mansfield's laptop – of dead cattle lying in the desert bush. The Janjaweed had slaughtered all of those animals that they couldn't loot or drive away, which was all part of the scorched-earth policy they were pursuing.

Even here, in the timeless peace of the rural Cambridge fens and in the bosom of my family, one half of me remained mired in the darkness that was Darfur.

NINETEEN

Believe passionately in the ideas and in the way of life for which one is fighting. Liberty deserves to be served with more passion than tyranny.
André Maurois

IT WAS THE FIRST WEEK OF JANUARY 2004 WHEN I FLEW BACK to Sudan. I was feeling partially refreshed by my break. No matter what trouble-torn part of the world I had been sent to, Christmas with my family in the Cambridgeshire fens was the one thing that I always did my utmost not to miss. And, somehow, my family seemed to know that, while I'd been absent so often, I loved them dearly and did my best to be there when it really mattered.

Yet, in truth, barely an hour had gone by when I hadn't found my mind wandering to Darfur. It had never been like this before. Even with Rwanda or Srebrenica, because the mass murder hadn't happened on my watch, I had been able to leave it mostly behind me. I was desperate for news from Darfur, and to get our people back on the ground.

One of the very first things I did upon reaching Khartoum was to seek an update from Roger. During my absence, he told me, there had been no rebel attacks on El Geneina. The specific threat that had led to us evacuating the entire UN presence hadn't come to anything. In fact, there had been few if any reports of fighting from out of that troubled region. With things being so quiet, Roger presumed that the conflict had died down to something like manageable proportions, and that was what all his sources were telling him.

Yet in the back of my mind I couldn't help but worry that somehow we had been duped. I had pulled out our painstakingly constructed relief effort, and all because of a feared rebel assault on El Geneina. I worried very much that we had pulled the UN out of Darfur for nothing –

for a chimera. I just had to hope that any harm done wasn't terminal. After all, it had been Christmas and New Year, and not a lot seemed to have happened anywhere during that time.

I had returned to Khartoum vowing to be more positive. In that spirit, I went to see Sulaf, to argue for us to be allowed back into Darfur. I felt almost genuinely glad to see him again, and I wished him a heartfelt Happy New Year.

'D'you know, Sulaf, I've missed our little chats, and none more so than those over Darfur. So, tell me, when can we go back to our work there? I'm sure there's much to be done.'

'Dr Kapila, it's been too quiet without you,' Sulaf returned my greeting. 'Rest assured, my friend, we'll get you back in very soon. But first, let me check on the security situation and then we shall see.' I sought a meeting with the deputy minister at HAC. Far better him than his objectionable boss, Hamid. Again, I asked when we would be allowed back in.

'You are the one who insisted you get out,' he reminded me, politely. 'Now you are out, we will think about letting you back in. But, first, have a cup of tea.'

Every day I kept agitating for our return, and I kept getting the same answer – *not quite yet*. This went on for a week or more before we started to receive worrying reports from our UN counterparts in Chad. Darfuri refugees were pouring across the border, and they were telling horrendous stories about attacks on villages and mass rape. I began to have the horrible suspicion that the very worst might have been happening while our backs were turned.

I issued warnings to the various government ministries in Khartoum. I did so face to face and in written démarches – formal diplomatic documents. I pointed out that if they continued to refuse us access, they would be 'obstructing humanitarians, which under international law is a crime against humanity'. This was little short of threatening my host government with war crimes, and it was a serious escalation in the dark game that we were playing.

But still, access was refused. Still I was told 'soon, but not yet'.

One of the few remaining sources from whom I hoped to get information on the ground was my rebel leader friend, Hassan. A few days after my return to Khartoum, my cell phone rang. It was two o'clock in the morning, and I snatched it up knowing instinctively that it was him. 'Hassan? Mukesh. What news?'

'It is very bad right now.' Hassan's words were rushed, his voice tight with tension. 'Everything has escalated. All the very worst things that we have spoken about over the last weeks – they are happening right now. We need...'

Boom! There was the unmistakable sound of a massive explosion on the far end of the line, and an instant later the connection went dead. I couldn't believe what had happened. I refused to let myself believe it. I kept dialling his number, but there was no reply. Eventually, I forced myself to face up to the dark truth. There had been a huge blast and that very instant the line had gone dead. I couldn't but think that my worst fears had been realised: Hassan, the rebel leader who had placed so much trust in me, had been killed.

After a sleepless night, I called Tim Mansfield. I told him what had happened, and he promised to check. A few hours later, he was back in touch. All the information he could gather pointed to Hassan being dead. A little later that day it was confirmed absolutely in a Khartoum newspaper. Several top rebel leaders – Hassan included – had been killed. Hassan had died while speaking to me on his satphone. More than likely, they had homed in on the signal to get him.

That evening, I headed over to Roger's place. In spite of our occasional differences over security, I trusted Roger absolutely, and he was as near as I got to a friend in Khartoum. I proceeded to rant and rave to him about Hassan's death and about what hidden nightmare might be even now unfolding in Darfur. I got the usual monosyllabic answers, but at least I felt as if someone was listening. 'It's a complete bloody mess, Roger,' I told him. 'We've been out since late December, and those bastards keep refusing to allow us back in.'

Roger took a slurp of his beer. 'Yes, sir.'

'We have several hundred thousand refugees in Chad, and more keep flooding in daily.'

'They do, sir.'

'In fact, there are Darfuri refugees scattered from Chad to Khartoum, to as far south as the Nuba Mountains.'

'Correct, sir.'

'With maybe 500,000 in Chad alone, that's a tenfold increase in a matter of months.'

'Pretty much, sir.'

'From the refugees, we hear horrific stories of mass rape. As the nightmare worsens in Darfur, the so-called peace talks in Naivasha stagnate. As the violence worsens, so the talks falter, but no one seems willing to recognise this or to act. Overall, it's a total bloody mess, isn't it, Roger?'

'You could say that, sir, yes.'

'A mess that I have presided over.' I took a swig of my own beer. 'In effect, the people of Darfur are being sacrificed on the altar of geopolitics, but that sacrifice is meaningless because no peace deal will ever be signed while the horror continues. Garang is immovable on that, and I suspect Khartoum won't sign either, not until they've finished their dirty work. Am I right or am I right, Roger?' 'Pretty much bang on the nail, sir.'

I lapsed into a silence, my mind a swirl of dark thoughts.

'Roger, there is only one option left open to me,' I began again, 'at least, as I see it. I need to go and speak truth to the world powers

– to present my analysis and alert them to their failures. Surely they can't plough ahead with a policy that is sacrificing so many innocent lives? Surely, Roger, when they're alerted to the fact that their policy is completely useless, they'll have to change?'

'You'd like to think so, wouldn't you, sir.'

'And if nothing else, I can lobby world governments to pressurise Khartoum to allow us back in. I'm getting nowhere here arguing for access. We're being stonewalled. It's the only sensible option, wouldn't you agree?'

'I guess, sir, it is.'

And so it was that, with Roger's help, my decision on my next course of action was made. I would go on a whirlwind tour, targeting those centres of power that could seriously influence Khartoum. London would be my first port of call, for London's backing was critical. Without it, I had little hope of achieving anything.

I knew, of course, that I had been down this road before. Four months earlier, I had trodden the corridors of power in an effort to get action on Darfur. But I owed it to the victims: to the woman who had spoken out in Nyala; to Idris, and the thousands of other disappeared IDPs around Khartoum; and now, also, to Hassan, the late rebel leader. I owed it to the people of Darfur to try again, and in my life I have never been one to take no for an answer.

Even after beating Freddy De Witt at the Big Kingsley, it had been a continual struggle to be accepted at Wellington College. My fellow pupils could tell that I didn't just want to be like them. I was proud of where I came from, and in 1970s British public school culture there were many boys who didn't much appreciate someone with a different skin colour and heritage. I reacted to their blind prejudice with a determination to beat them at their own game, and I never for one moment lost my sense of otherness.

In time, I did beat them at their own game. Just a year into Wellington College I was coming top of the year. I'd gone from being the Indian boy who didn't know if testicle-scrubbing was an esteemed English ritual, to being a school prefect, a skilful fencer and the most academically accomplished pupil. I felt as if I had shown them, but still I remained an outsider to all but a few.

One of the rare friends I made was a fellow pupil called John Loveless. When my father couldn't afford to fly me back to India for school holidays, the Loveless family's noisy, rambling house by the sea in Broadstairs became my refuge. John's father, Alan, was a general medical practitioner, and he used to take me on his rounds in the local hospital. Together, the Loveless family demonstrated the side of British society that in time would capture my heart.

Set against the mindless prejudice that I'd experienced from some at Wellington, there was an openness and a tolerance amongst many in Britain that was hugely refreshing. I never once regretted coming to England, because for me this was the educational chance of a lifetime. I had my heart set on going to Oxford University, but my interview there seemed to go badly, and in due course they declined to offer me a place. But yet again, I refused to take no for an answer. I wrote to the very top people at Oxford pleading my case. I pestered Harold Macmillan, the former British prime minister and then chancellor of Oxford, directly. I refused to give up until Sir Alec Cairncross, then master of St Peter's College, offered me a place, but only if I could achieve three A-grades at A-level and 2 S-levels at Grade One. This was in effect another 'no' – for to get those kind of grades was at that time all but impossible.

Yet at least I had a conditional offer, and I sensed in Sir Alec's behaviour a certain British sense of fair play. The odds were stacked against me, but at least I had been given a sporting chance. I had never worked so hard in my life as I did then, and in due course did achieve those grades and my dream of going to study at Oxford. The one thing that Mahatma Gandhi had always admired about the British was their sense of fair play and of giving people a sporting chance. It was something that I learned to appreciate as well. Some six years after getting into Oxford, I ran into my nemesis, Freddy DeWitt, once again. By then I was a fully qualified medical doctor, and I had applied for a job in Cambridge. I drove over to the interview and who should be sitting in the waiting room but DeWitt. He too had qualified as a doctor, and we were competing for the same job. He greeted me with a disbelieving stare, followed by a frigid politeness. I went before the interview panel, and the inevitable question was put to me. 'People here in Cambridge and the Fens are not used to coloured doctors. How will they react to you?'

'Well, they'll just have to learn to get used to me,' I blurted out spontaneously. 'Just like I've had to get used to bread-and-butter pudding, freezing weather and not to mention rugby!'

The interview panel seemed to find my answer really very funny. I was given the job, and I'd beaten Freddy DeWitt once again. In appointing me, they had taken a brave step towards defeating prejudice and ignorance. Their English sense of fair play had prevailed, and they had given me a chance. And all I was hoping for as I took the long flight from Khartoum to London was to appeal to the British sense of fair play, and to be given a sporting chance over Darfur.

Again, my key meeting was going to be with the Foreign and Commonwealth Office (FCO). I was scheduled to have lunch with Sebastian Hawkesley-Smith, one of the key advisors on British government policy towards Darfur. He was a tall, charming, suave individual and a consummate Whitehall mandarin, and we knew each other of old. He was also a man of great knowledge and learning, and if I appealed to his sense of fair play I hoped right would prevail. He took me to his plush London club. We sat on overstuffed leather sofas as he ordered a lunch that reminded me very much of my Wellington College days: roast lamb followed by bread-and-butter pudding and custard. I tried to force the very British ordered formality of the setting to the back of my mind as I prepared to take my host into the unfolding and chaotic heart of darkness that was Darfur. 'The situation in Darfur worries me greatly,' I told him, once the usual chitchat was done. 'I have to tell you that I have heard the Sudanese government use the term "the final solution" with reference to Darfur. I fear they are using that term deliberately and that Darfur is fast becoming a place of massive ethnic cleansing, and that they will finish the job by all possible means.'

In this English gentleman's club, where the furniture was from the time of Dickens and the cooking so very much old school, it seemed almost crass to go on about such brute prejudice and violence.

'The evidence we have is that almost the entire population is on the move,' I continued. 'From April 2003 to January 2004, an entire region the size of France has been upturned. I know of no single situation that has escalated so quickly. This is a war being waged by a government against its own people, using helicopter gunships and Antonovs, and Janjaweed militia against civilian villages.'

As I spoke, I could see him pushing his food around his plate in a decidedly uncomfortable way. I ploughed on regardless.

'Now, it is morally wrong to use Darfur as a trade-off against the Naivasha peace talks, which is what I believe is happening. But more to the point, that trade-off isn't working. It is wholly in vain. While we fiddle with Naivasha, Darfur is burning, and – make no mistake – Naivasha won't be signed while Darfur is in flames. Quite the reverse: John Garang has told me categorically that he will not sign.'

Sebastian fixed me with a pained look. 'Calm down, Mukesh, old boy, calm down. You're going at a million miles an hour, my friend. Help yourself to some more vegetables, why don't you. And have you tried the mint sauce?' He paused. 'Look, Mukesh, old chap, don't you think you're over-dramatising things a little? You do have something of a reputation for exaggeration, and you're behaving close to hysterical at the moment, which is far from convenient.'

I felt my blood boil. *Hysterical. Over-dramatising. Not convenient.* Who the hell was he to patronise me? Try telling that to the tens of thousands of women and children who'd been gang-raped. Or the husbands and brothers who'd been forced to watch those rapes, while they were taunted with cries of 'zurka' – nigger – and 'abeed' – slave. Try telling that to the Darfuri men whose wives and daughters were being given 'Arab babies'.

'Sebastian, please don't belittle this.' My voice had gone cold and quiet, and I was gripped by an icy calm. 'These are very serious war crimes that we are talking about in Darfur. We are talking about a regime that has deliberately manufactured ethnic cleansing and scorched earth to wipe an entire race and culture off the face of the earth, utilising extreme and brutal violence targeted at women and children. These are crimes against humanity on a massive scale.'

Sebastian half-choked on his lunch. 'Mukesh, that may or may not be the case. I for one would need an awful lot of convincing. But do keep your voice down, won't you, there's a good fellow.'

His toned softened slightly, becoming somewhat more cajoling. 'Look, Mukesh, as I'm sure you appreciate there are bigger geopolitical issues to consider here, and we really do have to take the long view over difficult issues like Darfur. That requires patience. Patience. We're discussing all of this with our international partners, and the one thing we mustn't do is paint Khartoum into a corner, don't you agree?' I bit back a suitable reply. 'Sebastian, you need to be aware of one thing. I have increasingly started to consider whether these crimes against humanity that I have witnessed in Darfur shouldn't be placed before the International Criminal Court, because they are certainly of a scale that warrants such treatment.'

'The ICC?' Sebastian let out a quiet chuckle. 'Surely, Mukesh, you're not being serious? It would require a United Nations security council resolution to refer it to the ICC, and that, trust me, will never happen. Even were the security council to agree to discuss it, which they will not, China would veto it, and anyway Sudan is not a signatory to the ICC. This is too far fetched, Mukesh, old fellow. Trust me, any ideas you may be entertaining about the ICC are really too implausible and are quite frankly destined to go nowhere.'

'I still believe that raised in the right way an ICC submission could get through,' I argued. 'Do you really think the Chinese would veto such a thing if Khartoum were publicly charged with crimes against humanity? It would be hugely provocative, even for the Chinese, and if we were determined enough it might just succeed.'

He placed down his knife and fork and gave this look. 'Perhaps, Mukesh, it is time for me to be clearer about things. Your stirring things up in this way doesn't help us apply the measured pressure that is necessary. Nothing personal, old chap, but really you should be careful. All this stirring things up will end very badly for you.' He paused, as if to emphasise the point.

'Well, how about at the very least a peacekeeping force?' I pressed on, ignoring his thinly veiled warning. 'It's working in the Nuba Mountains, so why not in Darfur? At least that way we could halt the worst of the violence on the ground and safeguard the remaining civilians in their villages.'

Sebastian fixed me with a withering stare. 'Peacekeepers? In Darfur? You wouldn't stand a chance, my friend, and not least because the Russians and Chinese would veto any such proposal. And are you really honestly trying to tell me the government of Sudan would allow them in? Come on, old boy... Peacekeepers – it's a pipe dream.' He waved his hand at the dish that had been placed in front of us. 'Now, on to more civilised matters, such as dessert. Have some bread-and- butter pudding. Invariably, the custard here is delicious.'

In an effort to conceal my rage, I took a helping of pudding and custard and forced it down me. But the remainder of that luncheon was occupied only by stilted and uncomfortable small talk. As far as I was concerned, this meeting had been a total waste of time. Beneath the polite civility, Sebastian's message was crystal clear: *no change on British policy over Darfur. And watch your step, old boy: causing all this trouble will not be good for your career.*

Is this what Sebastian and those like him really thought of me, I wondered – that a few nuanced warnings over a club luncheon would ensure my silence? If so, they had badly miscalculated. In appealing to my sense of self-preservation – my career – they were way off the mark. My moral compass would not be swayed, not when my very soul was on the line, as I believed it now was over Darfur.

Sebastian and I parted with a brief handshake. I ducked into a passing cab, feeling thankful that the grey London rain had given me ample excuse to hurry away. I told the cabbie to head for Heathrow airport. As we drove away I didn't look back. Instead, I consigned Sebastian to the growing ranks of those good men who had chosen to do nothing...

As my flight lifted off for New York, I didn't entertain any greater expectations of how things would go at UN headquarters.

But I would go ahead and present my case regardless.

TWENTY

The man who goes alone can start today, but he who travels with another must wait till the other is ready.
Henry David Thoreau

I MET FIRST WITH JAN EGELAND AND TOLD HIM OF MY conversations in London. Jan agreed that the situation was absolutely dire but told me again that I'd have to convince Kieran Prendergast if there was to be any hope of the UN taking political action. I went ahead and met with Prendergast, telling him what I'd told Sebastian and Jan. His response was in large part to tell me that I wasn't doing my job properly.

I was reminded that Darfur was first and foremost a humanitarian matter, and my role as United Nations resident chief was to deal with this as a humanitarian issue. In essence, I was being told to go stick an Elastoplast on a wound that would bleed the patient to death, instead of trying to save the patient's life.

'But we can't achieve anything much by distributing aid to people who are being bombed, raped and murdered in their thousands,' I pressed. 'Surely you understand that. How can we pursue a humanitarian mission in the midst of a war zone wherein a *"final solution"* is being perpetrated by a government against its own people? That's their choice of words, by the way – Khartoum's – not my own. Of course, you'll know that from reading all my reports.'

'That's as may be,' Prendergast replied. 'But you're straying way outside of your remit, which is what concerns me most. You're the resident and humanitarian coordinator for Sudan – that's your remit, and you need to stick to it.'

'So what about peacekeepers?' I demanded. 'If we had peacekeepers on the ground, at least then we could go about our humanitarian remit with some degree of security and some chance of doing some good for the victims.'

Prendergast choked back a chuckle. 'Peacekeepers? Surely you're not being serious? The UN is massively overstretched around the world on peacekeeping operations as it is. And in any case, Khartoum would never allow them in. You do know you need the consent of the government to send peacekeepers in, don't you?'

I didn't know what more we had to say to each other. I had just about managed to keep things civil thus far, but I was in grave danger of boiling over and telling him exactly what I thought of him. Instead, I bade my farewells to Prendergast and left.

My final meeting was with Mark Malloch Brown, my boss at UNDP and one of the key people who had recruited me to my post. Mark gave me the final piece of unpleasant news: effectively, a decision had been made within the UN to fire me.

'Mukesh, I'm afraid you're seen as causing too much trouble.' He had before him a large briefing paper, and I guessed it contained reports from all those who had been complaining about me. 'After the north–south peace deal is signed, I'm afraid you will no longer be the UN resident coordinator in Sudan. We're going to have to replace you. A new resident coordinator will be found.'

I remembered Sebastian's words of warning in London just the previous day: *be careful – it will end badly for you.* So be it: I was being cut loose by New York. I didn't fight this or try to object. In fact, I felt almost relieved. By my actions I had upset enough people to get myself fired. There was no need for pretence any more. I was free to do exactly as I saw it in my time remaining as UN chief, and I was gripped by an absolute determination to make every second count.

From New York I flew back to Khartoum, via my usual Frankfurt connection. But during that long and lonely journey I felt my sense of self and my determination slowly ebb away. Increasingly, it felt as if I had nowhere left to turn. The UN route was closed to me; world governments were deaf to me; Khartoum had turned against me. The world seemed determined to allow this dark horror to pass, and I felt at a loss and completely boxed in.

It wasn't just passive neglect that I was witnessing over Darfur; I was being actively blocked from doing anything that might achieve results. I had been fighting to stop the horror for so long now, and I felt almost as if I had reached the end of the road. A large part of me was tempted to pack it all in. I felt like resigning my post immediately, I was so demoralised and so low.

My flight touched down in Khartoum at dusk in the third week of January 2004. I was whisked through the VIP arrivals hall, knowing that my luggage would be sent after. Outside, Omer was waiting with my car, the UN flag fluttering on the bonnet as usual but this time seemingly as if to mock me. Before pulling away from the airport, Omer reached over and handed me the mail that had accumulated in the days I had been away.

I leafed through the usual UN circulars and diplomatic invitations until I came upon a plain envelope with a handwritten address. It was marked 'Personal' and was postmarked 'Khartoum'. I was curious as to what it might contain. As Omer whisked me through the darkened streets towards my residence, I ripped it open. Inside was a handwritten letter on a single sheet of paper torn from a ring-bound notebook.

Your Excellency, the UN Resident Coordinator for Sudan.

The writer is sorry to disturb Your Excellency, the head of the UN, but I would beg to be heard. I must tell you about what happened to my family. I had a large family, and my cousins and brothers and my entire clan in northern Darfur have been completely destroyed. Soldiers came to our village and several of my relatives – my nieces and sisters – have disappeared, and all of our houses were burned and all our cattle were taken away. All the harvests and even the wells were destroyed. They murdered many people, and those who survived had to flee from the land. Even my wife and daughters were raped by these soldiers. . . I write to inform you about the terrible things that are happening... Please, I beg of you, sir, as chief of the United Nations in Sudan, understand what is happening to the Darfuri people and hear me. And please, do whatever you can to help us, and the many other families across Darfur who are likewise suffering.

As I read that anonymous Darfuri man's words, I imagined how I would feel were this to have happened to my home and my family. Reading that letter I felt as if a bucket of cold water had been thrown in my face. How could I possibly think of giving up? This was not the time to crack or to throw in the towel. How could I stop now in light of what the writer was saying to me?

The writer of that letter hadn't asked for anything specific. He hadn't asked to speak with me directly or to meet me, possibly because he feared it would be too dangerous for him to do so. His was simply an appeal to be heard, which made it all the more poignant. That letter reminded me powerfully of how the people of Darfur needed a voice as never before, and maybe I still had it in me to be their champion.

During the drive to the house, a plan of sorts started to form in my mind. There was one option that I hadn't yet considered – *and that was of being the whistleblower*. Up until now, there had been little or no reporting of Darfur in the international media. It was hardly surprising: a conspiracy of silence was coalescing at the very highest level of governments and the UN; there were no aid workers there to issue any reports or alerts; there were no journalists on the ground to file any stories. But maybe I could.

As UN chief, I still had real credibility and standing, and maybe I could blow this thing wide open. There was no international media in Khartoum, so I didn't know exactly how best to access the world's press, but there had to be a way. By the time Omer pulled up at my Khartoum residence, my mind was made up. I would redouble my efforts to get the UN back into Darfur. I would ramp up my efforts to secure the evidence that I needed. I would get proof of the extent of the horror, and then I would press the nuclear button: I would go public, if that was the only option left open to me.

I climbed the stairs to my bedroom feeling in fighting spirit. I dumped my bags and decided to ask Isabelle over for dinner. It would have to be Ahmed's baba ganoush – again – and we wouldn't be able to eat in the garden, for a sandstorm was blowing. We'd dine inside, behind reinforced, shatterproof, wire-mesh-covered glass, as if we were imprisoned. But the setting wasn't important: it was the strategy that I wanted to discuss with her that mattered.

I served Isabelle a glass of wine before passing her the handwritten letter. 'This was waiting for me on my return to Khartoum.'

She read it quietly a few times over, then turned her horrified gaze on me. 'But this is just terrible... What are you going to do?'

'Well, there's nothing much I can do about this one case. I don't even know who the writer is – it's unsigned. But what he says is typical of what we fear has been happening while we have been excluded from Darfur. We have to get more serious about this. We need to raise our game to a new level. We need to get back in, and whatever it costs we have to secure the evidence that we need.'

'Of course we need to get back in.' Isabelle let out a frustrated sigh. 'But, Mukesh, we've been trying for weeks and to no avail. What more can we do?'

'I don't know,' I conceded. I stared into my wine glass, searching for inspiration. 'We simply have to try harder. Maybe I haven't personally tried hard enough. Maybe I need to raise the level of the dialogue myself. And when the evidence is secured, maybe I will need to go public with it myself, because I do not believe that anyone else will.'

Isabelle fixed me with her steady gaze. 'Mukesh, you should do whatever you believe is right to fight this unspeakable horror. You have the courage of your convictions. You should take whatever steps are necessary. And, rest assured, I will support you in fighting this evil in whatever way I can.'

I was tempted to tell Isabelle about my last meeting in New York and that my days as UN chief were numbered. But I decided not to. I didn't want to demoralise her, and I didn't want her to lose faith in our mission. I trusted her absolutely, and if I were to take the path that I had chosen I would need her by my side to strengthen and support me.

The following morning, I arrived at our office to find a large crowd at the gates. As Omer neared the barrier, figures surged in from all sides, banging on the roof of the vehicle and chanting. For an instant I gazed out at a sea of angry black African faces, before Omer whisked us inside. Once in my office, I sought out an interpreter who could tell me what the protesters were chanting. I had a pretty good idea, but I just wanted it confirmed.

Sure enough, they had gathered at the office of the UN to protest over the horrors unfolding in Darfur. I was amazed. It was all but impossible to mount protests on the streets of Khartoum, everything was so closely controlled by the Mukhabarat. The protesters must have come from the IDP camps, and I hoped that this was the start of something truly momentous and significant.

An hour or so later, I detected a change in the tenor of the chanting: it had gone from one of angry protest to fearful cries. There were a series of dull thuds, and a few moments later the familiar smell of teargas drifted through my open window. A moment later there was the sharp crackle of gunfire, followed by terrified screams. The Mukhabarat's thugs must have arrived to smash up the demo.

There was a knock at my door. It was Mona. Apparently, one of the demonstrators had managed to pass a bundle of letters to our gate guards. She gave it to me. Each letter had a handwritten address, and was marked: '*For the personal attention of Kofi Annan, United Nations secretary-general*'.

I could guess what those letters said. They would be similar to the one that my driver had handed me upon my arrival the previous day in Khartoum. The Darfuri victims were writing to the head of the UN, pleading to be heard.

It occurred to me that if Kofi Annan read such letters, perhaps that might move him to act. I bundled them up so they could be sent on to New York in the UN mail. I used the opportunity to pen a memo to UN headquarters myself, reporting on the demonstrations and their violent suppression. I pointed out that these were Darfuris protesting about the violence in Darfur. I pointed out that we had heard reports of widespread horrors, but with Khartoum refusing us access we had no means to independently verify anything on the ground.

Seeing the desperation on the faces of those demonstrators reinforced the sense of urgency I felt to get us back into Darfur. But after a round of visits to the usual suspects I was still being fed the same old line: *you took the UN out; we can't guarantee your security yet; we'll let you know just as soon as it's safe for you to go back in.*

This was hopeless. I needed something to force open access. I needed a Trojan horse to get us back in there, and I had just such an idea coalescing in my mind.

While working at DFID I'd helped set up something called the International Humanitarian Partnership (IHP). IHP was funded by the British, Swedish, Norwegian, Finnish and Danish governments to provide a surge capacity to respond to crises around the world. It consisted of aviation, logistics and communications experts, plus associated materiel, held 'on call' to respond to war, famine and disasters. Maybe IHP could be my secret weapon in the war I was now waging to open up access to Darfur?

I knew I wouldn't get Khartoum's clearance to get IHP into Darfur, but what if I simply got them into Khartoum? If I mobilised IHP, I could get a massive set of resources – aircraft, vehicles, personnel and all their medical and food supplies – flown directly into Khartoum. It would then start to look very, very bad if all of that sat on the runway doing nothing because onward access into Darfur was blocked. Key donor governments – the UK amongst them – would have to get involved. In effect, it might force HAC's hand.

When working with DFID, I'd taken IHP into Kosovo and East Timor. I knew how forceful their people could be when faced with a regime denying them humanitarian access. Right now there was no situation in the world as serious as Darfur, of that I was certain. They would be straining at the leash to get in there.

I spoke first to the Swedish IHP contingent, and just as I'd predicted they were raring to go. I told them to prepare to flood Darfur with internationals, so as to be the eyes and ears of the world community on the ground. I got them to plan for how many flights a day they'd need, where they'd land, and to get their aircraft, communications, vehicles and experts on standby.

That done, I paid a visit to HAC and submitted requests for 30-odd Swedish IHP people to fly a humanitarian task force in. I explained that IHP was a ready-made relief effort in a box and that it would make sense to route them directly from Sweden to Darfur. El Fasher airport was large enough to land their aircraft, so why not? HAC couldn't think of a reason to say no, so as a stalling tactic they told me IHP would have to route first via Khartoum.

'OK,' I said, 'let's get them into Khartoum.'

I had HAC on the back foot, and they had no option but to agree. The IHP Darfur Task Force mobilised immediately. Over several days, a massive team complete with all their state-of-the-art equipment flew in – including a fleet of Land Rovers, ballistic matting for mine protection, communications kit, a command-and-control centre, solar lighting, computers and innumerable crates of food aid and medicines. By the time IHP's in-load was complete, we had a warehouse stuffed full of humanitarian materiel at the airport and several dozen IHP staff billeted at the Hilton. We also had a giant Ilyushin transport aircraft parked up very visibly on the runway, waiting for clearance to fly onwards into Darfur. The IHP team consisted of firemen, search- and-rescue specialists, a disaster-management crew and health workers. Crucially, the entire operation was funded by the governments making up the IHP, and while they were brought in under UN auspices they could not be held hostage to internal UN power plays. By calling on IHP, I had outmanoeuvred HAC, the Mukhabarat that drove their obstruction, and the UN's impotence. Or so I hoped. The next few days would prove it either way.

Now I changed my tactics. I explained to HAC how bad it looked to have all these internationals sitting in Khartoum twiddling their thumbs. I warned them that the IHP people would get bored and speak to their people back in their home countries about how desperate they were to get into Darfur. The story would break in the international media, and it would quickly become one of how HAC was blocking access to Darfur.

I briefed William Patey and other friendly diplomats to help us up the ante. I got them to speak to their Sudan government counterparts in Khartoum and ask why IHP was trapped. I asked them to point out that IHP needed to be cleared to deploy into Darfur with all due haste. In no time, HAC was being hit from all sides, including the key governments who had funded IHP's deployment.

While I'd been unleashing IHP, more demonstrations flared at our offices and other key points around Khartoum. Then came the clampdown, and it was swift and merciless. Protests were violently crushed, and from the IDP camps we began to hear reports about renewed mass disappearances. But it wasn't only from around Khartoum that the IDPs were being removed.

News filtered in to us that Intifada Camp – the one that I had visited in Nyala – had been stamped out of existence. Apparently, the local authorities had blocked all aid, while promising 'proper food and shelter' in a new desert location. Most of the camp's occupants had refused to move to what they feared was a death camp and had quietly melted away. Trucks with mounted machine guns had arrived to forcibly carry off those who remained.

This was the first significant disappearance that we had learned about outside of Khartoum. It sounded horribly reminiscent of the trainloads carted off to the Nazi death camps during the Second World War. I felt it like a body blow, not only because it was so sinister but also because I had spent time listening to the stories of the families in Intifada Camp just a few months ago.

I sent a strongly worded alert to UN headquarters. In it, I detailed the forced relocation of 8,000 already badly traumatised Darfuris, many at gunpoint. I asked UN headquarters go to the world's press to publicise what had happened at Intifada Camp and our wider worries about Darfur. The only response from UN headquarters was silence.

I went to HAC and raised the issue with Sulaf, who passed me on to the minister of state for humanitarian affairs, Mohammad Youssef Abdalla. I told him that closing Intifada Camp was unacceptable and that we, the UN, were deeply concerned for the plight of the IDPs. In response, the minister told me that it had been a 'political decision to move the camp' and thus it didn't fall within my humanitarian remit.

'My government has dealt with those people,' the minister told me, with an air of finality. 'The decision is one that I back personally. And, Dr Kapila, please understand that if you continue to push this issue, the UN is treading a very fine line in terms of what is acceptable. May I remind you that the UN is supposed to work in cooperation with the host country government, and on humanitarian issues only.' It was another thinly veiled threat. I didn't particularly care. I knew that my days were numbered, for I'd already been given my notice by New York. I doubted whether Khartoum was aware of that yet, and in a way it gave me an edge. I had nothing to lose. They could do their worst, but they wouldn't silence or break me.

A few days later, my IHP weapon finally hit its mark. I was called to see the minister for foreign affairs, Dr Mustafa Osman Ismael. It was a rare thing to be summoned to a one-on-one at this level. Osman Ismael and I had met only once before, and I knew him to be one of the more acceptable faces of the Khartoum regime. The danger that news might break of the IHP being blocked must have weighed upon him heavily, especially as it was his job to manage the regime's international relations.

Today, he proved particularly affable. 'Dr Kapila, I have good news for you,' he announced, with a warm smile. 'On 14 February, you will be allowed back into Darfur. So get your people ready – you're going back in!'

The 14th of February was four days hence, so this really was a significant breakthrough.

'Well, that's fantastic,' I told him. 'But is something specific happening on the 14th to make this possible?'

The minister chuckled. 'By then, we're confident that our security forces will be firmly in control and we can guarantee your safety. The president made a statement on 9th February. Perhaps you missed it? He declared an end to all military operations in Darfur and that all is well.'

I wasn't aware of any such statement, but I figured I'd have to take it at face value for now and grasp this opportunity with both hands.

'Well, Mr Minister, this appears to be very positive. Thank you.' 'Not only are we declaring an end to military operations, but we are also granting an amnesty to all rebels. If they hand in their weapons within the month, we will give them amnesty. Plus we're opening up corridors to all relief agencies – first and foremost your IHP – and we're making plans for the displaced and the refugees to return home. We'll also implement a weapons collection and control system across Darfur, to disarm all parties. Perhaps your UNDP can help with that.'

It all sounded too good to be true, and I didn't quite know what to say.

'We are also planning a National Committee to be formed

from all sides – tribal chiefs, civil society leaders and the like – to promote reconciliation and the return of all Darfuris. We would like to count on the UN's support in all of this.'

'Of course,' I told him. 'We can start a weapons-for-development programme right away. Those who disarm can get priority assistance from the UN. I have vast experience of such work, and I can guarantee that we'd take a very active lead.'

I thanked the minister for allowing us back in. I told him that we now had much to do to prepare for our return, so I was needed back at my office. I returned forthwith and relayed the good news: IHP were to get their bags packed. In four days' time, we were going back in, and, if the minister was to be believed, all was well.

I issued instructions that at dawn on the 14th, all IHP and UN people we could muster should be at the airport ready to take to the air.

TWENTY-ONE

I want to live my life so that my nights are not full of regrets.
D.H. Lawrence

THE NEXT FEW DAYS WERE A WHIRLWIND OF ACTIVITY. I HADN'T necessarily believed all that the foreign minister had told me, but I had to presume that it wasn't a complete pack of lies. His proposals for dealing with the crisis had seemed entirely sensible, and what was the point of allowing us back in on a total lie? He would know that sooner or later the truth would out. In short, I allowed my natural optimism to trump all the dark rumours of recent days.

At first light on the morning of the 14th, we had a Beechcraft crammed full of our people, plus two Buffalo cargo planes lined up on the runway ready to go. The giant Ilyushin would follow shortly with all the heavy equipment. But our spirit of expectation was frustrated by the lack of a final green light from air traffic control. Seven o'clock became eight, and still we weren't cleared to get airborne. Eight became eleven, and we remained stuck on the runway.

I was getting regular updates, and I knew that shortly the window of daylight in which we could fly would close. I ordered the IHP team to stay in the aircraft and to sleep there if necessary: the only way they were leaving that runway was onwards into Darfur. I phoned the minister of foreign affairs and told him how bad it would look to have our teams camping out on Khartoum airport's main runway. Then I made the threat that I had been keeping in reserve.

'I'm sorry, Minister, but if they're not in the air by 12 o'clock midday, I am going to have to make a call to the BBC. You must understand I am under huge pressure both from the UN and IHP donor governments, and I will have no option but to release to the BBC the entire story of how we are all being held hostage on the runway. You will understand that I don't want to do this, but...'

'Yes, yes, Mukesh, I hear you. Give me an hour. One hour and I'll have you in the air.'

'You have until midday, Minister. You yourself said the IHP can go into Darfur, and now they are trapped in their aircraft. You know how bad this looks. I will be forced to put out some kind of statement, and what am I supposed to say – that a team of humanitarians is being held hostage by your government?'

'Mukesh, I understand completely. I'll have your answer within the hour.'

I got off the line to Osman Ismael and phoned my old nemesis, the minister at HAC. I gave him the same ultimatum. I would have preferred to get airborne with no hassles, but there was one part of me that was actually enjoying this. For once I was actually feeling somewhat empowered, and I loved the way that I had Mr Hamid squirming on the end of the line.

For the next hour, I sat in my office, with Isabelle popping in and out with anxious updates from the runway. I had my mobile phone by my side and my two landlines on the desk in front of me. I knew this was going to the wire, but I couldn't help but believe that we would win. My Trojan horse had been wheeled up to the very gates of Troy, and it was about to be taken inside.

At 11.55, there was a trilling on my mobile. I grabbed it. 'This is Mukesh.'

'We've just got the green light for take-off!' It was Rob Holden speaking from the airport. 'Shall we...'

'Yes! Go!' I practically screamed. 'For God's sake – go! Get off your butts, get airborne and get into Darfur.'

From then on, the airlift went without a hitch. All that week, supplies and personnel kept getting ferried in. I started to get emails and satphone calls from the IHP teams, reporting that landing zones and field offices were operational. My priority was to get them to fan out from their bases, doing recces into the rural areas. It was time to see just how much of what Osman Ismael and the others had told me might be true of Darfur.

As our teams fanned out, so the first worrying reports filtered in. Gradually, a pattern started to emerge. First, large swathes of the countryside were completely devoid of people. Second, the IDP camps around the three state capitals – El Fasher, Nyala, El Geneina – were full to bursting. Third, vast numbers had fled to refugee camps in Chad. Fourth, while large numbers of villages had been burned to the ground, others had been left untouched.

As the days passed and our teams spread further across Darfur, so my worst fears were confirmed. Mustafa Osman Ismael, the urbane and cultured foreign minister, had not told me the truth. Maybe the Mukhabarat had sold him a lie, which he had served up to me in all ignorance. In any case, I now gathered the facts about what had unfolded during the eight weeks that we had been excluded from Darfur.

Khartoum had used that time to ramp up the intensity of their ethnic cleansing and scorched earth to unforeseen levels. They had used our absence as an opportunity to commit massive crimes against humanity unobserved. Aircraft had bombed villages across the entire vastness of Darfur, following which the Janjaweed had committed an orgy of burning, looting and violence.

The stories our teams were hearing became ever more stomach- churning: they included babies being cut from their mothers' stomachs and of mass public gang-rapes. Females had been rounded up and raped ten or twenty times in front of their families. And in many of these instances, the military had accompanied the Janjaweed as they went about their business, working in clear partnership with each other.

While we had been excluded, a massive and systematic operation had got under way to cleanse the entire region. It had happened on a scale that I found inconceivable, for few areas had been left untouched. In eight weeks, they had carried out a mass campaign to terrorise and ethnically cleanse an area the size of France. The organisational and planning skills behind such an operation would try the capabilities of a superpower, as would the logistics required to achieve it. To do it in such a short time beggared belief. It was stupefying.

In short, we had been obstructed and blocked and lied to repeatedly so that Khartoum could pursue its 'final solution' to its ultimate end. Darfur had been turned into one giant killing field. Across this vast land, they had identified the targets, launched their attacks, terrorised and left a swathe of devastation where no one could return. It had been a monstrous and hugely efficient killing machine.

As I contemplated all of this, I was consumed by an unbearable sense of failure. I had failed in my duty. All the rhetoric about acting early and the responsibility to protect had proven empty. I had failed. I had allowed myself to be hoodwinked. My Trojan horse had won only a pyrrhic victory. All we had won was the privilege of being the first to witness and validate the true extent of the horror. *It had happened on my watch.*

I felt absolutely sick with outrage and consumed by a burning fury. I also felt severely disturbed in my own mind. I decided that I now had no choice but to mess them up in turn – all those responsible for doing this – and at the earliest possible opportunity.

There would be no holds barred now. Come what may, I would ensure that those who had planned and orchestrated this, and deliberately hidden it from world view – *from my view* – would face justice. It was too late to save the countless victims, but it was never too late for a reckoning.

I ordered my teams to shift to gathering data and hard facts. I needed numbers. I needed ammunition with which to strike back. With each village attacked, I wanted to know how many rapes, how many killed, how many abducted. I wanted the name of the village, the time of the attack and the exact make-up of those who had perpetrated it. I no longer wanted personal stories, horrific though those were. I wanted the precise, specific data to nail the perpetrators and get them put behind bars.

I asked for quality information, and almost immediately my people began to deliver. We were moving into the final act now. Soon, I would unleash my broadside. I would press the nuclear button, and damn all those murderous, racist, rapist bastards to hell. And I would not forget the United Nations. The role the UN had played in all of this was unconscionable. I would up my reporting to unprecedented levels, so that when the truth was out the UN could never claim the excuse of ignorance.

With Isabelle hammering away furiously on her computer, compiling our field data into urgent reports, we flooded New York with daily - sometimes hourly – alerts:

18th February: Janjaweed militia and associated forces attacked IDP camps at Nertiti and looted food aid and non-food items, including blankets.

23rd February: Janjaweed militia attacked Morni village and nearby IDP camp.

23rd February: Janjaweed militia looted and burned Digain Karro, 132 kilometres north-west of Nyala.

24th February: humanitarian staff witness a village burning in Nabagaya, 124 kilometres northwest of Nyala.

27th February: Janjaweed militia attacked a village in Gemeiza Korongo and looted IDPs' belongings.

27th February: humanitarian staff travelling through Tawila, 62 kilometres west of El Fasher, witnessed Janjaweed militia looting and burning a village.

29th February: consistent reports and eyewitness accounts of systematic attacks upon villages and IDP camps and the looting of humanitarian assistance. Urgent high-level political intervention to ensure the protection of civilians and to provide security is therefore required. At present the Janjaweed militia attacks are carried out with impunity.

And so it went on. I fired these reports into the blank

void of silence that was the UN, not expecting any response. I did so in order that the UN would be held to account when Darfur hit the world's attention like a whirlwind. I made it crystal clear that trying to mount a humanitarian mission in the midst of such horror and violence was impossible. Worse still, in our attempts to provide humanitarian relief we were often making it worse for the victims, because it brought the Janjaweed to loot them again.

2nd March: humanitarian actors agree that unless the pressing issue of protection of IDPs and other vulnerable population is resolved at the highest levels, no amount of humanitarian access to affected areas can bring genuine relief to those in need, as any assistance without adequate security is putting IDPs at additional risk of being looted, raped or killed.

Shortly after I filed that report, I was scheduled to speak at a conference in Khartoum to mark International Women's Day. What unspeakable irony. While tens of thousands of women and children were being gang-raped in Darfur, we in the nation's capital were supposed to celebrate 'Womanhood' at the grandiose People's Palace, a massive conference hall built by the Chinese.

Well, I was damned if I was going to play ball. Some days earlier, I'd been given a nice, polite speech penned by UNICEF, one mouthing all the usual platitudes. I tore it up and threw it in the bin. It was time for stage one of the fightback.

The day of the speech, I climbed the steps to the platform and gazed out over the ranks of seats arranged before me like an amphitheatre. The room was packed to bursting. All the usual government ministers were there, as were the ranks of various dignitaries, including a scattering of diplomats, aid agencies and others. There were also a number of local journalists gathered in the press area. I knew that my speech was going to be carried live by Radio Omdurman – Sudanese national radio – and I had warned not a soul of what I intended to say.

I faced the crowd and started to speak. 'On International Women's Day, it is important to celebrate the many achievements of women. Women hold up half of the sky, as Mao famously said. But, sadly, there is nothing to celebrate as far as Sudan is concerned. We can commemorate, certainly, but how can we celebrate when millions of women and girls are sat in refugee camps as the victims of war? We all know that women and girls suffer most in war. They are the first victims and they are hit hardest.'

I glanced at the ranks of ministers and dignitaries on the front seats, and mostly they showed a mixture of po-faced indifference or outright disapproval.

'Every culture teaches respect for women,' I continued, 'and their welfare and protection are a matter of pride for the whole of society. For men to be able to look after their womenfolk and give them respect, love, care and protection – that is central to every world culture. To do this for your mother, sister, wife and daughter is vital. Yet what we see around us here in Sudan is the opposite of all this, and especially what is happening now, in Darfur.'

At the mention of Darfur, a rumble of disapproval swept around the room. My speech was being translated into Arabic, so everyone here would understand exactly what I was saying.

'As I speak, thousands of women have been raped, abused and terribly humiliated in Darfur. So on this day we should soberly recall the challenges before us and dedicate ourselves to address this gender war. This is a war fought on many fronts, and it starts from birth, where girls are cut in female genital mutilation, which is a lifelong sentence.' I saw a shadowy figure step across to the Radio Omdurman crew and gesture for them to cut their broadcast. That was it then, my words had just been silenced from the airwaves. I continued speaking against a growing rumbling from around the hall. From some quarters there were cheers and wild bursts of applause, but from others there were cries of outrage, and fists were raised angrily.

'When a young girl closed up by FGM is raped, the rape and the sheer physical effect – imagine raping someone whose genital area is scarred up from the FGM; you have to force your way into a young virgin girl – when you rape such a female, the pain and mutilation that follows is in another category, another league. The laws of this country forbid this practice, yet it continues under the very noses of the authorities.'

Howls of outrage competed with enthusiastic cries of support to drown out what I was saying. The noise was becoming deafening.

'Clearly, then, we cannot celebrate today,' I battled onwards. 'The best we can say is that we have a huge amount of work to do to protect the human rights of women and their integrity everywhere in Sudan, and particularly in Darfur...'

From somewhere just in front of me there was a commanding cry, and all of a sudden the girls' choir standing beside me broke into song. It was a clear attempt to drown out my words.

'In Darfur, women and children make up fully two-thirds of the victims,' I yelled above the singing. 'Some 80 per cent of northern Sudanese women suffer FGM, and it is the most severe form possible – Pharaonic FGM, wherein all is sliced off and sewn up. Many, many of these women have been raped in the Darfur crisis... So, you will understand that we have little to celebrate here in Sudan on International Women's Day but much work to do.'

I ceased talking and made my way down from the stage as the noise of the choir swelled in volume. The dignitaries were looking in any direction they could to avoid me, as if I had the plague. It was only Isabelle who had the fortitude to step forward and help me back to my seat.

'So brave,' she whispered into my ear. 'Bravo, Mukesh! It had to be said...'

I felt a tug on my sleeve. Nimal Hettiaratchy, the head of a small UN agency – the UN Population Fund

(UNFPA) – leaned over.

'Fantastic, Mukesh,' he declared. 'Thank you for taking a stand.'

Other than that, no one else spoke to me at all. It was as if I had suddenly become an untouchable, and I realised then how lonely the course that I had chosen was going to prove. I didn't particularly care. I felt as if I had done right by the women of Darfur, and that was what mattered. And in spite of the Radio Omdurman broadcast being cut, at least I had got some of my message out on the airwaves. I waited anxiously for the newspapers the following day, in the hope that they would carry more of my speech, but there was nothing – not a single mention of it anywhere. The Mukhabarat had done such a fine job of suppressing any media reports that it was as if I had never spoken. If I needed any reminding that the place to blow the whistle wasn't here in Khartoum, this was it. I would get no access to a free or fair media in this country.

As if in horrible vindication of all that I had said in that speech, I received an urgent email from Daniel Christensen. It was marked 'Confidential' and only circulated to myself, Isabelle, Rob Holden and one or two others. On 27 February, UN staff had witnessed the looting of Tawila town, an event that I had duly reported to the UN. A week later, Daniel had been able to lead a team into Tawila, and his email concerned what he had found there.

In the attack on Tawila town, some 85 villagers were killed. All the houses were burned. 100 women were raped, six in front of their fathers who had then been killed. 150 women and 200 children had been abducted by the Janjaweed. In the wider Tawila district, some 30 villages had been burned. People were fleeing in all directions. Of the 94,000 residents of Tawila District, some 18,000 now remained, as IDPs. Those IDPs had gathered in a camp, where we heard the stories of a 13-year-old and 15-year-old girl. They left the camp to gather firewood and were attacked by men in uniform and plain clothes and raped. The attackers view the non-Arabs as being 'deserving of only the worst of what this world has to offer'. Those we spoke to in Tawila stated that helicopters had been providing ammunition to the Janjaweed during the attacks, and that Janjaweed were using Land Cruisers provided by the Sudan government. Any wounded on the Janjaweed side were taken away by Sudanese Army ambulances to get treatment. Looting continued even as we spoke to the victims, and no police or military were posted to restore peace and security.

In short, Daniel and his team had been eyewitnesses to the Sudan military's involvement in rape, pillage and murder. He named the local Janjaweed leader as being Musa Hilal. The Janjaweed had said they took instructions only from him and that he had 'ordered the attack'. I knew of Musa Hilal by reputation, and from what Roger had briefed me. He was one of the most feared Janjaweed leaders, and he reportedly received his orders direct from the Mukhabarat.

This attack would subsequently become known as 'the Tawila Incident'. What set it apart from countless other such atrocities in Darfur was that it had been witnessed by UN and IHP staff from its very inception and until the 'mopping-up' operations. It had continued with impunity, in spite of our people being on the ground. It struck me that Daniel and those with him must be under a huge amount of stress, but for a humanitarian it was far better to be doing something than to be trapped in Khartoum.

Tawila shocked and sickened me. It was also unique. It was the first time that our people were able to provide direct eyewitness evidence. This was no longer us hearing reports from the victims. Now, we had seen it for ourselves. If ever we needed one, Tawila was the smoking gun. Daniel's report warned that the same group of Janjaweed were moving on to attack nearby Korma town in the same way that they had Tawila.

Tawila proved that the UN had zero ability to help or protect people. There was nothing that humanitarian actors could do to stop such deliberate, targeted violence and brutality. As I had been arguing for months, Darfur needed urgent international political intervention, and it needed peacekeepers to go in on the ground with the arms and the mandate to take action.

Darfur was a sea of flames, and nothing else now would stop the killers.

TWENTY-TWO

We should every night call ourselves to an account. What infirmity have I mastered today? What passions opposed? What temptations resisted? What virtue acquired?
Seneca

AS I READ AND RE-READ DANIEL'S TAWILA REPORT, I WAS reminded so powerfully of Rwanda and Srebrenica. In Rwanda, the UN had a peacekeeping mission on the ground when the killings began, but the lion's share were withdrawn once the Belgian peacekeepers were murdered. UN headquarters refused repeated requests for reinforcements, even as the killings began.

In Srebrenica in 1995, some 10,000 Bosnian civilians had sought protection in a UN 'safe haven', garrisoned by 400 Dutch UN peacekeepers. The Serb Army had surrounded the safe haven and demanded that all Bosnian Muslims be handed over. The Dutch force commander had requested air strikes, to force the Serbs to withdraw. He had also asked for permission to defend the safe haven. All of this had been refused on the basis that it would provoke the Serbs, with whom the UN was 'building bridges'. As Kofi Annan was then the UN head of peacekeeping, the decision was taken in part by him. The Dutch commander was forced to open the gates to his base and allow the Bosnian Muslims to be loaded upon buses and driven away. Some 8,000 of them were subsequently massacred, their bodies dumped in hedges and ditches. I was sent to Srebrenica to deal with the immediate aftermath of the massacre – the largest in Europe since the Second World War. Most of those killed were men and boys, and my job was to help trace the survivors.

We set up a massive programme to help the widows, one that also focused on gathering the evidence we needed to prove just who had committed the war crimes. From the get-go, we had legal and forensic experts involved, and the evidence we gathered went to support the International Criminal Tribunal for Yugoslavia – the court in which those responsible were tried.

Arguably, had the Dutch force commander refused his orders and fought it would have forced the UN's hand. But he was a military man and he obeyed his orders. After Srebrenica, the sense of national shame in the Netherlands was such that the Dutch government fell. But the key failure to protect had been the UN's, and no one from that august body was ever held to account. Those at the top of the UN – Kofi Annan included – got away scot-free.

In Rwanda, there had been no force on the ground empowered to prevent and protect. In Srebrenica, a well-armed UN force had been ordered to stand by and do nothing, so choosing not to prevent and protect. In Darfur – *in Tawila* – we had people on the ground, but they were tiny in number and they were unarmed humanitarians. There was nothing they could do to prevent and protect. Despite our presence, we were powerless to stop the rapists and the killers.

Having read Daniel's Tawila report, I took all the usual actions. I briefed the Khartoum diplomats. I fired in reports to the UN. I wrote démarches to the Sudan government, putting them on notice that they were responsible for war crimes. I wrote personally to Mustafa Osman Ismael, the foreign minister, plus my old adversary the minister at HAC. I told them that the UN had uncovered prima facie evidence of crimes against humanity in Tawila, and I warned them that we had credible information pointing to an impending attack on nearby Korma town.

Our reports point to gross violations of human rights and international humanitarian law. Your Excellencies, rape conducted during military operations is considered a war crime; given the severity of these reports we would appeal to you to investigate these attacks and bring the perpetrators to justice. In thanking Your Excellencies may I also express my regret to have to draw to your attention again such happenings.

In essence, I was writing to the architects of the mass murder, warning them to cease and desist. But it was all to no effect. Nothing happened either on the level of the Sudanese government or internationally. The attack on Korma town went ahead and was documented in an urgent email sent through to me from the field.

At 6.00 p.m., ten vehicles attacked Korma village, resulting in 22 rapes, seven on children, and several in front of their families. The rape victims were abducted, and a week later only 16 had been returned. Unspecified numbers of men and boys were abducted and forced to herd looted livestock. A second attack took place wherein the market was burned and looted and 8 more people killed. Reports make reference to the use of helicopters to resupply the attackers.

The day after the attack on Korma had been confirmed, I was sitting in my office on an airless afternoon banging out a new report to the UN with little hope of it making any difference. I detected a clamouring from the corridor outside, which grew in volume. It sounded as if a fight had broken out in the reception area. There was a knock on my door, and Mona's head appeared.

'Mukesh, there is this crazy woman here who keeps demanding to see you. The guards keep trying to get rid of her, but she just won't go away.'

'Well, let her in,' I said. 'Tell her she can come and see me.'

A minute later, Mona led this figure into my office. She was a tall, black African woman with the most incredibly fine features. She moved with an extraordinary poise and grace, and had she lived in Paris and not Khartoum she could no doubt have graced the cover of *Elle* magazine. Her clothes were dirty and torn, but they did nothing to detract from her presence, which was captivating. Nothing about her struck me as being remotely 'crazy', that was for certain.

'Please,' I indicated one of my leather armchairs, 'take a seat.'

Mona translated my words into Arabic, but the woman

shook her head and spoke some words in reply.

'She doesn't want to sit in your beautiful chair,' Mona translated. 'She fears she will spoil it. She is from Darfur, and she has come a very long way. She apologises for her appearance.'

At that, the woman lowered herself until she was sat cross-legged before me on my carpet.

'Would you like some tea?' I asked her. 'Mona, bring some tea and plenty of digestive biscuits.'

McVitie's Digestives were my favourite, and I used to stock up on supplies whenever I was back in the UK. The Darfuri woman accepted the tea and biscuits, then rearranged the bright blue headscarf she had draped around her head and shoulders. She started to speak as Mona translated.

'I come from north Darfur,' she began. 'I lived in a village near a town called Tawila.'

At the very mention of that name, my blood ran cold. I gripped my desk with both my hands, for I knew instinctively what was coming.

'One afternoon on the market day, I was in Tawila with my family, buying some things,' the woman continued. 'These people on horseback and vehicles came – loads and loads of them, hundreds – some in uniforms, some in blue and white robes – and they ran around and captured all the women in the market who couldn't escape.'

She paused, as if gathering her strength. 'They lined up the women and got them to squat on the ground, with guns pointing all around. The men had been rounded up also, and those in uniform and the Janjaweed, they started to rape the women. They did this systematically, from number one, to two, to three... They ranged in age from young girls of six or seven to grandmothers of sixty-five.'

She paused again, her eyes staring at the floor and unable to meet mine. She had been speaking in a soft and gentle voice, and I could tell that Mona – a cultured, motherly city girl – was having difficulty translating some of the more troubling details.

'Tell her to go on, Mona. Tell her I'm listening. And, Mona, please don't hold back on any of the details.'

'Yes, Mukesh,' Mona replied. 'I'll try.'

'I was one of them,' the woman continued. 'They raped me. I could see my father and my husband watching as they did it, and my two boys were somewhere in the crowd. I was raped repeatedly. I cannot remember all the times, but it must be a dozen at least. Finally, I passed out. Or it was more like I wished I could pass out, but I couldn't – I was in some kind of a stupor. All around me there was screaming, especially from the little girls.'

The woman continued speaking in Arabic for a minute or so more, but at the end of it Mona seemed lost for words. She gave me this look of total shock and revulsion, as if the words just wouldn't come. I knew this wasn't Mona's job. She was my secretary, not my translator. But I had to hear.

'Please, Mona, find the words to tell me. I know this is difficult for you, but this woman has come a long way to speak to us.'

'I was in the dust on the ground, my head pushed into the dirt,' Mona translated. 'They hitched up my robes and one man took me and raped me as the others held me down. The first one was done in a minute or so, and then the next took his position in line. At first I tried to struggle and fight back, but then they beat me and shoved me even harder into the dust. As they violated me, they insulted me. They kept calling me "zurka" and "abeed", and telling me they would give me "fine Arab babies". I was violated again and again. All around me they did the same to others, like it was a production line in a factory.

'Once the rape was done, the militia set fire to everything. Huts, trees, the market place – all was set alight with torches and petrol. They started looting, and some of the women and boys were put in their Land Cruisers and driven away. A sudden quiet descended on the place – apart from the noise in my head, and the crackling of the fire, and the crying. We were worried the fire would spread and we would be burned alive. I couldn't see my husband or my father or my two boys anywhere, so I fled to my village. What else was I to do? I gathered my few possessions – I am a teacher, you see – and I didn't know what to do.'

She looked at me then, a quick flash of her gracefully arched eyes – eyes that were dark and brimful of tears that were yet to be shed. 'I couldn't find my family,' she continued. 'I couldn't find my children. My boys were ten and twelve years old. I couldn't find my brothers, even. No one from my family remained anywhere. So I gathered my few possessions and I got a lift on a truck, and other trucks after that, and I travelled to El Obeid, and from there to Khartoum. I have some relatives in the city. I reached here this morning, but first I made my way here, to the UN, to reveal what is happening in Darfur.'

All through her incredibly traumatic testimony, the woman had not shed a single tear. Nothing like this had ever happened to me in my life. The raw shock and trauma was so real that this woman remained entombed within it, her emotions locked down, the pain internalised. Yet somehow she had made her way over one thousand kilometres to this city, fought her way through the barbed wire and several cordons of UN guards, and found me. Anyone else would have given up long ago, but this woman from Tawila had nothing left to lose. 'I cannot thank you enough for what you have done today,' I told her. 'You are incredibly strong, and I admire your bravery and your courage so greatly.'

The words were inadequate. They were inadequate then, and they are now. But I didn't know what else to say. I was myself in a state of shock, and I was on the verge of tears. It was one thing reading reports; it was another entirely hearing it direct from one of the victims. But I couldn't show how much her words had shaken me. I was afraid of breaking down in front of her, for I had to appear as if I knew what I was doing. For her especially – for this unbelievably brave and courageous Darfuri woman – I had to appear as if I was strong.

I had to appear as if I knew how to deal with such horror. I had to make it seem as if I knew what to do. I had to maintain the mask of control. But inside I was bleeding and burning up with rage. Over and above the pain I felt for this woman, I was gripped by an all-consuming fury. My mind was consumed by this one thought: *The evil people who did this to her, and so many like her – we'll get them.* But first, we had to find a way to help this woman and to protect her. 'I would like to properly document what you've told me, and I would like to ensure that we can help you.' I glanced in Mona's direction, and I could see she was close to finished. 'But Mona, I think, is exhausted. And you perhaps need to spend some time with your relatives, at least before we do any more?'

'I have cousins here in Khartoum, and I would like to see them,' she said. 'I will be staying with them.'

'Perhaps you can come back tomorrow?' I asked. 'In the morning? We'll have some of my human-rights people here to document your story, plus we'll have our medical people on hand so you can be helped. You'll need to re-live your story again, but are you OK with that?'

'I am.'

'What is your name? And do you have an address here in Khartoum?' 'My name is Aisha,' she said. 'I don't know the exact address. I know where to find my cousins, that's all.'

'How did you manage to find me?' I asked her. 'And why me?' 'Who else could I turn to?' Aisha asked, simply. 'The police, the soldiers, the authorities – they are in on this. They are doing it. I know there is a UN operation under way in Darfur and that you provide help. You are the only person I could come to. There is no one else. And the United Nations is powerful, so it can do something about what has happened. That's why I am here.'

'Is there anything you need now? Immediately?'

'No, nothing. I will stay with my relatives and rest and return tomorrow. It is enough that you have heard.'

It was then that I made the single greatest mistake of my entire life: I allowed her to walk out of my door. I have relived this time and again since then. I should never have allowed her to leave. I should have insisted she take asylum in my office, but she appeared so calm and composed, and so eager to go find her family. A part of me thought she needed to be with them, to find comfort with her own people. Aisha was a teacher – a woman of education and learning – and I figured she knew her own mind. And so I allowed her to go.

I sat alone in my office thinking over all that she had said. As I reflected upon the unspeakable barbarity of the mass public rape that she and so many had suffered, my mind drifted to a similar encounter, one that was burned forever into my soul. Five years earlier, I'd paid a visit to Freetown, the capital city of Sierra Leone. I went to visit Connaught Hospital, for health was one of the key programmes that DFID was funding in the country.

I was taken directly to the hospital's women's ward. I stepped inside, and right in front of me was one of the most stunning women that I had ever seen. But it wasn't that which had so transfixed me. It was her eyes. They were enormous golden pools of liquid pain, brimming with unshed tears. My gaze flickered to her lap. She cradled this tiny child who was a carbon copy of herself, and both had had their left arm amputated at just below the elbow.

In Darfur, rape was being employed as a weapon of mass terror. In Sierra Leone, the RUF rebels had specialised in amputations – chopping off arms and legs with machetes – as the means to spread total fear. The mother was cradling her child with her one surviving hand. I was mesmerised: such incredible grace juxtaposed with such mindless brutality.

I tried to speak to the woman, but not a word would she say. The nurses explained that she had been rendered mute by whatever had been done to her. But her eyes spoke to me: they were far from empty.

There was a person in there haunted by demons and by

235

ghosts. Yet what struck me most was the lack of anger in her face, the absence of any hatred. Somehow, she was Madonna with child.

I reached out and touched the child, stroking her one good hand. I felt this unbearable sense of loss. I would have given anything to turn back the hands of time and give them back the hands that they had lost. And again I felt that surge of anger boiling up from the pit of my stomach. How could anyone have done this? What could they possibly hope to achieve? What was their end? It could only be terror – terror and control. How could they live with themselves?

That woman had had the same unshed tears as the woman from Tawila. Both had been crying inside. As with Aisha, she had presented this incredible picture of dignified calm. The child in her lap was wriggling around and sucking her thumb, but the mother was this statuesque figure embodying dignity in the face of evil. I was so moved I never even took a photograph. I felt I couldn't. It would have been hugely powerful, but it would also have been an affront to her grace and her dignity.

I learned nothing more about what had happened to that Sierra Leonean woman, because she was unable to speak. Likewise, I was to learn nothing more about Aisha, the woman who had come to my office to tell her story from Tawila. The morning after Aisha's visit we were ready and waiting, but by midday there was no sign of her. In my heart of hearts, I knew she was never going to come.

I summoned Roger and ranted and raved. I railed at how she had come to me to speak and in so doing had walked into a nest of vipers, for the UN was hopelessly infiltrated. I ranted about how she had lost everything – her home, her job, her parents, her siblings, her husband and her children – and now she had likely lost her liberty and possibly even her life. And I demanded that Roger try to track her and find her and safeguard her in any way that he could.

Roger took a deep breath. 'Sir, with respect, it will be very, very difficult. And if I do try, I may just make it worse. I may draw the authorities' eyes to her, which won't help.'

In spite of the fact that I was on the very edge now, the rational side of me had to accept Roger's words.

Quietly, we used our contacts to try to get news of her, but there was no sign. To all intents and purposes, the woman from Tawila had disappeared. The terrible irony of this moment was devastating. Here was I, the chief of the UN, tasked with protecting millions, and I had failed to safeguard the life of one brave soul. There were no mitigating circumstances that I could think of.

I had failed personally at this most basic of levels – that of saving one life.

TWENTY-THREE

Two roads diverged in a wood, and I – I took the one less travelled by, and that made all the difference.
Robert Frost

HAVING LOST EVEN THIS BATTLE, I TOOK STOCK. MORE REPORTS were coming in from the field of daily atrocities. At first I had thought it was all over – that the regime had done its worst while we had been locked out of Darfur. Now I knew that 'mopping-up' operations were still very much under way.

Daily alerts winged their way from my office to New York, but they disappeared into an echoing void. I was making ever more blunt démarches to the government, but here too I was largely being ignored. I felt totally exhausted and utterly, utterly finished and demoralised.

I was scheduled to fly to Nairobi, on some UN business to do with the Naivasha Peace Accords. I asked Isabelle if she would accompany me if I went early, so that we could be there for the weekend. I didn't know exactly what I intended to do, but I felt the desperate need for some time away from Khartoum.

On Friday, 16 March, we took a flight to Nairobi and checked in to the Windsor Country Hotel, an old-style establishment set in green and rolling hills on the outskirts of the city. I didn't know exactly why I had come. All I did know was that I was desperately in need of sleep and to clear my head. I hadn't slept well for weeks now, and the darkest hours were plagued by horrible nightmares.

Isabelle set up an office in one room, so she could keep tabs on our Darfur teams. I gave her my mobile phone, so she could take my calls. Then I went to my room and for the first time in an age I slept for 12 solid hours. That sleep was one of the most refreshing that I have ever had. It was completely dreamless. I awoke the following morning feeling as if my head was crystal clear.

I was surprised by how good I felt, and I couldn't understand how I could feel this calm and collected. It was as if my subconscious mind had already settled on the course of action I was going to take and had nothing more to agitate itself over. It was just my conscious mind that hadn't quite realised it yet.

After a late breakfast, I told Isabelle I was going for a walk in the woods. She understood instinctively that I needed to be alone. The Windsor Country Hotel is set within acre upon acre of lush green woodland. I felt as if I was taking a stroll in the New Forest back in England, except that above me were chattering troops of monkeys. I walked and walked, and as I did so my mind went over all that had happened to me since I had taken up my post in Khartoum.

No channels of action over Darfur seemed open to me any more. The diplomatic community, world governments, Khartoum, the UN – all were closed. The more I thought about it, the more this seemed like the end of the road. There was not the slightest hint of a plan to stop the slaughter, no hint of a peace process, no hint of a peacekeeping force, no hint of a plan to re-establish security. Quite the reverse: everyone with the responsibility to do otherwise was ignoring Darfur.

There was no recognition of the magnitude of the crisis, yet no one could claim that they didn't have the information on which to act. In short, there was a concerted conspiracy of silence over Darfur. I walked and thought until it was approaching dark. I didn't have my mobile with me, so Isabelle couldn't check to see if I was all right. By the time I returned, she had grown quite worried, and she was visibly agitated.

After an early supper – and having reassured Isabelle that I wasn't suicidal, or at least not quite yet – I went to an early bed. I couldn't sleep, so I stayed up surfing the Internet. I re-read – online – the reports of the UN inquiries into Srebrenica and Rwanda (my own were back in the office). I was struck again by how it was my high responsibility to act personally to stop mass murder, no matter what others around me might think. The higher one's position, the higher the responsibility.

There was no way I could seek any guidance from New York. All I would be told was more of the same: *best keep quiet, old boy, and concentrate on your business – humanitarian work.* As I surfed the Internet, I was hit by a sudden realisation. The tenth anniversary of the Rwandan genocide was but a few days away. Here we were, ten years on from Rwanda, and what had we learned? The same mistakes and worse were being repeated in Darfur. So what had changed? And who was there willing to step forward and act? No one, it seemed, apart perhaps from me.

I surfed and read and pondered and debated my course of action until I was tired, and then I slept. I was up with the dawn the following morning, and I went for another walk. This time the woods were bathed in early sunlight, and I was struck by how stunningly beautiful they seemed. One image of beauty fused into another, and I remembered the beauty and dignity of Aisha, the woman from Tawila who had come to my office to tell her story of gang-rape.

How could such beauty exist in this world in such close proximity to evil, I wondered? I no longer felt tired. In fact, I felt full of energy, but with the return of my energy came again my anger. My mind began to play back images, like a movie spooling scenes from my life. Again and again I saw Aisha's face and heard her voice as she spoke. The image fused with that of the UN building in New York – a dark symbol of inexcusable indifference and impotence.

That fused into one of Sebastian warning me over bread-and-butter pudding in his London club: *It will all end badly for you, Mukesh, old boy.* That image faded into one of Tim Mansfield's laptop, showing me the graphic evidence of the scorched earth and devastation being wreaked across Darfur. The image of a burned-out hut merged with my own bird's-eye view of burning villages as my UN flight powered me through the airspace above Darfur.

Over and over, my mind played this kaleidoscope of images in which the architects of the evil merged with the perpetrators, plus that handful of 'good men' who had done nothing. As I wandered through that magical, sunlit forest, I felt as if I was in some heightened state of being – almost as if I was in some mild hallucinogenic trance. Fingers of sunlight probed the thick canopy above me, making patterns of light-and-dark, light-and-dark on the forest floor.

As I passed from one to another, I thought back over all my visits to the dark places of the earth. I thought of Rwanda, and of the visit to Ntarama church and the heaps of dead bodies that we had found there. I thought of the Indian sisters who, with their frail bodies and their faith, had saved so many. I thought of poor General Dallaire, the commander of the UN peacekeeping force in Rwanda – he who had sent cable after cable to New York, asking for permission to disarm the Hutu militias and to raid their arms caches, each of which had been denied.

The lesson from Rwanda was clear: when you suspected those on high of issuing the wrong orders, it was beholden upon you to defy those orders. Dallaire had done that for as long as possible, and he had hung on against orders and saved thousands of lives. But as a military man, Dallaire had known that ultimately he had to withdraw his peacekeepers when ordered by the UN to do so, and for that he would carry a heavy burden for the rest of his days.

As for me, I had no orders as such, although I had been told repeatedly and in no uncertain terms to stick to my humanitarian remit and not to rock the boat. Already, I had in effect been sacked from my post for refusing to play the game. But as a humanitarian I felt few such constraints to follow orders or heed warnings. I was a maverick civilian facing superiors who had lost my respect and my trust.

For a moment, I paused in a beautiful clearing flooded by sunlight. It was then that I consciously made my decision. I had no troops, so I couldn't order anyone to open fire to defend the people of Darfur. I had few staff, and those I did have were unarmed. There was only one thing that I could do now, and it would be driven by the cold rage I felt that these unspeakable crimes were being allowed to happen unchecked by those in power.

What I was about to do was far too important, with far too many lives at stake, to be driven by my emotions alone. I needed to coldly calculate the course of action on my part to achieve maximum impact, for nothing actually mattered now but stopping this evil. I turned back towards the hotel. It was midday, and I went directly to my room, from where I dialled the mobile phone of the UN press officer in Nairobi.

I'd had dealings with Ben Parker before, for he'd issued the odd press release about the north–south peace negotiations. Ben was entrepreneurial and opportunistic, and he had a sharp nose for a story. He was your archetypal likeable rogue, and how he had made it into the UN I couldn't imagine. He was a wolf to their sheep, and more importantly he was a fantastic media guy who was absolutely right for what I had in mind.

I asked Ben if he could come to the hotel after lunch, for I had some urgent business I needed to discuss. He told me he'd be there. After speaking with Ben, I went to find Isabelle. We took lunch on the lawn, from where we could see the golfers strolling through the distant greens. It was such an incongruous setting in which to strategise the future of Darfur. Ironically, it reminded me of Wellington College – a genteel place where norms were supposed to be observed. 'Isabelle, I made the call to Ben Parker.' We'd ordered food and we were waiting to be served. 'He's coming after lunch for a chat.'

She stared at me for a second. 'You've decided? Your mind's made up?'

'It is,' I told her. 'Isabelle, you know exactly what I'm about to do, so there's no need for me to tell you. And this way, when you are held to account by your bosses in New York – as no doubt you will be – you can honestly say that I told you nothing about what I planned to do. That way, you can exonerate yourself when the witch-hunt begins, which trust me it will.'

'I don't actually give a damn about any of that, Mukesh.'

'I know. And I treasure you for it. But trust me, it's better this way.'

Ben arrived promptly. We ordered tea, plus a beer for Ben, and got down to business.

'Ben, I want you to arrange for me to speak to the BBC, live and exclusive,' I told him. 'And, precisely, I want to speak to the BBC Radio 4 *Today* programme, in the morning slot between 7.30 and 8.30 a.m. I won't give advance notice of what I want to say, but trust me it will be well worth their while. And it has to be live, so I won't be edited. I won't give any more details about this before I do the interview. I don't want to discuss it with them beforehand. Just get me that slot, live and exclusive, and I promise you they will not be disappointed.'

Ben smiled this wolfish smile. 'Just one question: is it Darfur?'

I spread my hands. 'Ben, you're a clever guy. You can draw your own conclusions. Just get me that slot, OK?'

'Fine. It should be doable. I'll call you to let you know.'

Ben's eyes were glinting, and I could tell that he was relishing the challenge. At last, a real juicy story to get his teeth into. A typical UN press officer would check first that a UN official of my standing knew what he wanted to say and whether the interview had been cleared via New York. Ben asked none of those things. From past interactions, he knew Darfur was my passion, and he knew instinctively that this was about Darfur.

That evening, he called. 'It's fixed. At 9.30 a.m. Nairobi time tomorrow – 7.30 a.m. London time – you're to be at the BBC's Nairobi studio. You'll be hooked up direct from there live to Radio 4.'

'I'll be there,' I replied. 'And Ben – thanks.'

Over dinner, Isabelle asked me what I would say. I warned her that if I told her, she could no longer claim the defence of ignorance. She said to hell with that, she needed to know.

'Well, then, I will say it all, and tell it as it is about Darfur.'

'All?'

'There's no point in holding back. If the world's leaders will not listen to us, I will go direct to the world's peoples. I will blow this thing wide open and go above and beyond the heads of those who should have acted.'

'Mukesh, this is going to be very serious, with huge ramifications,' she said. 'But you're right – yours is a moral duty to speak out, as a human being and as head of the UN in Sudan.' She seemed happy at the decision that I'd made, but daunted at the same time. 'If you are decided, then you must go for it. You know what you have to do.'

I took courage from her support. We shared the same convictions, which put steel in my backbone. And so we raised our glasses and toasted my breaking the silence.

That night, I lay in bed feeling suffused with a calm resolve. I knew that I was on the brink of something momentous – for me and for Darfur. My days were numbered anyway, so in a sense I had nothing to lose. But I did fear that I would be at risk from all sorts of crazies, especially when I had to return to my post in Khartoum. Yet my real preoccupation was how the wider world would respond and what they would do to me. How would my own government, the Brits, react? What would the UN do? How would other global powers respond?

If there was a code of conduct to protect whistle-blowers within the UN, I for one had never heard of it. I knew that I would be hung out to dry, and that my UN days were over. For a while, I thought about my family. Ever since our Christmas break, I had been phoning them every other day, but I had told them little or nothing about my disquiet over Darfur. I didn't want to burden them or darken their lives. All I could think right now was this: *we have three girls at high school, and what will I do to earn a living? Thank God my wife has a well-paid job.*

I was only 48 years old. I was one of the youngest resident coordinators that the UN had ever appointed. I had achieved a high post, and I had bags of global experience in the field. I had been earmarked as a high-flyer destined for a lofty position in the international humanitarian system, with friends in the major world capitals. Now, all of that was about to come crashing down.

I had no doubt how the United Nations and world governments would react to the course of action that I was set upon. Once I pressed the nuclear button, I would have 'gone feral' in their eyes. I would be ostracised, spurned and rendered potentially unemployable. Overnight, I would have gone from being the privileged, high-flying insider to being the outcast.

For an instant, my conviction wavered, my sense of self-preservation almost trumping my will. Then a voice in my head – the Kapilesque rebel within me – told me not to be so weak-willed. For the tens of thousands of Darfuris who had died in the bloody bush, there were no such indulgences. Those who had survived would live with the horror for the rest of their lives, and most would doubtless prefer to be with their loved ones who had perished.

For a moment, I thought back over the stories that Grandma used to tell me on the hot nights in Chandigarh, ones of gods and devils. In her tales, against all odds good had always triumphed over evil. Perhaps, after tomorrow, I might do likewise.

Underlying all my emotions was a cold fury. In my mind, those responsible for Darfur were both the Khartoum genocidaires *and* those 'good men' who had chosen to do nothing. I made little distinction between the two now, and in my mind both had blood on their hands. My anger was all-consuming, and mostly it was directed at the so-called world powers by whom I felt so enormously betrayed. The Tawila massacre had taken place barely two weeks ago, and how many other Tawilas had we failed to witness or to stop? The rage I felt was because we – *I* – had failed to act to prevent them all. If we had acted early enough, we could have prevented the worst, of that I was certain. If we had spoken with a powerful and united voice, the world community could have prevented countless Tawilas from taking place in Darfur.

In spite of their anti-Western rhetoric, the mainstream politicians in Khartoum wanted the economic and other opportunities that went with better relations. If the Western powers had intervened, we could have forced Khartoum to rein in the Janjaweed. We could have stopped the worst of the horror. Tawila – and so many other Tawilas – could have been prevented. Yet we had failed.

Tomorrow, I would speak first and foremost to my own country – to Britain – via the BBC. This was the country that I had married into and adopted as my own. This was the country whose government I had faithfully served during all my years with DFID. The BBC was still the voice of the establishment in Britain, and the Radio 4 *Today* programme was iconic. At 7.30 in the morning, most decision makers would be tuned in over their breakfasts.

It was them that I intended to reach and hit when I went live over the airwaves.

TWENTY-FOUR

There comes a time when silence becomes betrayal.
Rev. Dr Martin Luther King

THE ENTRANCE TO THE BBC NAIROBI STUDIO WAS
unprepossessing – a narrow concrete stairwell in between a
couple of run-down shops leading to the first floor. During
the car journey that morning, my brain had been feverishly
trying to work out exactly what I wanted to say. The
interview would not be long, and I would only get the one
chance.

I was ushered into the studio, a glass of water was placed
in my hand, and a set of headphones over my ears. The
show's producer asked me a few simple questions about
what I'd had for breakfast as a sound test.

Then: 'Dr Kapila, you're through to the studios in
London.'

I suddenly felt suffused with an all-embracing calm. I knew
that I was going to give the interview of my life. I had no
script and no notes, but very few times in my life had I ever
felt such a pure clarity of mind. Tawila was the smoking gun.
No going back. I had all the facts that I would ever need. I
felt utterly certain this was the right thing to do. I had the
proof: I had to expose it to the world.

I heard the voice of the BBC anchorwoman come on the
air. 'Now, we're going live to our studio in Nairobi, to
speak to the United Nations humanitarian coordinator in
Sudan, Dr Mukesh Kapila. Welcome, Dr Kapila. Stories
are coming out of Darfur, a remote region of Sudan, of
horrific goings-on. Who is fighting whom?'

'There are two main groups,' I replied. 'On one side are
Arab militia – the Janjaweed – supported by and allied to the
government of Sudan. On the other side are the Sudanese
Liberation Army and Sudan Liberation Movement. And in
my view, and I have seen many conflicts around the world

247

in the last few years, this is currently the world's worst crisis. Well over a million people are affected – displaced internally within Darfur or pushed into neighbouring Chad. We have eyewitness accounts of systematic scorched-earth policies being put into effect, along with mass rape, torture, and looting of villages. One of the worst aspects is how these tactics are being used to spread systematic terror.'

'Have the aid agencies got any access?' she interjected.

'We have access to about a quarter of the affected region, but even that is ad hoc and temporary. This is because of continued insecurity. There are attacks on trucks carrying food and other aid, and deliberate government obstacles put in our way – bureaucracy and procedures that are followed at a snail's pace... Obstructing humanitarian access is a crime against humanity.'

'There is little coverage from international journalists,' the interviewer remarked. 'They are not allowed in. You say aid is urgently required. Is there anything more the international community should do?'

'Absolutely. Of course aid is required to relieve the desperate suffering. But much more than that, we need a settlement to the conflict... We have called for a ceasefire and for all sides to get together face to face to find a long-term solution.'

'But that isn't happening?' she prompted.

'No. Not at all.' I paused for an instant. *Now to do it.* 'Those are the facts as we know them. But let me make three things absolutely clear. First, this is the world's greatest humanitarian crisis happening right now, and I don't know why the world isn't doing more about it. Second, this is a human-rights catastrophe on a par with the Rwandan genocide – the only difference being the numbers involved, not the means nor the aims. Third,' and now I was pressing the nuclear button, 'the government of Sudan is responsible for this, and they are guilty of ethnic cleansing on an inconceivably vast scale.'

I took a second to catch my breath. It was as if I could

hear a pin drop in the studio in London.

'Right now we are approaching the tenth anniversary of the Rwandan genocide,' I continued, 'and I do not know why the world is refusing to act over Darfur. The world community has stood by and done nothing, and this is the greatest scandal and the greatest tragedy of our time. There has been blatant and systematic obstruction by the government of Sudan of humanitarian agencies trying to get access to the victims and to investigate what is happening on the ground in Darfur, yet world governments have done nothing to intervene or to act.'

I glanced at my watch. My time was almost done. Now to finish it. 'No one can claim ignorance, for we know the facts and have done for some considerable time. In short, the government of Sudan has deliberately attempted to hide what is going on in Darfur and to hide the war crimes that are being perpetrated there. And the world community has silently colluded in that obfuscation and chosen to do nothing in defence of the people of Darfur.'

'Dr Kapila, thank you for speaking so frankly.'

I removed the headphones and shook hands with the Nairobi producer.

'Great report,' he remarked, as he showed me to the door.

Isabelle and I left, descending the concrete steps. It took us a few seconds to do so, and by the time I reached the bottom there was a trilling on my mobile phone.

'Dr Kapila,' I answered.

'Dr Kapila, this is the BBC World Service in London. We've just heard your report on the *Today* programme, and we'd like to do an interview.'

'But I've just spoken to you,' I said, a little confused.

'No, this is the BBC World Service, not domestic. We want to do our own report.'

'Fine,' I said. 'I can do it here and now if you like.'

I proceeded to do my second interview, presenting the facts and making the three key points. Then the presenter had a series of questions for me. I sheltered in the concrete stairwell from the road noise, as I did my best to answer.

That interview done, Isabelle and I got into the waiting car. No sooner had I shut the door than my phone rang again. It was Voice of America radio, asking for an interview. So I sat in the car as we nudged through the Nairobi traffic and spoke to them. Just as soon as VOA was off the line, Reuters called. Reuters was followed by Associated Press, then the South African Broadcasting Corporation (SABC), and after that the *Johannesburg Times*. All throughout that car journey, I was taking calls and giving interviews: the *Financial Times*, followed by newspapers from as far away as Holland, Hong Kong and my native India called. By the time we had reached the UN's Gigiri compound on the outskirts of Nairobi, I'd given a dozen or more interviews. It was astounding.

Isabelle and I rushed inside. I had an office put at my disposal, and I switched on my laptop. She and I had yet to exchange the barest of words. I went straight to the BBC's homepage on the web. At the top was a banner headline: 'Breaking news: the head of the UN in Sudan, Dr Kapila, calls the crisis in Darfur a Rwanda-like genocide...' I turned to speak to Isabelle, but my mobile rang again. This time it was the *Frontier Post*, a Pakistani newspaper asking for an interview.

I'd told Ben Parker to give out my number to any press that might call. I'd told him I would speak to any media, no matter who they were, but none of us had quite expected this level of response. I was astounded. And then I suddenly had a thought. It was 12 o'clock midday Nairobi time by now, so five o'clock in the morning in New York. In four hours' time, UN headquarters would open for business and stumble into the whirlwind.

I turned to Isabelle. 'Oh my God, what do we do about New York?' 'Of course! They'll be awake soon...'

'I'll dictate a memo.' I paced back and forth behind her. 'Address it to Iqbal Riza, chef de cabinet of the secretary-general. Say: "Please draw this memo to the personal attention of Kofi Annan. It is my considered duty to inform the secretary-general that I consider the situation in Darfur to be ethnic cleansing for the following reasons..."'

I went on to reiterate what I had said in my press interviews. I ended the memo by stating that I had spoken to the media and that there might well be questions directed at UN headquarters, so New York needed to be prepared. I asked Isabelle to copy the memo to Kieran Prendergast and Mark Malloch Brown. Once the memo was done, she emailed it directly to New York. It would be on their desks as soon as they got into the office.

I thought of this as my 'blood memo'. It was the one in which I revealed to New York just what I had done: blowing the whistle to the world's media over all the blood that had been spilt in Darfur and just who was responsible. To them, this would be unthinkable, but, to me, enough blood had been shed in Darfur to last until the end of time.

But it was also my blood memo in that I had drawn blood with New York: I had smashed down the wall of silence, and hopefully this would force them at last to act. I had shown that I could fight, that I had teeth and claws and would use them.

Ben Parker was hovering on my shoulder. 'Great interview, Mukesh. Very impressive. But listen, CNN want an interview. So do the BBC, SABC and a host of other TV channels. I reckon we do a press conference this afternoon so you can kill all birds with one stone. What d'you say?'

'Let's do it,' I told him. 'In for a penny, in for a pound as they say.' At three o'clock, we gathered in the meeting room adjacent to the office. It was jam-packed, standing-room only, with news cameras and lights in every corner. Ben had asked one of the reporters to start with a 'trigger question' – *what's going on in Darfur*? In answer, I ran through the same points as I'd raised in the previous interviews.

Then it was thrown open for questions.

'Why are you saying this now?' a female reporter queried. 'Why not before?'

'That's a good question,' I answered. 'The statements I've

made today could only be made once we were sure of all the facts. We were excluded from Darfur from December to February, and only recently were we allowed back in. And in the last two weeks, we've collected the evidence which allows me to say all this – like the crucial Tawila incident, for example.'

A barrage of questions followed about Tawila, and I gave a detailed account, including Aisha's testimony given to me at my office in Khartoum.

Next question: 'Why didn't you say all this in Khartoum?'

'Well, there's really no independent or international press there. I didn't feel I could speak as openly and freely.'

Question: 'What should happen now?'

'Personally, I believe those who are committing these crimes against humanity, which are backed and organised by the Sudan government, have to be held to account and brought to justice. This matter should be referred to the International Criminal Court, these crimes should be investigated and the perpetrators brought to justice. The ICC is the only place to do that.'

The questions and answers went backwards and forwards for a good half an hour. I finished off with this:

'It is a disgrace that Africa's longest-running conflict, which has generated the world's largest numbers of displaced people and refugees, has now generated the first genocide of the twenty-first century, and that it remains off-radar in terms of any formal discussions in the UN security council, the world organ for peace and security. One would have to ask what is the relevance of the security council to today's main security problems? What is the point of it, if it can't even discuss the main issue of the age?'

After the press conference proper, I went out into the garden to do one-on-one interviews with CNN, BBC News and several others. It was six o'clock that evening by the time I was done – mid-morning New York time. I had been bracing myself for the reaction from UN headquarters. I had been expecting explosive phone calls and emails: *Mukesh, have you gone stark raving mad?* Instead, there was nothing. I could only presume that they were so outraged as to be totally lost for words.

But what did it matter? The story was out, and they could do nothing to stop it. In any case, I knew I was right. The facts were incontrovertible, and they had been repeated ad nauseam in all my briefings and alerts. I had gone public and outflanked the UN machine, but they could hardly counter by saying that I was crazy. They had all the evidence before them that what I was saying was true. And if they did try to paint me as a madman, they would look as if they were siding with a regime that had engineered a genocide.

In short, they were damned if they did and damned if they didn't – which was just where I wanted them. As far as the media saw it, I was the UN's man on the ground. In the eyes of the press, no one else had higher credibility. They had the man on the ground giving them an explosive, revelatory story. No one in New York could undermine that. For the media, it mattered as much who said something as what was said. I had more legitimacy than New York, and I had wrong-footed them all.

At midday every weekday, there is a press conference in New York by the UN secretary-general, or his spokesperson. Midday is seven o'clock in the evening Nairobi time, by which point the press furore had died down a little. Isabelle and I were back at the hotel, wondering what the UN would have to say. Darfur had made headlines around the world, and there was no sign of the media storm abating. The press in New York had taken up the cudgels and would be demanding answers.

In my memo to New York, I had laid out exactly what the UN now needed to do. It was a repetition of what I had been asking for in so many of my previous reports:

1. The issue had to be debated in the UN security council.

2. A security council resolution had to be agreed, followed by a peacekeeping operation on the ground.

3. An inquiry into Darfur and the UN's own failings was urgently needed.

4.Darfur needed to be referred to the International Criminal Court.

5.A truce and eventually a fair peace agreement needed to be negotiated between the Darfuri rebels and Khartoum.

I had suggested a course of action to be followed, and I was hoping the secretary-general would announce something similar in his New York press conference. Today's would prove to be one of the most popular UN news briefings ever. Kofi Annan did not put in an appearance. Perhaps he was out of town.

It was left to his press spokesperson to make a statement expressing Annan's 'grave concern' over Darfur and urging the government of Sudan to investigate. It was hardly as much as I'd hoped for, but it was a start. At least the issue had been recognised and the wheels were starting to turn. Notably, this was the first clear expression of concern that Kofi Annan had publicly made over Darfur.

Late into the night, there were still stragglers from the media getting in touch. I had calls from the *New York Times*, the *Washington Post* and the *Seattle Inquirer*, as American newspapers woke up to the story. I took a cold Tusker onto the lawn and continued to give interviews. I felt in a buoyant mood. I would now have to face whatever the consequences would be for me personally, but the silence had been broken. It was out, and no one could put the genie back into the bottle. The following day, I awoke to the aftermath. In the hotel lobby, I found the local Kenyan and world papers full of the story. I checked email and voicemail, and still there wasn't a squeak from New York. The wall of silence was oppressive and somehow ominous. In contrast to the absolute quiet from UN headquarters, my email in-box was flooded with messages from well-wishers.

'Hey, buddy, fighting words! Well done – goin' out with a bang!' That email was from John Prendergast, one of the key human-rights campaigners on Darfur. I knew him well, and it was great to read his support.

But best were the emails from Darfuris and other Sudanese. 'May God bless you and keep you safe and well,' read one. 'You have given us a voice when we had none. You have given us hope when we were hopeless. You have shown us that there is light at the end of the tunnel.'

There were countless others like that – signed with names like Abdul Abdullah or Zainab Al-Nasir – clearly Sudanese, and some, I presumed, Darfuri. Then there were the emails from UN staffers from all over the world. Mostly, I had no idea who these people were, and probably I had never even met them.

'Our hearts are with you, Dr Kapila. We are so proud that someone from the UN has finally had the courage to speak out over Darfur.'

Many of the aid agencies that had worked alongside us in Darfur had also emailed.

Médecins Sans Frontières wrote: 'Mukesh, we're shocked and impressed. We didn't think anyone in the UN had it in them to speak as you have. We're so grateful for your efforts and also for getting us access to Darfur.'

I took huge courage from these friends and strangers sending in their heartfelt support.

Mid-morning, I took a call from one of my few remaining allies in New York. He proceeded to brief me regarding the fallout over what I had done. Apparently, there was total consternation at UN headquarters. Those in power were 'running around like headless chickens', he told me, somewhat gleefully.

They were accusing me of breaking all the rules. I had gone feral, they were saying. Worse, as far as they saw it, I had caused a major diplomatic incident by my actions. They viewed my press statement as being a direct accusation of the Sudan government, which is exactly what I'd intended it to be. And it was also seen as having put the UN itself on the block for having taken zero action over Darfur, which was my other chief intention.

The modus operandi within the UN is that no one ever speaks out or steps out of line. If you blow the whistle, you're finished within the UN. Those are the unwritten rules. So be it: at least my actions had had the impact I desired. Overnight, Darfur had gone from being a non-issue to making world headlines. The logjam was broken.

As for the reactions from Khartoum, these would not be long in coming.

TWENTY-FIVE

Convince your enemy that he will gain very little by attacking you. This will diminish his enthusiasm.

A Chinese proverb

WHENEVER I, AS UN RESIDENT CHIEF, WAS AWAY FROM Khartoum I appointed a temporary stand-in. This time it was Nimal Hettiaratchy, my Sri Lankan colleague who headed the UN Population Fund. I had told him nothing about what I might do in Nairobi, for I hadn't known myself when I left Khartoum.

He called to brief me on what had happened. After my story hit the press, he had been summoned to the foreign ministry and asked to justify my actions. The only response he was able to give was: 'Speak to Dr Kapila about it when he gets back.' He had received a very strongly worded protest about my 'outrageous and indefensible statements'. I told him to batten down the hatches and that I would return shortly.

I couldn't just slink away. I was still UN resident chief and I had a job to do. But I was afraid now for my personal safety. I knew that Khartoum would counterattack, using their media to smear me, whereupon sanctioned or rogue agents could seek to do me harm with the regime's implicit backing. I was truly fearful.

It wasn't in Khartoum's interests to turn me into a martyr. But there were those extremists who might take matters into their own hands, and then the regime could say: *well, this wasn't us, of course, but what does he expect after all that he has done?*

I put a call through to the one person I felt might be able to protect me if my life was put in any danger in Khartoum – the British ambassador, William Patey. After all, no matter how much grief I was no doubt causing my own government, I was still a British citizen.

William answered my call with a simple but heartfelt greeting: 'Brave words, Mukesh. Brave words indeed!'

'Thanks, William. I'm returning to Khartoum shortly, probably tomorrow, and I'm a little concerned for my safety. If I need to make a dash to the British Embassy, will you be ready?'

He laughed. 'Yes, yes, we'll be ready. Mukesh, come over any time you need us.'

Twenty-four hours later, I found myself sitting next to Isabelle on a British Airways flight to Khartoum. The aircraft touched down just after dusk, and as usual Isabelle and I were whisked through VIP arrivals and into the waiting car. Omer handed me my mail, and his attitude towards me was as professional as ever. It almost felt as if I had been away on any normal trip and that nothing had changed.

He drove me to my home, from where I put a call through to William Patey.

'I'm home,' I told him. 'All seems fine and I'm going to try to get some sleep. Maybe it's all going to be OK.'

'Nice to have you back, Mukesh,' he replied. 'Whatever happens, keep me posted. We're here for you.'

I slept well, and the following morning I headed for the office. Not a thing was said by anyone about what I had done. All the IHP people and my UN teams were out in the field, so I hadn't exactly been expecting a chorus of 'well done'. But there was a brooding anticipatory stillness about the office, as if this was the quiet before the storm.

Roger was first in for his early-morning briefing. We turned first to the local press cuttings, from which it soon became clear that the storm was already starting to break. The most vitriolic material was in the Khartoum Arabic – as opposed to the English-language – press. 'Kapila – pack of lies!' screamed one headline. 'Kapila – runs away and talks outrageous lies to the world!' screamed another. The reports railed that I was in league with the enemies of the Sudanese state, in particular 'the Jews'. Worse still were the calls for 'jihad' against me and statements that I deserved to be killed.

'Sir, I figure you know this already,' Roger remarked, 'but I will really have to look after you now. You'll need close protection. I will stick very close to you, and I'll re-deploy our people so there is more watchfulness around you.'

'I understand, Roger, and thanks.'

One Khartoum newspaper appeared to have been reasonably fair towards me. 'Kapila is both a hero and a villain: he is a hero for speaking out, and a villain for not speaking sooner, so as to protect his own job...' It was fair criticism, if untrue. The reporter was right. I had spoken out too late. But I had lost my job weeks back, so I had no job to protect. Roger pointed out that that particular newspaper had been shut down that morning. Any Khartoum media that were intending to be even remotely fair towards me were likely to face the same fate.

As Roger and I talked through the ramifications of all that I had done, it became increasingly clear that the security issues made it impossible for me to stay on in Khartoum. The media storm was unlikely to die down. Quite the reverse. As Darfur continued to claim world headlines, pressure upon the UN and the Khartoum regime was bound to keep rising. This would only bring me into further and more serious confrontations, for I was duty-bound to keep exposing and accusing both the regime in Khartoum and the machine in New York. After discussing this with Roger, I had a quiet chat with Isabelle.

I would prefer to fall on my own sword and resign, I told her, than have the Khartoum regime declare me *persona non grata* and expel me, or the UN recall me. Isabelle told me that whatever course of action I chose to take, she would be leaving with me.

'But you'll be needed here by whoever replaces me,' I objected. 'Mukesh, my heart will go out of this when you leave. And anyway, I am closely associated with you, and I would find it impossible to serve another UN chief. So, I will prefer to finish my time with you.' We argued about it for a while. Finally, she told me that I had brought her to Sudan and to Darfur, and she would leave with me.

It was as simple as that. I was deeply touched by her loyalty.

'Well, in that case, book us two flights to leave on 31 March,' I told her. That was barely a week away, and it would mark the one-year anniversary on my taking up my post as UN chief, which seemed a fitting date to depart.

Next, I called a meeting of my UN heads of agencies. 'Friends,' I told them, 'I want to thank you for all your support over the year. I think we've come a long way in terms of what the UN can do for all parts of Sudan. But as for me, my usefulness to you is over, and it's best that I go. Therefore, I will be leaving at the end of this month.' My announcement was met with a shocked silence. I didn't sense any enormous regret from many in the room, but it was clear that they hadn't expected me to go so swiftly. As I went to leave the room, the heads of several UN agencies came hurrying after me.

'We will miss you very much, Mukesh,' Nimal, the head of UNFPA, told me.

'Thank you so much for your spirited leadership,' said Arachi, the head of the United Nations Industrial Development Organisation (UNIDO), who had been one of my few steadfast supporters.

'It will be as if a light has been switched off,' remarked the head of UNOCHA.

I thanked them for their kind words but told them what I guessed they knew already: I really couldn't stay.

I returned to my office and shuffled some papers absent-mindedly as I tried to think about packing. It was then that I heard a wailing cry from just outside my door. I wondered what on earth it might be. I went to investigate, and Mona, my assistant, was nowhere to be seen. I could hear a woman's voice coming from the toilet, crying out in distress. I guessed it had to be Mona, and I asked Isabelle to go investigate.

Isabelle hammered on the door to the ladies: 'Mona, come out!

Come out! Come on, Mona, come out!'

The only response was a rise in the volume of her

hysterical wailing. 'But he's leaving! Oh, Allah, no! Why does he have to go?'

I realised then that I was the source of her distress. I wandered over to the door. 'Hey, Mona, I'm OK!' I yelled through it. 'I'm not dead yet!'

Eventually Mona emerged, red faced and dabbing her eyes. I asked Isabelle to make her some tea and to try to calm her down.

I returned to my office and penned an email to New York, announcing my resignation as United Nations chief in Sudan and my imminent departure. I sent it off right away, but by the end of that day I still had not received a word of response from UN headquarters.

The following morning, I received yet another interview request, this time from the Arabic TV station Al Jazeera, to be carried out with their crew in Khartoum. I accepted, and in doing so I knew that I'd be taking the fight right into the lions' den. To speak out in Khartoum would be a hugely provocative act, but it was crucial that I speak to the Arab – as well as the Western – world.

The Al Jazeera crew came right over and set up in my office. I proceeded to say the same as I'd said before, only now I decided to up the ante still further. I focused more on crimes against humanity and who exactly had committed them. I fingered the Sudanese government directly and explained why the regime should go before the International Criminal Court.

'Let me make one thing very clear,' I told the interviewer. 'The president of Sudan, Omar Al Bashir, should be included amongst those individuals referred to the International Criminal Court to face charges of war crimes and crimes against humanity. He may be a serving president, but that doesn't make the crimes any the less reprehensible or justice any less of an imperative.'

I could see the interviewer's eyes light up at what I was proposing. He realised the enormous power, not to mention the sensitivity, of someone in my position saying such a thing, and especially here in the UN's headquarters in Khartoum. He and his camera crew finished the interview shortly, packed up their camera and lights and rushed back to their studio to file their story.

Al Jazeera screened the interview that very day, with explosive results. The Al Jazeera Khartoum bureau was immediately shut down, and their news crew expelled from the country. The first threatening phone calls came in to me directly after that Al Jazeera broadcast, which must have been like a red rag to a bull.

My cell phone rang – *caller unknown*. 'This is Dr Kapila,' I answered. 'You have insulted our country!' It was an Arabic-sounding male. 'You are a liar in cahoots with the Jews and the enemies of Sudan.

You deserve to be punished...'

The line went dead. Half an hour later it rang again: *caller unknown*. I felt I had to take it, for I was still getting regular calls from the media.

'Dr Kapila,' I answered.

'You have insulted our country!' Another male Arabic voice, more sinister sounding. 'You deserve to be treated in the worst of possible ways.'

Click. The phone went dead.

Bizarrely, chillingly, the words he'd used conjured up a disturbing memory for me, a vision of the hell of Tawila. The phrase he'd spoken echoed those the Janjaweed had used when speaking to Daniel Christensen of the black African inhabitants of Tawila: *they deserve only the very worst this world has to offer...*

A few hours later, the phone rang for a third time: *caller unknown*. It was this one that would disturb me the most, for it was from an Arabic-sounding woman.

'Dr Kapila, you have insulted our country!' That same phrase again, almost as if the callers were reading from a script. 'You will be found dead one day soon, and thereafter you deserve to go to hell!'

I told Roger what was happening. He figured the regularity, coupled with the similarity in the phraseology – *you have insulted our country* – pointed to these not being crackpot calls. Roger felt certain this was a well-orchestrated campaign, and there were no prizes for guessing by whom it was being waged. In response, he increased the security presence around me still further, and he warned me that from now on he would not leave my side. He would be my permanent shadow, 24/7, and he would even sleep in my house at night.

I had received death threats before, or at least something similar. I had even been tried in absentia in Iraq and sentenced to death. But nothing had ever felt to me remotely this immediate or sinister. The fear I felt was anchored in the knowledge of who exactly was driving this: it was the same agency as had orchestrated the 'final solution' in Darfur.

As news filtered out of my impending departure, so the responses started to come in, though there was still a blank wall of silence from New York. The key diplomats in Khartoum decided to issue a joint press statement in support of all that I had done. It was sent out to the world's press and governments by the US chargé d'affaires.

We of the British, French, Dutch and American diplomatic community in Khartoum wholly commend the stand taken by UN resident coordinator Dr Mukesh Kapila, and endorse what he has said about the serious events now unfolding in Darfur...

I was hugely encouraged by the clarity and strength of their backing. In their eyes at least, the action that I had taken was the right one. A similar strongly worded statement of support was put out from Geneva, by experts at the office of the UN High Commissioner for Human Rights. That, too, was heartening. But still there was not one word of response from New York.

In spite of this – perhaps because of it, even – I decided that I would not let up on New York during my last few days in post. Despite the storm of media coverage, the horrors were ongoing in Darfur. Even as the world's press turned the spotlight on Khartoum, the regime seemed unwilling or incapable of reining in the mass murderers.

There was much still to do, and I kept firing in my alerts to UN headquarters.

19 March: Janjaweed militias attacked, looted and burned villages... 21–23 March: Janjaweed militias attacked, looted and burned...

23 March: Janjaweed militia forces attacked and looted... 27 March: armed horsemen attacked, looted and burned...

In response, only silence. Not one single word did I receive from New York. No one upbraided me. No one commended me. No one so much as commented on my resignation. But worst of all, no one issued any kind of acknowledgement of my reports. The troubles were ongoing in Darfur, the darkness spreading like a cancer, and yet from New York I received not one word of recognition of this or of what the UN intended to do about it.

It was from my diplomatic contacts in Khartoum that I was finally given an insight into what was going on within UN headquarters. Facing an escalating media assault, the international community – the UN first and foremost – felt under siege. Hounded by intense criticism, the UN security council had finally moved to act and called a meeting to formulate an urgent course of action on Darfur.

Yet still the press interest in Darfur showed no sign of abating. Quite the reverse, in fact. The international media had taken up the cudgels and were even now getting news crews and their top reporters into Chad, from where they could access the refugee camps. The focus of the news had become the scope of the genocidal violence in Darfur, as graphically illustrated through those refugee stories.

As for me, my focus had shifted away from the media, which had gained a momentum all of its own. I was turning my attention towards the future and to my one consuming priority. I'd blown the whistle. Now it was time to ensure that justice would be done. I needed to record and document the exact process via which ethnic cleansing and genocide had taken place in Darfur, identifying who was responsible. My final days in Khartoum were going to be consumed with gathering evidence and working out how best to preserve it.

I realised that I wouldn't feel at all safe carrying that evidence out of the country on my person when it came my time to leave. So I compiled everything I had onto a zip drive and arranged for a friendly diplomat to send it out in his embassy's diplomatic pouch and deliver it into a safe pair of hands. Once that was done I knew there would be no stopping the quest for justice – for the evidence of these massive war crimes, plus the names of those who had orchestrated them, had been put well beyond the reach of the Mukhabarat and Khartoum.

With just a day or so to go before my departure, a round of farewells began. I was still getting the threatening phone calls, and if anything their frequency had increased. Roger was working all hours and even sleeping in my bedroom on a camp bed, and I was forced to travel everywhere with a phalanx of security. It felt as if the United Nations office in Khartoum and my residence were themselves under some kind of siege.

The French ambassador hosted a goodbye dinner on behalf of the diplomatic community. He had beautiful menu cards printed up:

Dîner du mardi 23 mars 2004 en l'honneur de M. Mukesh Kapila. Entrée: Velouté d'épinards; Brick aux herbes. Plat: Eventail de volailles aux champignons; Pommes dauphines; Salade aux pignons...

Dinner was served with a selection of fine French wines. The starter was accompanied by a Chablis William Fèvre 2002, followed by a Domaine des Salices Syrah 1998, with a Monbazillac 1996 to go with the dessert. At the end of the meal, I was presented with a menu card, one signed by all present:

'I am now wholly in favour of UK–France collaboration – after six months of careful consideration and review,' wrote one of the French contingent.

'Mukesh, I sincerely hope your efforts are built upon by whoever comes after you. You did a fantastic job,' wrote one of the Americans. 'Mukesh, you leave the Sudan before us,' wrote the Dutch, 'but you must be sure we will try to follow the path you have opened.'

And, typically, the Brits signed off with humour. One had circled the dessert – 'Biscuits fondants au chocolate' and written: 'Beware! Butt- enhancing diet!'

But perhaps the most meaningful for me was the message from one of the Sudanese guests:

'I hope what you started last week in Kenya will be built upon; I would thank you from the Sudanese and Darfuri people from the heart.'

TWENTY-SIX

This is the first teaching of the Knights; you will erase everything you had written in the book of your life up until now: restlessness, uncertainty, lies. And in the place of all this you will write the word 'courage'. By beginning the journey with that word... you will arrive wherever you need to arrive.

From the breviary of a medieval knight

THE DAY OF MY DEPARTURE WAS 31 MARCH 2004. I SPENT THE morning tidying up my office, but all the while I was feeling this burning impatience to get myself gone. My work here was done; the silence broken; the evidence spirited away to safety. And although I had regrets, I knew that I had done the right thing. My continued presence was simply causing everyone a headache, especially those tasked with safeguarding and protecting me.

Just before lunch, an email popped into my inbox. It was from a contact within the European Parliament in Brussels, and it concerned a resolution that the Parliament would pass on the Sudan the following day, 1 April. They had sent it to me to check and to give any feedback before the Parliament went public.

We note with utmost concern the March 22nd statement made by the UN's coordinator for Sudan, Mukesh Kapila, stating that the situation in Darfur is akin to the biggest humanitarian and human rights crisis in the world today... We strongly condemn the reported provision of financial, logistical and other support given to the Janjaweed militia by the government of Sudan, including the indiscriminate bombing of civilians.

It went on in a similar vein, stressing how the use of sexual violence, rape and abductions as a weapon of war amounted to very serious war crimes and calling for a no-fly zone to be put into place over Darfur and for peacekeeping troops to go in on the ground. It was the first official statement by a government, or group of powerful governments, over Darfur. It had taken a little over a week since my breaking cover for this to emerge. The conspiracy of silence had been well and truly broken, and the dam of inaction was starting to break. I returned to my Khartoum house and ate a late lunch with Isabelle, plus my permanent shadow, Roger. As a last act of closing down my residence, I had to distribute my few domestic possessions. I gave Ahmed the freezer, the one in which he had managed to destroy all my insulin. He wanted to start a restaurant – *some hope,* I thought – hence his desire to have my white goods.

To Mary, my wonderful housekeeper, I gave the rest of my domestic things – toaster, kettle, microwave – and I was so very pleased that Nadia, my former special assistant, was taking Mary on in her own household. To Mona, I gave my DVD player and TV, and to Omer, my driver-cum-spy, I gave my fridge. That done, I asked Ahmed to cook for me his speciality one last time: that evening, we would feast on baba ganoush.

Isabelle, Roger and I had just sat down to enjoy a last meal when there was a ringing on my mobile phone. I had started to dread such calls due to all the death threats I was receiving. But this time the call was coming from the ministry of foreign affairs of the Sudanese government. I stared at my phone with a growing sense of disquiet. Were they going to make one last effort somehow to try to frustrate or to sink me?

I glanced at Roger. 'Foreign affairs. Do I take it?' He nodded. 'It won't help not to.'

I punched answer and placed the phone to my ear. 'Yes?' 'Dr Kapila?' a male voice enquired.

'It is,' I confirmed, somewhat guardedly.

'I'm calling from the ministry of foreign affairs. Before you leave Sudan, Dr Mustafa Osman Ismael would like to invite you to his personal residence, for tea. If you would like to accept, do you know how to get there? If not, I can give your driver instructions.'

The invitation had come from out of the blue. I considered it for a moment. My flight wasn't leaving until past midnight, so there was plenty of time to have tea, if that was truly what this was all about.

'Just one minute,' I told the caller. I placed one hand over the phone. 'Roger, Osman Ismael is asking me to his place, for tea supposedly. What d'you think? Do I go?'

Roger shrugged. 'I figure he's a straight player. If you want to go, go.'

I told the caller that I would be delighted to accept the invitation and asked that he give my driver some directions.

Omer drove me out to the foreign minister's residence, set in a peaceful location on the outskirts of Khartoum and on the banks of the Nile. Osman Ismael came out to greet me in person and led me into his living room. He was dressed simply in a pair of Western-style trousers and shirt, and his house was furnished equally plainly but tastefully. He offered me tea, and then we began to talk.

'I hear with deep sadness that you are leaving,' he told me. 'The president has asked me personally to convey his regrets that it ended this way. I want to emphasise it was not my own government that requested you to leave. This is the United Nations' doing.'

'Well, actually, I resigned my post of my own free will,' I remarked. 'I jumped before I was pushed, as it were...'

'That's as may be, but it is the United Nations, not my government, that would have been doing the pushing.' He paused and fixed me with a direct look. 'It is a great pity to be losing you, for while we know you are a difficult man, we believed we could work with you. We know you are an honest man and you say what you think, and that you're not in the pocket of anyone.'

He smiled, wryly. 'In fact, the reason you are in so much trouble right now is perhaps for the very reason that you are your own man, and you have run out of friends. When you are in no one's camp, Dr Kapila, then there is no one there to protect you.'

'Well, I have tried my best to be true to the principles of the UN,' I told him, 'which is to behave impartially and not take orders from any single government. You know, we've been fixated on Darfur, and of course my going is all to do with that, but we also worked well together on many other issues.'

'Yes, I know. You are the first UN country chief to argue so strongly for development aid for Sudan and for long-term programmes of infrastructure and human development. And you've helped to open constructive dialogue with the SPLM in the south. This we know. You are a sincere man with a vision, and we know that your heart is with the Sudanese people.'

'It is. Absolutely. I have no quarrel with the people of Sudan. As I think you know, I first came here as a medical student many years ago and fell in love with your country.'

The minister paused, his expression growing graver. 'Dr Kapila, we know that terrible things have happened in Darfur. Very bad things. A lot of people have suffered and so many Darfuris have been forced to flee their homes...'

'Yes, but the question is did your government not engineer this?' I broke in. 'I feel as if you have badly misled me, because on the one hand your government organised and masterminded this, while on the other doing their best to hide it. Surely, you're not trying to deny this any more?'

'Well, personally, I can tell you I am ashamed of those elements inside the government that were involved or who failed to control events in Darfur. There are many others in my government who are ashamed at what transpired and...'

'Perhaps there are,' I interjected. 'But think of all the things I personally warned you and other ministers about: Intifada Camp, Tawila, Korma – to name but a few. You had every warning from me, you had every evidence necessary to hand, and you had every opportunity to act to stop it.'

The minister spread his hands, almost as in a gesture of surrender. 'Dr Kapila, it is not my government's policy per se that these terrible things happened. But it is true that some parts of my government have acted unconscionably, and I can understand your frustration and your anger.'

'Mr Minister, it is well known that it is the military and

the security people who have led these things. But surely you're not trying to tell me that your president isn't able to keep those elements under some form of control?'

The minister remained silent for a long second. I waited for an answer, but none was forthcoming, and his silence was enough for me. Yet still I couldn't help but warm to this man. I felt he was at heart a decent individual, one placed in an impossibly difficult position by his own government.

'Dr Kapila, we are worried there will be a United Nations security council resolution against us, one imposing sanctions,' he ventured. 'Do you have any advice on how we can handle this and maybe try to avoid it?'

'Well, the only way you might possibly do so now is by convincing the world you are bringing the violence to an end immediately and in a genuine manner. And start taking measures to bring the refugees home and to provide real security in the area so they can go back and resume their daily lives.'

For a while, we talked around what measures the regime might take to try to rectify the situation, and then he remarked, 'If you go to New York soon, as I presume you will, will you give the Sudan ambassador to the UN a call? Perhaps you might provide some advice on what line he should take in any security council discussions.'

I practically fell out of my chair. This was all so bizarre. Was he really reaching out to me – to the regime's greatest detractor – and asking for help?

'You know, you can always count on my advice for the overall welfare of the people of Sudan,' I told him, 'and for the peace and stability of the country. I'll always work for that.'

The conversation meandered on, going this way and that, before I glanced at my watch. It was eight o'clock, and I really needed to be getting home.

'Forgive me, Minister, but I do need to be leaving. I have a flight to catch...'

'Of course.' He smiled. 'I've appreciated having this rare

opportunity to talk so frankly.'

He walked me to my car and we shook hands. 'Dr Kapila, you are a man we could work with still,' he told me again. 'Never forget that.' 'Mr Minister, as I said, my heart is with the people of Sudan. Please, always remember that.'

I got into the car, and Omer drove me away. I turned around and glanced out the rear window. Osman Ismael was standing by the roadside, waving goodbye. I waved back, and then he was out of sight. I settled into my seat, feeling an odd frisson of regret. Doubtless, he was a man I could have worked with. If only I'd been liaising with him and not the Mukhabarat people at HAC.

Yet even if I had been, I didn't believe that any of these front people really mattered much. Behind men like Osman Ismael, at the centre of the malevolent state machine sat the Mukhabarat, and it was they who were the architects of the unspeakable evil that had engulfed Darfur, they who had made of the 'final solution' a terrible reality.

From home I hurried directly to the airport, along with Isabelle and Roger, for time was pressing. In contrast to my arrival a year earlier, there was no pomp and ceremony surrounding my departure. All those who had been there to greet me were absent at my parting. This was the cost of my breaking the silence: I was now the outcast I had feared I would become. But compared to the people of Darfur, my suffering was as nothing.

Omer my driver and I parted outside the terminal building, for he wasn't allowed into the VIP area. I said a peculiarly emotional goodbye to him. In spite of his double-agent role, I had grown fond of him over the year that he had driven and, strangely enough, protected me. 'Sir, it has been an honour,' he told me, as we shook hands for the last time.

I was tempted to say something like: *Omer, I've known all along who you really are. You're a Mukhabarat agent, aren't you?* But it seemed like a cheap shot. I'm sure he knew that I knew, and in many ways he'd done his best to warn me – for example with his text message: *Oh trouble, what a big God I have.*

I settled for something cryptic. 'Omer, it's been a pleasure to have you watching over me. Do as well for my replacement, won't you?' Isabelle and I hurried through the VIP area, as we were late already.

Roger escorted me to the very foot of the plane's steps – a true professional to the last. I figured that he was making absolutely certain that I left alive and in one piece, and that I was safely off his patch. I paused on the steps and turned. 'Thanks for everything, Roger. Sorry for all the trouble.'

For a moment his laconic mask almost cracked. 'Sir,' he said, 'wherever you go now, stay safe.'

We mounted the aircraft steps, they were rolled away and we were soon airborne.

I gazed out of the aircraft's window. There was a full moon suspended above us, and the African sky was a kaleidoscope of stars. As Khartoum receded from view, the Nile became visible for a magical moment – a silvery streak threading through the dark desert – before the night claimed it. We jetted onwards, and I wondered if I would ever set foot again in Sudan, a country that I truly loved and that had changed me forever, even as I had tried to change it.

I ordered a beer, but before it had even arrived I drifted off into an exhausted sleep.

EPILOGUE: 'THE WORLD'S MOST SUCCESSFUL GENOCIDE'

EVEN AS I LEFT MY POST IN SUDAN, MY ACTIONS AS whistleblower over Darfur were taking effect. Within days of my departure from Khartoum, the United Nations security council met for the first time ever to formally discuss the situation in Sudan. It issued its first-ever statement on Darfur, expressing 'deep concern at the large-scale violations of human rights and international humanitarian law, including indiscriminate attacks on civilians, sexual violence, forced displacement and violence of an ethnic dimension' and urged 'that those responsible be held accountable for the atrocities taking place in Darfur'.

Further concrete action to halt the bloodshed followed shortly afterwards. The first peacekeepers – from the African Union – were on the ground within four months of my departure, tasked with re-establishing law and order and safeguarding Darfuri civilians. Notably, these were Rwandan soldiers – with the searing experience of their own country's genocide to motivate their efforts in Darfur. Never before had the international community been forced to move so fast and so far from its original stance, which had been to do nothing. The world powers and the UN leadership that had poured such scorn on my desperate pleadings just a few weeks earlier had been forced to recant thanks to media pressure and the worldwide outrage that followed.

I continued to play a focal part in this. My role was to compile a detailed report – with the help of Isabelle and Humayoun, a human-rights specialist I'd worked with in Sudan – presenting all the evidence we had gathered on the abuses in Darfur. That report prompted the UN to commission a formal inquiry into the allegations of war crimes in Darfur and who ultimately was responsible. Those files we had spirited out of Khartoum in a diplomatic bag provided crucial evidence that would help to identify those accused of war crimes.

The UN's formal inquiry reported back to Kofi Annan that there was prima facie evidence of 'crimes against humanity and war crimes including acts with genocidal intent' having occurred in Darfur. That forced the security council to refer the matter to the International Criminal Court in The Hague. The ICC started its investigations in June 2005 and went on to indict several members at the top of the Khartoum regime, including the Sudanese president himself, Omar Al Bashir. He was charged with five counts of crimes against humanity, two counts of war crimes and three counts of genocide. His charge sheet – the first ICC indictment of a serving head of state – reads like the plot of a horror movie: murder, extermination, torture, rape and more.

In short, a little over a year after I blew the whistle over Darfur, the three major factors that I had called for – UN security council resolutions on Darfur, peacekeepers to go in, those responsible to be referred to the ICC – had come to pass. At long last, the humanitarian relief operation also geared up, as donor governments rushed to fund life-saving food, water, shelter and healthcare. All of this came too late to halt the worst of the suffering in Darfur, because the killings had already happened and the Darfuri way of life been all but exterminated. But even peacekeepers late in the day are better than no peacekeepers at all. As to war-crimes indictments, although Al Bashir did all he could to make life more difficult for the international humanitarian organisations working in Darfur, it was never too late to see that justice was done.

I mention all this not in an effort to take any credit – I have no truck with self-aggrandisement in the face of one of the greatest failures of the world community in recent times. I do so simply to demonstrate a crucial point, perhaps even the central message of this book: *one person's actions can make a difference.* It is possible to stand in the face of unconscionable evil, however high the stakes may be personally and however frightening it may be to do so. It is possible to stand alone; it is possible not to be one of those good men who choose to do nothing.

Death threats against me continued long after I left Khartoum, and indeed increased in severity. I ignored them, as I did my continuing critics in the UN system. Meanwhile, the stress and trauma of what I had endured in Sudan worked its course through my mind, body and spirit. My harsh self-judgement of what I saw as a personal failure added to my malaise. There was an inevitable personal toll in terms of my closest relationships.

As I struggled to adjust to my new life, what kept me going was a determination to see the architects of the 'final solution' in Darfur brought to trial – including the Sudanese president, Omar Al Bashir. So, I remained one of the foremost voices speaking out over Darfur and agitating for justice.

After leaving my post as UN chief in Sudan, some kind of 'disciplinary action' was mooted against me. However, I was still a DFID employee seconded to the UN, and the British government defended me resolutely. DFID argued that if disciplinary action were to be considered by the UN, then the exact nature of my wrongdoing would need to be made crystal clear. In essence, the British government demanded to know why the UN wished to shoot the messenger. In the final analysis, no formal action was taken by the United Nations against me for my stand over Darfur.

Others were less fortunate – most notably those who had stood resolutely at my side. Isabelle, my special assistant – my support and confidante during the toughest times – paid a high price indeed. Although she returned initially to the UN in New York, and even received an award for her exceptional service to the organisation, her days were numbered. One of her bosses warned her that as long as he remained in power she had no future there. Sudan was a sovereign country, he told her, and its government had the right to do as it willed. 'Even when it comes to killing its own people?' she'd countered. He told her to keep quiet and to stop supporting me. Isabelle struggled on, writing powerful poems inspired by her experience in Sudan, but eventually she left New York and found work elsewhere.

As for me, after having taken the stance that I had I might have thought that I had left Darfur behind, but it never left me. It remained a raw and festering sore, and for no greater reason than that little had improved on the ground. Based in Geneva and working first for the World Health Organisation (WHO) and then for the International Federation of the Red Cross and Red Crescent Societies (IFRC), I found myself continuing to follow events as they unfolded in Darfur with dismay. In spite of the peacekeepers going in, and despite the peace agreement between north and south Sudan, little had changed for the better for the Darfuri people.

More than two million Darfuris were displaced across Darfur and the rest of Sudan, or forced into refugee camps mostly in Chad. Few, if any, had been able to return to their devastated villages, because those areas remained horribly insecure. In spite of the peacekeepers, the security situation was abysmal: the Sudanese military continued to target Darfuri civilians, aid workers and even the peacekeepers themselves. While Khartoum had apparently bowed to the international community and allowed the peacekeepers in, in truth those soldiers wearing the distinctive UN blue beret were ill-equipped to keep the peace, and they were hampered and obstructed at every turn. Khartoum ensured they were unable to do their job, using force of arms where necessary.

Thus, Darfur had reached a situation of stalemate: the refugees remained in the camps, few could go home, and even in those camps they were prey to attacks by government forces and the dreaded Janjaweed. Women and children were raped when out collecting firewood. Men were murdered. Boys were abducted. So what in truth had changed? The level and scope of the violence was less, because the genocidaires had largely done their job, but, crucially, the violence was still of the same nature as before. Only its geographical focus had shifted – from the villages to the IDP camps and the refugee camps in Chad.

I began to realise that in spite of all the international resolutions and condemnation, in spite of the peacekeepers going in on the ground, in spite of the war-crimes charges at The Hague, Darfur had actually become 'the world's most successful genocide' – to coin a chilling phrase that came to mind in one of my darkest moments in Geneva. In Rwanda, more people had died – some 800,000 – but at least the genocidaires were deposed from power, the killing stopped overnight and many of the key figures responsible put behind bars. Crucially, justice was seen to be done. There was a reckoning, reconciliation and Rwanda had made a start on the long road to recovery.

In Srebrenica, before Rwanda, NATO forces had driven the Serb genocidaires out, stopped the killing overnight, and the International Court for the Former Yugoslavia was formed to hold accountable the architects of the war crimes. Teams of elite soldiers flew snatch missions into remote areas, seizing suspected war criminals so they could be brought to trial. In Srebrenica and the wider Balkans, there had also been a reckoning and the hope of reconciliation with time.

Not one of those things had come to pass in Darfur. The chief architect of the genocide – Omar Al Bashir – remained president of Sudan; his key cohort – Ahmed Haroun, the operational commander on the ground – was promoted to high political office. The Janjaweed were still very much at large, their chief – Musa Hilal – growing ever more powerful. In short, not only had there been no reckoning but the architects of the 'final solution' in Darfur had been rewarded financially, personally and politically for their heinous crimes. As for justice, reconciliation and recovery – they remained a chimera.

As my awareness of all this – and my deep unease – grew, I encountered one remarkable Darfuri woman in a London meeting that would prove fateful. Halima Bashir had written a book called *Tears of the Desert*, recounting her terrible suffering in and escape from Darfur. It turned out that she – like me – was a medical doctor trained in Khartoum Medical School. She had been targeted by the Janjaweed and government soldiers for treating the wounded and trying to save lives. She had been 'punished' by being sent to a clinic in a remote outpost in northern Darfur.

As I read her story of how the Janjaweed and government forces went on to attack that village outpost, raping women and girls during their raids, I realised that the account had to refer to *the Tawila incident* – the very same attack that my UN staff – Daniel Christensen foremost amongst them – had witnessed and that Aisha, the extraordinarily brave woman who had come to speak to me in my office, had told me about. Tawila had been the crucial tipping point for me: it had galvanised the action that I went on to take in Nairobi in blowing the whistle.

I went to meet Halima, now living as a refugee in London. I asked her what she wanted most. Two things, she said: one, justice; two, she very honestly told me that she wanted revenge. I told her I hoped we could turn revenge into reconciliation and recovery, but justice she must absolutely have.

Shortly after meeting her, I flew to the Netherlands, to give a long interview to Radio Dabanga – a kind of Radio Free Darfur. After my interview, the show would be thrown open to questions and comments from Darfuris around the world, including those in the refugee and IDP camps. It is illegal to listen to Radio Dabanga in Sudan, but many were doing so in secret and at very real risk to their lives.

I recounted the story of my time in Sudan and how I had been forced to blow the whistle over the world community's failure to act. That done, the journalist opened the lines for comments and questions. I took a few, and the discussion revolved around the prospects for a peace process and the possibility that Darfuris might return home. But then an old Darfuri woman came on the line, speaking on a mobile phone from one of the IDP camps inside Darfur. From the moment she started talking, her voice was suffused with a remarkable passion as well as an absolute, unshakeable determination, and I was electrified.

She told me that her father, brothers and sons – all the menfolk of the family – had been killed. She was living a miserable life in the camp with her surviving daughters, unable to leave for fear of rape and worse. Then she really went for it: 'The blood of our menfolk has soaked into the desert sands, and for what? Are we now to accept the Arab theft of their lives and our land? Has the struggle been for nothing? We must continue to resist by all means possible, to the last woman if needed, until we get our livelihood and our pride and our dignity back. Thank you for what you did in speaking out – you gave us hope. But what now? We are still here suffering. Our struggle is not over. *Mr Kapila, your job is not done.*'

The connection cut as abruptly as she'd come on the line, but what she had said left me speechless. Her words hit me like a lightning bolt. I felt more awake than I had done in an age. Over the past few years, I had directed major programmes for the IFRC and lived the good life in Geneva – in a reality far removed from the heat and dust of Darfur. But every day when I had gone through the motions of working, I had actually been in something of a daze. After hearing first Halima's story from Tawila and now the old lady from the IDP camp, I knew with an absolute clarity what I had to do.

I had learned from her that, although they had been crushed, Darfuris were still resisting. The resistance remained spirited and strong. It suddenly struck me that the architects of the 'final solution' in Darfur hadn't won completely. The Darfuris were united in their determination not to allow the genocidaires to declare total and absolute victory. And if they could remain so absolutely resolute and determined, why had I stepped aside from the path? Why had I been content to say I'd played my part and that my time in Darfur was done?

It was then that I realised something really quite shocking. After my year in Sudan, I had accepted a high post at WHO, and in doing so I had effectively allowed the UN to buy me off – the WHO being part of the UN system. Many had told me that the UN was afraid of me after what I had done over Darfur. Those at the top had quietly decided that 'a Mukesh inside the UN system was far better than a Mukesh outside of it'. They'd given me a high post and kept me a part of the UN machine, the quid pro quo being that I was sidelined from my agitation over Darfur. That was why I had felt so empty and aimless in the last few years.

In January 2012, I stepped off the Air France flight into the cool night of the Chadian capital, N'Djamena. A few months back, I had been given the chance to pick up on that Darfuri woman's challenge: *Mr Kapila, your job is not done*. A UK-based genocide prevention charity, the Aegis Trust, had asked if I would like to return to the region to meet survivors from Darfur now languishing in refugee camps in eastern Chad. The world appeared to have forgotten Darfur, and Aegis argued that someone with my profile and track record could catalyse international attention – but only if I could get into a position from which to speak again with impact and authority.

Hence my flight into N'Djamena. That morning, I had filed my resignation letter with my boss at the IFRC, secretary-general Bekele Geleta. I had resigned as his under-secretary-general because I knew the trip I was about to undertake could be seen by some as jeopardising the neutrality of the Red Cross. My intention to speak out in public on behalf of the forgotten Darfuris could be construed as being incompatible with my leading role in the Red Cross and Red Crescent Movement. I'd resigned with real regret – I had grown to love the organisation and found the work hugely fulfilling. And I could never forget how the Red Cross had once saved my family during Partition in India, and how it had rescued me again by taking me in when I had been forced out of the UN. I hoped the strong commitment of my friends in the Red Cross and Red Crescent Movement to the suffering people of the world would help them understand why the call of Darfur – *your job is not done* – was irresistible to me.

While planning the trip with Aegis, I'd spoken to David Loyn, the BBC world affairs correspondent whom I knew well and respected hugely. I'd explained to him my plans to return, to expose how Darfur had become 'the world's most successful genocide'. David's reaction was immediate: he wanted to come with me to film a BBC report. The very concept of 'the world's most successful genocide' had sent a terrible chill down his spine. If he and I could return to the region, we could expose this to the world in a powerful and compelling way.

However, matters in Chad were to prove somewhat less straightforward.

I already had my permission to travel to the border area where tens of thousands of Darfuris lived a pitiful life in desert camps, unable to return home. But our flight in a UN aid aircraft wasn't scheduled to leave for 24 hours. In the interim, we gathered as a team: myself, David Brown and Mike Shum of Aegis, David Loyn and the BBC cameraman, Duncan Stone. That evening, over dinner in N'Djamena, we received an unexpected phone call, informing me that my permission to travel east had been withdrawn.

While the BBC team and Mike Shum started out on their own to the camps, I was asked to pay a visit to the Chadian minister of the interior and public security. I didn't feel entirely encouraged by such a summons. We gathered at his office, where green tea, dates and almonds were served with great formality.

'Your Excellency, welcome to Chad,' the minister greeted me. 'We are honoured to have someone of your eminence here. We know who you are, but there was a misunderstanding about your paperwork and now there is simply not enough time for you to travel east before you are due to leave. We therefore think it would be more convenient for you to return home on the earliest available flight.'

Politely but firmly I told him that my trip was to draw

attention to the plight of the Darfuri refugees so more money could be donated to address their needs. I also pointed out that there was a UN flight going out the following morning that could still get me into the Darfuri refugee camps. So what was the sense in preventing me from going? I saw the minister waver. My argument was hitting home. 'Very well, Dr Kapila, I see no reason why you shouldn't take that flight.' But then a shadowy figure sitting beside him – from the Chadian Commission for Refugees, their equivalent of my old nemesis, the Sudanese HAC – sprang into action. 'But, minister, this is surely a matter on which we need to consult many others.'

The expression on the minister's face changed. 'Ah, yes – quite right. Well, Dr Kapila, please return to your hotel and we will be in touch with you tomorrow.'

The meeting had had a veneer of civility and politeness, but beneath the surface I could tell they were determined to prevent me from going any further towards those Darfur refugee camps. If I was to be prevented from doing so, we desperately needed a plan B.

The focus of David's story would now have to shift completely: it would become a story about a well-known senior humanitarian being refused access to the refugee camps and kicked out of Chad. And in fact, this would make it a stronger story for the BBC. It had gone from being a strong humanitarian story to a fantastic tale of international geopolitics and intrigue. As far as David Loyn saw it, the Chadians had played right into his hands.

The priority now was to play for time. I needed to stop them kicking me out of the country for long enough for David to return from the refugee camps, so we could wrap up this new angle on the story. I argued truthfully that my flight ticket had restrictions, which meant that I couldn't leave for two or three days. Hopefully, this would give David time to return with all his footage, so he could play to me the evidence of the world's most successful genocide.

Against all the advice of his Chadian government minders

– and with warnings of murderous bandits and night
ambushes ringing in his ears – David Loyn and his team set
off from the camps on an epic two-day drive across the
deserts back to N'Djamena.

While we were waiting for them, we decided if we couldn't
get me to the Darfuri refugees, we'd try to bring them to
me.

Noresham, a Darfuri widow, volunteered to give the slip to
the guards around her camp and drive to N'Djamena to speak
to me. She told me: 'Our situation is very bad. We are just like
prisoners sitting in our camps. It is not only me. My people
are all imprisoned. We keep hearing from our homes in Darfur.
The killing is still going on there. The rapes are still going on.
You go to the market and can't go back to your house – either
you get raped or killed. So it's far from finished.'

'What would you like the world to do?' I asked her.

'We have been abandoned. We want the international
community to come and see. We also want our children
educated and food for our bellies. But more than that, we
don't see the perpetrators brought to justice as was
promised.'

Her voice was clear and uncompromising, the tone
honest and determined. My encounter with Noresham
would form a key part of David Loyn's story.

He reached us just a few hours prior to my flight taking
off, but it was time enough for him to show me what he
had filmed and to shoot a final interview with me. As I
flew out of the country that had expelled me, escorted by
my Chadian minders, David and his cameraman were
editing and voicing their final news report. It would make
world headlines: 'Former UN Sudan chief expelled from
Chad. Refugees continue to flee as Darfur burns'.

My overnight flight got me back to London as the news
was breaking around the world. From Heathrow, I went
direct to the *Today* programme – the same outlet with which
I had broken my silence in 2004 – to give them a live studio
interview. I told them that the Darfur situation was not
solved: millions were in the camps, the Sudan government

continued to bomb and to burn, and Bashir and his henchmen were still evading justice. Why had the world community again dropped the ball, I asked? And why was I getting kicked out of a country simply because I wanted to draw attention to the ongoing plight of the Darfuris?

Darfur had been a dead story for an age. The focus had become south Sudan's vote to secede from the north, on independence for the south and peace. But now Darfur was back in the headlines. I made sure to give an interview to Radio Dabanga, describing all that we had done in the hope that the old lady who had challenged me so directly might be listening. *Mr Kapila, your job is not done*, she'd told me. *I know. I heard you. I am back on the case. And this is only just the beginning. I failed to get to your people one way, but I will keep trying.*

Three months hence found me seated on another flight headed for the world's newest country, South Sudan. Since breaking the story from Chad, I had become immersed once again in issues Darfur. And one thing had struck me more powerfully than any other. Arguably, the world's most wanted war criminal was Ahmed Haroun – the operational commander of military forces (and, by extension, the Janjaweed) in Darfur and one of the ICC's key indictees. If Bashir was the architect of the Darfur genocide, it was Haroun who had put his plans into practice on the ground. And having succeeded so comprehensively in Darfur, Haroun had now turned his cruel mind to another long-suffering part of the Sudan.

Horrific news had started to filter out of the remote and closed Nuba Mountains, which sit on the very border of Sudan and South Sudan. Khartoum had incorporated the Nuba Mountains into the state of South Kordofan, a vast area stretching from the border with the South up to Darfur itself. Indeed, the Nuba Mountains had been one area to which Darfuris had fled during the worst days of the killing. The Nuba people being fellow black Africans – and fellow victims of Khartoum's wars of ethnic cleansing – they had offered the Darfuris sanctuary, and perhaps it was that which had led Haroun to turn his focus towards the Nubans. His orders to his soldiers had been captured on film broadcast by Al Jazeera: 'You must hand over the place clean. Swept, rubbed, crushed. Don't bring them back alive. We have no space for them.' An army commander had added: 'Don't bring them back, eat them alive.'

Other sketchy news reports had emerged that Khartoum was using Antonov aircraft to drop fire-bombs on Nuba villages, after which armed men followed – burning, looting and raping. In one notorious incident, UN peacekeepers had stood by – well-armed troops wearing the blue UN beret – as the killers went on the rampage. Nuban villagers had fled to the UN base seeking sanctuary, whereupon the so-called peacekeepers had closed their gates, leaving the villagers trapped outside. They had been gunned down in their hundreds before the very eyes of the UN soldiers, who had done nothing.

It was a scandalous and burning shame on the UN – yet another, after Rwanda, Srebrenica and Darfur. As the Nuba Mountains were closed to all journalists, reports had filtered out about this incident mostly via Nuban refugees fleeing the horror. There were chilling stories of mass killings and of victims being buried in mass graves. With no media able to go in and investigate, the Sudan Sentinel Project – a George Clooney-inspired satellite-monitoring initiative designed to keep watch over such atrocities – had detected evidence of those mass graves. But as of yet there had been little reporting on the ground.

Cue my flight into the area, along with Peter Moszynski, a respected Sudan analyst, James Smith, the chief executive of Aegis, and Inigo Gilmore, an independent journalist and cameraman.

It was the knowledge that Haroun had transferred his evil intent from Darfur to the Nuba region that had compelled me to go. If we could get into South Sudan, cross the border into the Nuba Mountains and secure the evidence on the ground, we could expose this new chapter in Haroun's – and Khartoum's – ongoing genocidal intentions. I had asked David Loyn to accompany me on this trip. David had been very keen but feared the BBC wouldn't sanction it. To cross an international border illegally into an active war zone was not something he figured he could get cleared by his employer – perhaps understandably. But if a freelance cameraman could go in and secure footage, David could use that on the BBC, and we could release it worldwide. That, at least, was our plan. *Mr Kapila, your work is not done...*

My first sight of the Nubans was a sprawling makeshift refugee camp in Yida, South Sudan. Some 30,000 had fled the horrors inside the Nuba Mountains and were gathered here in absolute hopeless squalor. More were arriving every day. One grandmother, who had hobbled across the border with her two disabled grandchildren, spoke to me in graphic detail about what was happening right there and then a few dozen kilometres across the border.

Her son and the father of her two grandchildren, their mother, plus five other children had been rounded up by the Popular Defence Force (PDF) 'militia' – Haroun's new model for the Janjaweed here in the Nuba Mountains – and disappeared. Others had vanished at the militia's hands, and finally she had decided to flee. It had taken two weeks to trek out, hiding in the bush whenever she heard Khartoum's bombers flying overhead. She was now living under a plastic sheet stretched over a hole in the ground, yet even here they were far from safe.

A few days previously Khartoum's air force had bombed the refugee camp, which was within the territory of South Sudan. At the refugee camp clinic, I saw a long line of emaciated mothers and children who had been brought to the brink of starvation by the attacks. Khartoum's policy – *Haroun's policy* – was twofold: one, to attack, bomb and burn to force the Nubans to flee; two, to spread such terror that the Nubans couldn't plant their crops and so would die a slow death of starvation. What I was seeing and hearing had all the hallmarks of a repeat of Darfur, almost a decade later and perpetrated by the same individuals.

It was chilling, and it made my determination to head across the border all the more strong. The journey across was beset by risks. The only route in was via a battered Toyota Land Cruiser with no windows and broken suspension, escorted by a contingent of Nuban resistance fighters – those who had once been commanded by my old acquaintance, John Garang. Sadly, I would have no chance to rekindle our friendship this time. Garang had died in a tragic helicopter crash not long after signing the Naivasha Peace Accords, and before South Sudan finally achieved its independence.

As we set off on a dirt track through the bush, I learned that the fighters escorting us were half Nubans and half Darfuri. Those who had fled the horrors in Darfur a decade earlier had joined the Nuban resistance, to fight against this newly opened chapter in Khartoum's 'final solution'. When I'd first heard that chilling phrase, I'd little realised that, in reality, it referred to much of the country under Khartoum's sway, not just Darfur. There was no other way to interpret the evidence that was now unfolding before our eyes.

A few miles down the dirt road, we crossed the border – marked by no more than a thin and ragged rope – and the foothills of the mountains rose up before us. But all around lay the remains of abandoned and burned-out villages. The very earth itself was scorched and blackened where Antonov bombers had dropped their firebombs, just as they had done a decade earlier in Darfur.

We reached a clearing and saw a lone water pump where a few nervous-looking women were queuing to fetch water. Via an interpreter, they began to tell us their stories, but no sooner had they started to speak than a loud droning filled the air.

The noise struck me as being terrifyingly familiar: it was the drone of an approaching Antonov. I'd heard it so often before on aid missions, as the Russian Antonov cargo plane is the workhorse of such operations. But in Sudan, of course, it had become the workhorse of firebombing sorties and the machine of ultimate terror. Everyone started to run, mothers shouting for their children, and kids screaming in fear. I felt rooted to the spot. I searched for our vehicle, only to see it disappearing in a cloud of dust.

It made sense for the driver to abandon us in an attempt to hide the Toyota, for without it we were stuffed. But there was no shelter for those of us remaining, apart from some small hills a few hundred yards away. Meanwhile, smoke could be seen rising in dense pillars over the fields where the Antonov had dropped its bombs. By now, Inigo had gone into action: he had his camera on his shoulder. At least he had something to do, to help him filter out the fear. I was petrified. I felt a hand grab my shoulder and a voice yelled in my ear. It was one of the Nuban women who'd been at the well. 'They're coming! They're coming!' She urged me to run in the direction of the foothills. I looked more closely and realised that what I had first taken for a bald, rocky mountain was actually alive with human beings. Every nook, cranny and shallow cave had been transformed into a makeshift home, as the Nuba had moved out of their villages and into the rocks in an effort to hide from the bombs. The grandmother in Yida had told me how people were being forced to live like this: now I was seeing it for myself.

The Antonov finished its bombing run, turned away and set a course north for Khartoum. We recommenced our interview with the women. A familiar story began to unfold: their villages had been firebombed from the air; mile upon mile of crops were burned; the survivors moved into caves, where they survived on berries and other wild foods. Some of the women spoke of how they were savagely beaten by the PDF – Haroun's new model of the Janjaweed – and of younger girls being taken away to the bush to be raped.

Having heard these stories – ones so darkly reminiscent of Darfur – we remounted the Toyota and pushed on, climbing into the hills. We reached Dar village – a deserted, smoking ruin, one that must have been firebombed very recently. What struck me most was how even the large earthen grain stores had been burned to the ground. Normally, the villagers would store their grain here, to tide them over from one harvest season to the next. Not any more. Haroun's strategy was blindingly clear: to bomb and burn the Nuba out of their villages and starve any who remained.

We drove on, reaching a place called Taroji, the forward base of the Nuban resistance movement. The fighters here were part of the umbrella Sudan Revolutionary Front (SRF) – which brought together those from Darfur, the Nuba Mountains, and areas like the Blue Nile and other marginalised parts of the country. The common thread that ran through the SRF was their non-Arab identity and their shared experiences at the hands of Khartoum: this was a black African resistance movement, and all of its peoples had suffered ethnic cleansing at the hands of Al Bashir's Arab supremacist, totalitarian regime.

In this large Nuban village that doubled as the resistance headquarters, we were taken to a hole in the ground, which had been dug as a kind of rubbish pit. Now it was littered with cluster bombs -- shiny brass cylinders looking like cans of Red Bull, with yellow and orange ribbons attached. The previous day, two children had been killed while playing with a cluster munition. So, the rest had been gathered up and dumped here in an effort to dispose of them 'safely' or as safely as possible. This was proof of the technological sophistication of Haroun's war against the Nubans: his Antonovs were dropping cluster bombs alongside firebombs, to deliver a double whammy.

Nearby were cases full of landmines. Each was marked with Farsi writing, being of Iranian manufacture. The SRF had overrun a Sudanese army base and captured the landmines. They were being planted around burned-out villages – near water sources and on pathways so as to stop people returning to their homes. During my time in the British government, I had helped negotiate the signing of the Ottawa Treaty banning landmines – the campaign of which Princess Diana was a figurehead. Sudan was a signatory to that treaty, yet here their forces were blatantly using landmines to wage war against civilians.

Littering the floor of a building next door were the largest artillery projectiles I had ever seen in decades spent visiting war zones: they were three or four metres long. These were precision-guided munitions, I was told, which were being used against specific targets. For me, these kinds of weapons – landmines, cluster bombs, precision rockets – were new to Sudan. Haroun had refined his techniques of ethnic cleansing in Darfur and added high-tech weapons of destruction here in the Nuba Mountains. This was no genocide of machetes and Kalashnikovs: this was high-tech mass murder.

I was shocked. What had taken me months to piece together in Darfur – via my own visits, the reports of my staff, Tim Mansfield's investigation and then Aisha's eyewitness account as a victim of Tawila – here I had witnessed in some 48 hours. It was as if Khartoum wasn't even bothering to hide the evidence of its gross misdeeds. It was blatant. Brazen. It was almost as if having been branded as genocidaires and arraigned as such by the court in The Hague, Bashir, Haroun et al. had decided to more than live up to those charges.

Haroun, for one, had a long pedigree of genocidal acts. Back in the 1990s, he'd earned the nickname 'The Butcher of the Nuba', when – prior to Darfur – he had waged a first campaign of ethnic cleansing in the Nuba Mountains. He had doubly earned that epithet now.

Our SRF minders advised it was too dangerous to stay longer than 24 hours. The Khartoum regime now possessed high-tech surveillance systems, including low-level radar to prevent relief flights going into the area illegally, and the ability to intercept mobile telecoms. That evening we retraced our route across the border, reaching Yida at nightfall. From there we headed to Juba, the capital of South Sudan, and thence to Nairobi. I booked myself into the same room in the Serena Hotel where Tim Mansfield had revealed to me the evidence from his secret mission into Darfur, plus I paid a short visit to the Windsor Park Hotel, to revisit the woodlands where I made my original decision to speak out.

That done, I called a press conference. Thankfully, we had a good turnout. I spoke about the simple truths that our Nuba mission had revealed: that a second genocide was now underway in Sudan, this time in the Nuba Mountains; that a humanitarian disaster was now inevitable, with hundreds of thousands of Nuban people facing imminent starvation; that the people orchestrating it were the same as in Darfur – namely Haroun and Bashir; and, finally, that the killing machine had been modernised and was far more high-tech and efficient than in Darfur.

I stressed how vital it was to put into effect the international arrest warrants against Bashir, Haroun et al. Just prior to the press conference, the ICC had issued an additional warrant, for the Sudanese defence minister, for crimes against humanity in Darfur.

After the press conference, I flew direct to London and did a dozen back-to-back interviews with CNN, BBC, Al Jazeera and others, describing what I had seen and making the point that this was Darfur redux. The failure of the international community to act decisively to stop the genocidaires had led to this – a second war of extermination against another innocent people in Sudan.

From London, I travelled to New York, for further press and other briefings. Shortly thereafter, US Congressman James McGovern proposed a Sudan Accountability Act, in which he called for sanctions against the country and real concrete efforts to get the ICC arrest warrants actioned.

'The former top UN humanitarian in Sudan, Mukesh Kapila, issued a warning to the world,' he told the US Congress. 'He said the government of Sudan military is carrying out crimes against humanity in the country's Nuba Mountains... Kapila said he saw military planes striking villages, destruction of food stocks and a scorched- earth policy. He said the attacks reminded him of what he saw in Sudan's Darfur region in 2003–04, when the predominantly Arab government in Khartoum targeted black tribes... We need to let our government and the world know people care and that we demand protection for these people from Khartoum's murderous policies.'

Nicholas Kristof of the *New York Times* also made it into the Nuba Mountains, emerging with similar stories and eyewitness testimony. Then, a few days later, George Clooney himself made it into the Nuba area, and his presence there helped push the Nuba issue even further up the agenda. But in spite of all of this action, the nightmare continued in the Nuba Mountains, and more and more refugees fled across the border into South Sudan.

This left me in a dark and hopeless mood. So many times, we – *I* – had failed to stop the killing: Srebrenica, Rwanda, Darfur and now the Nuba Mountains, not to mention elsewhere. It was then that the Aegis Trust people persuaded me to make one more journey – this time to return to the darkest moment of all in a life spent in conflict: Rwanda.

Rwanda. I had never wanted to go back, to face all of that again. But with gentle persuasion, a few months after my Nuba visit I flew into Kigali, the Rwandan capital. Over the days that followed, I returned to each of the key scenes from two decades earlier: the deserted Kigali house where bodies had been lying in the gardens; Ntarama Church – the church of the massacre; and the Missionaries of Charity orphanage in Kigali, where the nuns had stood firm against the genocidaires.

At each place, I witnessed something like redemption. Accountability, justice and a healing of the terrible wounds, coupled with reconciliation, were making the Rwandan nation whole again. The Rwandan government was absolutely determined that no one would ever forget, so as to ensure genocide could never happen again.

The attempt at forgiveness and reconciliation was epitomised by my visit to the Kigali Central Gaol, a place I had first seen in 1994, when it was stuffed to bursting with thousands of genocidaires. In order to visit the gaol, I had to get permission from the head of the Rwanda Correctional Services. He decided to tell me his story. He was a former member of the genocidal regime and had fled to the then Zaire as Paul Kagame's Rwandan Patriotic Front forces liberated the country. But he had chosen to return to face justice and, in a remarkable demonstration of trust and healing, the government had appointed him to the most sensitive job of running the country's prisons.

In the gaol, I saw what was being done to rehabilitate, through education and training, the mass murderers who remained, and I learned how former killers and their victims were trying to come to terms with each other while working together to rebuild the country. This was very much work in progress. While most said the right thing when asked, and did seem genuinely remorseful, I also encountered a darker aspect: the chillingly open unrepentance of some.

'Do you regret what you were involved in?' I asked a solidly built convict hard at work in one of the prison's workshops. He was serving 30 years for genocide.

'No,' he said, with as little concern as if I'd just asked whether he liked cheese. 'No... No.' He repeated the assertion almost cheerfully. Thankfully, Rwanda's future is in the hands of a new generation, even as the toxic legacy of genocide leaves them with massive internal challenges and tensions with neighbours. How they shape that future depends on how they deal with a past most are too young to remember. As we see all over the world, mass atrocities create cycles of violence that endure for centuries. They cannot be healed if ignored. But the cycle is not inevitable: it is either broken or it is cemented in the minds and hearts of each generation. To forestall the possibility of genocide happening again is a continuous and permanent task.

My return to Rwanda proved something vital to me. It showed me how a country so bedevilled could pull itself out of the heart of darkness and rise phoenix-like from the ashes.

It showed me that though ordinary people can be easily led astray by wicked leaders, the basic human instincts of love, compassion and the desire for peaceful co-existence are ultimately more resilient than the opposite – also human – inclination towards evil.

My return to Rwanda gave me hope. My journey back to see the victims of the Darfur genocide, plus seeing similar atrocities unfolding in the Nuba Mountains today, renewed my determination not to be a bystander. Al Bashir, Haroun and their cohorts cannot be allowed to get away with these hideous crimes against humanity. The survivors, and those who continue the struggle for justice and dignity, gave me the courage to keep going. They lifted me up and gave me something to keep striving for.

Mr Kapila, your work is not done. Indeed. But maybe one day, it will be.

*

Printed in Great Britain
by Amazon

74502164R00182